THE HISTORICAL DICTIONARY OF GOLFING TERMS

THE HISTORICAL DICTIONARY OF GOLFING TERMS

From 1500 to the Present

PETER DAVIES

Illustrations by Fran Carson

MICHAEL KESEND PUBLISHING, LTD.
New York

Illustrations by Fran Carson
Cover Design by Jackie Schuman

Library of Congress Cataloging-in-Publication Data

Davies, Peter, 1940-
    The historical dictionary of golfing terms: from 1500 to the
present/by Peter Davies; illustrations by Fran Carson.
        p.   cm.
    Rev. ed. of: Dictionary of golfing terms.
    ISBN 0-935576-44-4
    1. Golf – Dictionaries.   2. Golf – History.   I. Davies, Peter,
1940-   Dictionary of golfing terms.   II. Title.
GV965.D37   1992
796.352'03 – dc20   92-27571
                                                      CIP

FOREWORD

No game has a richer array of terms than golf. Five hundred years of golfing have built up an extraordinary vocabulary. Aside from the word *golf* itself, which is the sole vestige of remote and still controversial Dutch origins, three nations and only three have shared in creating the modern golfer's large lexicon: Scotland, England, and the United States. The Scottish stratum is the basic one, dating mostly from the centuries before 1850 when the Scots had the game to themselves: *bunker, caddie, divot, links, putt, stance, stymie,* and *tee* are purely Scottish words, and such straightforward but technical terms as *drive* and *stroke; match* and *medal; drop* and *lift; head, shaft,* and *whipping; ballmaker* and *clubmaker* were already in standard golfing usage in Scotland in the 18th century or before. The relatively brief period of English dominance in the late 19th and early 20th centuries is commemorated by such words as *par* and *bogey; fairway* and *rough; dogleg* and *hog's back; handicap; explode; golf widow;* and *Vardon grip.* The latest stratum, still actively being laid down, belongs to the modern period of overwhelming American prowess and influence on the game, including *birdie* and *eagle; Mulligan* and *Nassau;* hitting *thin* and hitting *fat; chip* and *wedge; charge* and *whiff; duck-hook, pull-hook* and *snap-hook; winter rules* and *preferred lies; swingweight; sweet spot;* and *swale.*

As new golfing terms have accumulated, old ones have changed or faded away. The golfer of 100 years ago spoke of the *fair green* not the fairway, of *swiping* from the tee, *sclaffing* the ball, *missing the globe, stealing* a long putt, and *playing the like* or *the odd.* Words such as *course* and *hazard* were in familiar use, but they did not then mean what they do now. The old hand-crafted clubs have been superseded by the factory-made matched set, but the old names linger on in the twilight usage of obsolescence: *baffy, brassie, cleek, mashie, niblick, spoon* (all Scottish) may be quaint or meaningless words to many of today's casual golfing millions, but they will always be held in affectionate regard by those who love the game (including most professionals), by collectors of golfiana, and by readers of the immortal golf stories of A.W. Tillinghast and P.G. Wodehouse.

In this dictionary, historical development and continuity are shown by the copious use of dated citations. Etymologies, where appropriate, are given in brackets before the definitions. "Scottish" refers to the form of English used in Scotland since 1700; "Old Scottish" refers to the period before 1700. The origins of most of the words have been more or less cleared up, but a few classic cases remain, not surprisingly, lost in the mists of golfing antiquity. Perhaps the most notable of these are *dormie, foozle, Mulligan,* and *tee.*

7

No attempt has been made to cover the huge category of slang, except for well-attested words that are now or have been in widespread usage.

The editor will be grateful for emendations, earlier citations, corrections, and additions. They may be sent to him in care of the publishers, and whenever possible should be supported by dated quotations of actual usage, whether from printed sources or from personal knowledge or recollection. Such citations, which are the foundation of all sound dictionaries, should be given in the following form, ideally on a 4-inch-by-6-inch index card:

---

stymie   *verb trans.*

[in wide unofficial or slang use meaning "to block or obstruct a player's way ahead"]

It was a hook, not vicious, but wide enough to stymie him behind a bush in the rough.

—Mark McCormack
  Golf Annual 1975 77.

The dictionary has been compiled from sample readings in the vast printed literature of golf, including newspapers and magazines, instruction books, fiction, poetry, and the numerous codifications of rules. The definitive and irreplaceable bibliography is Joseph Murdoch *The Library of Golf 1743–1966* (Detroit 1968, with supplement for 1967–1976). An indispensable collection of the early codes of rules is in C.B. Clapcott *The Rules of the Ten Oldest Golf Clubs from 1754 to 1848* (Edinburgh 1935), which has been quoted in the dictionary as "Clapcott 1935." The Badminton Library's volume on *Golf* (London 1890) has been quoted as "*Badminton Golf.*" A few quotations from the great historical dictionaries, especially *The Oxford English Dictionary*, *The Scottish National Dictionary*, and *The Dictionary of the Older Scottish Tongue*, have been used; these are given as O.E.D., Sc.N.D., and D.O.S.T. respectively. The authors and titles of all other sources are given in full without abbreviations.

I am happy to record my gratitude to Miss Janet Seagle, Librarian and Museum Curator of the United States Golf Association, Far Hills, New Jersey; to Dr. Archie Baird of Edinburgh; to Sir Alistair Denny, Bart., of the Royal and Ancient Golf Club of St. Andrews; to the late Eddie Thompson, Director of Golf of the Sea Island Golf Club, Georgia, and Mrs. Freda Thompson; and to Tommy Kukoli, Lyle Palmer, and Davis Love, also of the Sea Island Golf Club.

The drawings were made by Fran Carson from original specimens in the collections of the United States Golf Association, Dr. Archie Baird, and the late Eddie Thompson, and from new equipment lent by Tommy Kukoli.

THE HISTORICAL
DICTIONARY OF
GOLFING TERMS

A

ace n. & v.   **1** n.   A hole in one.

1926   Norman Minturn *Golf Illustrated* (Dec.) 47:   Last summer he did the 12th hole in one stroke and then on consulting his diary found that the year before, almost to the exact hour, he had scored an ace at the 10th hole.
1969   Eric Brown *Knave of Clubs* 98:   Never can an 'ace' have been so welcome to the player who achieved it.
1977   Michael Katz *New York Times* (June 9) D17:   Gerald R. Ford . . . got the first ace of his life.

2 *v.trans.*   To play (a hole) in one.

1970   Dick Schaap *The Masters* 32:   The only par-three that has never been aced.

address v. & n.   **1** *v.trans.*   To take one's stance and prepare to hit (the ball).

1867   H.J.M. *The Golfer at Home* (in Clark *Golf: A Royal & Ancient Game* repr. 1975, 186):   The moment a man begins to "address" his ball, as it is called, he expects that . . . everybody near him will become dumb and motionless.
1913   Horace Hutchinson *Country Life* (Apr. 12) 542:   . . . when we address the ball with one foot almost touching the disc.
1922   P.G. Wodehouse *A Woman Is Only a Woman* (in *The Clicking of Cuthbert* repr. 1956, 35):   James, who had the honour, shook visibly as he addressed his ball.
1963   Bob Rosburg *The Putter Book* 97:   I am addressing a short putt with a slight left-to-right break.
1976   *Rules of Golf* Definition 1:   A player has "addressed the ball" when he has taken his stance and has also grounded his club, except that in a hazard a player has addressed the ball when he has taken his stance.

2 n.   The action and position of addressing the ball.

1896   *Baily's Magazine* (Sept.) 244:   . . . in every case where a ball moves while a player is addressing it the question will arise whether or not the movement was due to anything done by the player in his address.
1944   Bernard Darwin *The Immortal Bobby* (in Wind *The Complete Golfer* 1954, 180):   He had as brief a preliminary address as Duncan himself, but there was nothing hurried or slapdash about it.
1977   Tom Watson *Golf Magazine* (June) 52:   Notice in my address position at right . . . that my left arm is extended and in line with the clubshaft.

3 at address

1941   Patty Berg *Golf* 13:   Try to form the habit of "waggling" once or twice just after assuming your position at address.
1977   Robert Halsall *Golf Magazine* (July) 112:   At address the left shoulder should always be higher than the right.

advice n.   Counsel to a player during a game, relating to play of the game.

1824 *Rules of the Thistle Golf Club* 50: The player is at liberty at all times, to ask advice from his partner or cady, but from no other person.

1976 *Rules of Golf* Definition 2: "Advice" is any counsel or suggestion which could influence a player in determining his play, the choice of a club, or the method of making a stroke.... Rule 9.1.a: A player may give advice to, or ask advice from, only his partner or either of their caddies.

aggregate *adj. & n.* —*adj.* (Of a stroke score) made over two or more rounds of play, or by two or more players playing as partners. —*n.* An aggregate score.

1887 Charles Chambers *Golfing* 79: ... the Glennie Medal for the best aggregate score during the two meetings was won by Mr. Leslie Balfour.

1907 Harold Hilton *My Golfing Reminiscences* 118: ... he required a total of 77 for the round to supplant my aggregate score.

1930 O.B. Keeler *The Golfer's Year Book* 127: ... his stroke aggregate for the 40 rounds is 2968, an average of 74.2.

1946 Frank Moran *Golfers' Gallery* 6: Hagen ... had handed in a grand round of 72, and his aggregate of 300 was generally taken as the winning figures.

1963 Arnold Palmer *My Game and Yours* 78: We were playing low ball and aggregate and if he lifted out of the water we were bound to lose the aggregate.

air shot A stroke that misses the ball entirely.

1967 Michael Green *The Art of Coarse Golf* 19: Although ten strokes better than you he won't concede any. May be pedantic about little things like not counting air shots.

1977 Angela Uzielli *Woman Golfer* (Nov.) 38: I made an utter air shot on the fourteenth.

albatross *n.* A score of three under par for a hole.

1975 Henry Cotton *History of Golf* 109: That 235-yard spoon shot had put him down in two—a double eagle (or albatross).

all square. See **square**[1].

amateur *n., often attributive.* A golfer who is not paid for playing; a nonprofessional. [*Note:* in golf as in other sports the nature of amateurism has been a subject of controversy since the emergence of professionals in the middle of the 19th century, and the quasi-legal definitions formulated by governing bodies have fluctuated widely from period to period. For full current rulings, see *Rules of Amateur Status*, appendix to the *Rules of Golf.*]

1853 *Unidentified newspaper clipping* (in Allan Robertson's album at the R. & A.): ... the Captain ... doing the whole round in 86. This number has been rarely, if ever, equalled by an amateur.

1870 Charles MacArthur *The Golfer's Annual* 140: Fourteen professionals and twelve amateurs started ...

1886 *Rules of the [British] Amateur Championship* (in Geoffrey Cousins *Golf in Britain* 1975, 39): An amateur golfer "shall be a golfer who has never made for sale any golf clubs, balls, or any other articles connected with the game, who has never carried clubs for hire after attaining the age of 15 years, and who has not carried clubs for hire at any time within 6 years of the date on which the competition begins each year; who has never received any consideration for playing in a match or for giving lessons in the game, and who, for a period of five years prior to the 1st of September, 1886, has never received a money prize in an open competition.

1901 Caspar Whitney *The Outing* (June) 333: The conduct of Messrs. Travis and Lockwood in receiving free hotel board and railroad transportation this spring, during a Florida golf campaign, makes them obviously ineligible to rank as amateurs.

1902 Horace Hutchinson *Golf Illustrated* (Nov. 28) 172: ... everybody knows in their minds what we mean by a professional, and what by an amateur; the trouble is to find words to define the idea.

1921 Andrew Kirkaldy *Fifty Years of Golf* 20: It often strikes me as wonderful what very intimate acquaintances an amateur golfer and his caddie are during a match.

1936 H.B. Martin *Fifty Years of American Golf* 129: At the same meeting that saw the disbarment of Ouimet the golf architects, a number of whom were amateurs, also suffered humiliation by being listed among the non-eligibles in championship competition.
1976 *Rules of Golf* Rules of Amateur Status 83: An amateur golfer is one who plays the game solely as a non-remunerative or non-profit-making sport. (See following four pages of exposition.)

American ball. The golf ball as officially specified by the U.S.G.A., having a diameter not less than 1.68 inches and a weight not more than 1.62 ounces.

1978 John M. Ross *Golf Magazine* (Oct.) 98: Australia has joined the growing list of countries that have adopted the 1.68-inch American ball for pro tour and open events. . . . The American ball is used by the British P.G.A. pro tour, as well as the British Open, and the Japanese P.G.A. also endorse it for their events.

amphitheater or **-theatre** n., *usually attributive.* (Of a putting green) situated in a bowl-shaped hollow.

1977 Johnny Miller *Golf Magazine* (July) 43: . . . a 427-yard dogleg left to an elevated amphitheater green.

approach v. & n. **1** *v.trans. & intrans.* To aim or play a relatively short shot from off the putting green onto it; play to (the green); play from off the green to get close to (the hole).

1867 "H.J.M." *The Golfer at Home* (in Clark *Golf: A Royal & Ancient Game* 1875, repr. 2975, 182): . . . while they (they flatter themselves) recompense him by the deadly accuracy with which they approach the hole.
1901 Findlay S. Douglas *The Outing* (June) 360: . . . the usual deadly accuracy of Taylor's approaching was marred by the poor condition of the ground.
1931 Joyce Wethered *The Game of Golf* 89: Good approaching without good putting to back it up is merely wasting good effort.

2 *n., also* **approach shot.** A relatively short shot aimed onto the putting green.

1890 Horace Hutchinson *Badminton Golf* 110: 'An approach shot' . . . means a stroke played with the intention of heaving the ball, which is as yet not on the putting-green, certainly on the putting-green, and possibly somewhere near the hole.
1908 W.W. Tulloch *Life of Tom Morris* 125: Tom's long game and approaches could not be surpassed.
1937 Henry Longhurst *Golf* 130: One may go for days, perhaps even weeks, without playing two approaches that could truthfully be termed identical.
1977 *New York Times* (June 27) 37: . . . a birdie 3 on the 14th, where he stuck an approach three feet from the cup.

approach putt, putting. A long putt aimed at getting close to the hole rather than into it; the playing of such putts.

1890 Horace Hutchinson *Badminton Golf* 135: Putting is commonly and conveniently divided into two heads—'approach putting,' and 'putting out,' or 'holing the ball.'
1901 Findlay S. Douglas *The Outing* (May) 240: With the general improvement of putting greens and their increase in size, the wooden putter will be found an excellent club for approach-putts.
1931 Joyce Wethered *The Game of Golf* 91: In the older works of instruction, therefore, it is not surprising to find that approach putting and holing out were regarded as two distinct branches of the game. The dividing line has now practically vanished.
1969 Jack Nicklaus *The Greatest Game of All* 241: [Bellerive] . . . its colossal greens. It was nothing unusual to have an approach putt of a hundred feet.

apron n. The narrow zone of close-cut grass surrounding a putting green, cut shorter than the fairway and nearly as short as the green.

1950 Gene Sarazen *Walter Hagen* (in Wind *The Complete Golfer* 1954, 169): Once again, mine found the corridor between the traps and finished on the apron.
1967 Michael Green *The Art of Coarse Golf* 26: . . . he hits a nice five iron to the apron.

architect n.   A designer of golf courses.

1912   Harry Vardon *How to Play Golf* 31: At the seaside the architect usually finds ideal sites for short holes staring him in the face.

1926   *Golf Illustrated* (Sept.) 11:   Golf course architects are studying contours and scientific methods of designing courses.

1959   Howard O'Brien (in Milton Gross *Eighteen Holes in My Head* 74):   The architect of Pebble Beach must have derived his inspiration from Dante's account of a trip through hell.

architecture n.   The theory and practice of golf course design, or the nature of the design of a particular golf course.

1907   W. Herbert Fowler (in Leach *Great Golfers in the Making* 154):   Links Architecture (title of article).

1931   T. Simpson *The Game of Golf* 170: To the efforts of Mr. Colt, Mr. Fowler and Mr. Abercrombie we owe what may be reckoned the five pioneer courses of modern golf architecture—Sunningdale, Walton Heath, Worplesdon, Coombe Hill, and Swinley Forest.

1954   Robert Trent Jones (in Wind *The Complete Golfer* 298):   The influence of British architecture was also felt in the next era of our golf-course design.

1968   Richard S. Tufts *Golf Digest* (May): The average golfer is inclined to become emotional when talking about golf course architecture.

attack v.trans.   To play (a hole or course) purposefully, especially aggressively.

1931   Joyce & Roger Wethered *The Game of Golf* 54:   Each hole may have to be attacked in a different way.

1962   Sam Snead *The Education of a Golfer* 212:   From then on I *attacked* the course instead of fearing it.

1978   Neil Amdur *New York Times* (July 17) C6:   But Nicklaus knew . . . You did not attack the menacing par-4 "Road Hole." You finessed it.

away adj.   (Of a ball or its player) lying farther or farthest away from the hole, and therefore to be played, or to play, next.

1913   Bernard Darwin *Country Life* (Sept. 30) 401:   It takes a day or two for the English onlooker [in the U.S.] to understand that "Who's away?" means "Who plays?"

1929   W.H. Faust *Golf Illustrated* (Apr.) 24: Both balls were on the putting green with Bill's away.

1948   Ben Hogan *Power Golf* 165:   . . . let him outdrive you for once on a short par four. As you are away you will then have the honor of making your second shot.

1966   Gary Player *Grand Slam Golf* 112: We both hit probing drives down the centre of the fairway. Lema was away.

B

back[1] *adj.* (Of a teeing ground) placed farthest from the hole, so that the hole is played at its longest distance.

1931 T. Simpson *The Game of Golf* 174: For myself, I have always refused to lay out a course that measured more than 6350 yards from the back tees.
1971 Tommy Bolt *The Hole Truth* 150: They can expect to see sixty or seventy of the world's greatest golfers climbing back tees some of the members didn't even know were on the course.

back[2] *adj., adv. & n.* **1** *adj.* Designating the last nine holes of an eighteen-hole course.

1977 *New York Times* (June 13) 43: . . . Geiberger was two shots down at the turn but rallied with a back nine four-under-par 32.

2 *adv.* Onto or into the back nine holes.

1969 Jack Nicklaus *The Greatest Game of All* 23: . . . made the turn in 32 . . . I started back with a bogey and a par.

3 *n.* The back nine holes.

1977 *Golf Digest* (Aug.) 29: He was six under on the back.

backspin *or* **back-spin** *n.* Backward rotation of the ball in flight, causing it to fly in a relatively steep upward trajectory, and tending to stop it from rolling on landing.

1890 Sir Walter Simpson *Badminton Golf* 204: Loft and backspin are the result of describing a small ellipse with the club.
1916 P.A. Vaile *The New Golf* 312: Underspin is practically a misnomer for any spin that a driver can communicate to the ball. Back-spin is a more correct term, for any spin of this nature is obtained, not by hitting *under* the ball, but by hitting it *behind*, as the club is descending.
1931 Joyce & Roger Wethered *The Game of Golf* 54: The loft on the club helps to get the ball into the air off the fairway, and also to apply backspin where it is needed.
1977 Davis Love *Golf Digest* (July) 46: A wood shot produces less backspin and more sidespin, giving you a more consistent curve.

backstroke *n.* Backswing.

1964 Julius Boros *How to Win at Weekend Golf* 11: Once I realized what was wrong I went to a lower, more compact backstroke.

backswing *n.* The movement of taking a club back and up to the point at which the downswing begins.

1915 A.W. Tillinghast *The Outcasts* (in *Cobble Valley Golf Yarns* 26): But his stroke

was just the same as ever—a short, cramped back swing, with a lunge of his body and a dig at the ball.
1978 Ben Crenshaw *Golf Magazine* (Oct.) 68: . . . you'll never get a good downswing from an incomplete backswing.

baff *v.trans. & intrans.* [*Origin*: Scottish, from Old Scottish *baff*="a blow made with something soft"; related to Flemish *baf*="a slap in the face" (Sc.N.D.).] *Obsolete.* To hit or scuff (the ground) behind the ball.

1857 H.B. Farnie *The Golfer's Manual* 49: The ball must not be hit clean; the club-head on the contrary, must hit or *baff* the ground immediately behind the ball, thus causing elevation without any fear of distance.
1881 Robert Forgan *The Golfer's Handbook* 59: BAFF—To strike the ground with the "sole" of the clubhead in playing.
1908 Arnold Haultain *The Mystery of Golf* (repr. 1965) 74: What duffer can tell beforehand whether he is going to slice or to pull, to baff or to top?

baffing-spoon *or* **baffy-spoon** *n.* [*Origin*: approach shots with this club were played somewhat in the manner of the modern wedge; see **baff** *v.*] A wooden club, no longer in use, that was the shortest, stiffest, and most lofted of the set of spoons, and that was used primarily for approach shots.

1862 Robert Chambers *A Few Rambling Remarks on Golf* 15: The BAFFING-SPOON is shorter still, and very much spooned.
1875 Robert Clark *Golf: A Royal & Ancient Game* 270: Previous to about 1848 or 1849, short wooden clubs, the baffing, or short-spoons, were used for this important stroke [i.e., approach shot].
1895 W. Dalrymple *Handbook to Golf* 54: There used to be a very valuable old club, known as the Baffy spoon; but since Allan Robertson introduced iron play through the green the use of it has died out.

baffy *n.* [*Origin*: from *baffy-spoon*.] **1** A small-headed, steeply lofted wooden

baffy
Spalding Gold Medal, 1906

club, no longer in use, developed from the baffing-spoon and continuing in limited use well into the 20th century.

1890 H.S.C. Everard *Badminton Golf* 385: . . . was particularly accurate with the baffy —a club to which he clung affectionately long after iron play had been introduced.
1907 *Army & Navy Stores Catalogue* 1000: Short-Headed Deep-Faced Spoons . . . No. 3, MSD Baffy equivalent to a pitching mashie.
1922 P.G. Wodehouse *Sundered Hearts* (in *The Clicking of Cuthbert* repr. 1956, 65): "I got a good tee-shot straight down the fairway, took a baffy for my second . . ."
1946 Bernard Darwin *British Golf* 32: He remained a fine player till he was old himself, and a great wielder of the baffy of his younger days.

2 Alternate name of the number four wood.

1972 *Encyclopaedia Britannica* 10:557: Wood clubs . . . Number Four (Baffy).

bag *or* **golf-bag** *n.* **1** A receptacle for carrying clubs, made of canvas, leather, or synthetic material, having a shoulder strap and a handle, and often separate compartments for balls, tees, gloves, etc.

1897 Horace Hutchinson *Country Life* (Jan. 23) 80: ". . . as the world gets more and more full of duffers, and their golf-bags get more and more full of iron clubs!"
1898 M. Gertrude Cundill *The Outing* (Oct.) 17: It was an exceedingly pretty girl who confronted him, and she carried a bag of the latest pattern, full of new clubs.

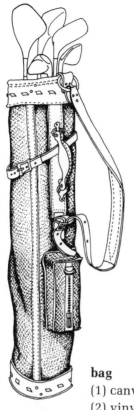

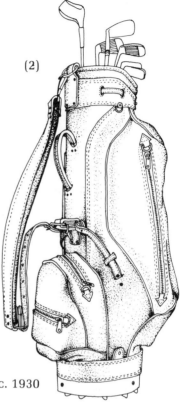

bag
(1) canvas and leather, c. 1930
(2) vinyl, 1979

1915   Alexander H. Revell *Pro & Con of Golf* 6:   An ordinary golf bag will cost from two dollars and a half up.
1933   John Ressich *Thir Braw Days* 92:   . . . as lang's he's stoot enough tae drag roond this great muckle portmanty that they ca' a gouf-bag.
1967   George Plimpton *The Bogey Man* 5: A golf bag is such an immense symbol of fri-volity in these parlous days, so much bigger than a tennis racket.
1973   *Bartlett's World Encyclopedia of Golf* 375:   There are three major bag classifica-tions: *Men's Bag . . . Ladies' Bag . . . Sunday Bag.*

2 *also* **bagful.**   Used as a metaphor for the whole array of a player's clubs or the repertoire of a player's shots.

1905   Frederick Upham Adams *John Henry Smith* 50:   "I wish I could make as good an approach with any club in my bag as he did with that improvised cane."

1915   A.W. Tillinghast *Once to Every Man* (in *Cobble Valley Golf Yarns* 108):   Clarence Miggs didn't have a stroke in his bag that would have stopped Tucker playing his fool head off today.
1921   Andrew Kirkaldy *Fifty Years of Golf* 101:   He has a bagful of shots and plays the whole game with ease and brain.
1956   Herbert Warren Wind *The Story of American Golf* 163:   . . . believing that in his bag lay one last parade of winning shots.
1979   *Savannah Morning News* (Jan. 4) 1c: . . . the good-looker with the bagful of precise shots and the precise putter.

bail out *phr. v.*   To retrieve or improve (a poorly begun hole) with good approach-ing or putting, or both.

1962   Sam Snead *The Education of a Golfer* 35:   Even after muffing 2 or 3 wood shots, you still have a 60–40 chance of bailing out

the hole with a 1- or 2-over-par score.
1978 *New York Times* (June 18) S5: [Gene] Francis said: ". . . I've been bailing out with a hot putter the entire tournament."

balata /ba-*la*-ta/ or /*bal*-a-ta/ n. [*Origin*: from Spanish *balata*, from Carib *balata*.] A hard, resilient substance derived from the gum of the bully or balata tree (*Manilkara bidentata*) of northeastern South America and the West Indies, and used to make the covers of rubber-cored golf balls.

1929 *Spalding's Athletic Library* n.p.: All golf ball covers are made chiefly of balata.
1968 J.S. Martin *The Curious History of the Golf Ball* 85: . . . balata (bully-tree gum, imported from nearby Latin America instead of far Malaysia), which Stoughton had found to be less frangible than gutta.

ball n. **1** or **golf ball.** The hard and resilient spheroidal projectile used in golf; before the 17th century made of wood or of compressed wool in a leather cover; from the 17th century made of boiled compressed feathers in a leather cover; after 1848 of solid gutta percha or a mixture of gutta percha and other substances; after 1900 of strip rubber wound around a core, with a cover of balata; now also of solid compressed synthetic rubber; usually colored white; and now always having several hundred indentations on the surface.

1506 *Accounts of the Lords High Treasurers of Scotland* (Feb. 22) (in Clark *Golf: A Royal & Ancient Game* 1875, 123): Item for xii golf ballis to the King . . . iiii s. [i.e., 4 shillings].
1568 *Edinburgh Testaments* I.153: Thre dozen of golf bawis, price thereof xxiii s.
1585 *Correspondence of Sir Patrick Waus* II.341: Ye will remember to bring with you ane dossen of commoun golf ballis.
1629 *Register of the Privy Council of Scotland* 2nd Series III.174: [The Council] grants license to John Dickson of making gouff balls within this burgh.

1638 Henry Adamson *The Muses' Threnodie* (in *Badminton Golf* 1890, 21):
And ye, my clubs, you must no more prepare
To make your balls fly whistling in the air.
1672 Sir John Foulis, Bart., *Notebook* (in J.C. Irons *Leith and Its Antiquities* 1897, 406): March 2. For three golfe balls . . . 15[shillings].
1743 Thomas Mathison *The Goff* 21:
The pond'rous club upon the ball descends,
Involved in dust th'exulting orb ascends.

1744 *Articles & Laws in Playing at Golf*: 1. You must tee your ball within a club length of the hole.
1790 *Hoyle's Games* 289: The Balls . . . are made of Horse Leather, stuffed with Feathers in a peculiar manner, and boiled.
1808 *Minutes of the Musselburgh Golf Club* (June 26) (in Clark op. cit., 90): The Secretary was authorized to give the boys at Mr. Taylor's two dozen of golf-balls.
1849 Charles Roger *History of St. Andrews* 79: [footnote] For about a year, golf balls . . . have been constructed of gutta percha, but whether this material may be ultimately preferred, time alone can determine.
1872 John Henry Walsh *British Rural Sports* 636: Balls are used about five quarters of an inch in diameter, and weighing from 26 to 30 drachms avoirdupois.
1902 Horace Hutchinson *Country Life* (Dec. 13) 767: . . . the rubber-cored balls can be bought freely at 25s. or so the dozen.
1936 H.B. Martin *Fifty Years of American Golf* 130: When we are in Great Britain we play with their ball, and when they are over here they play with our ball.
1976 *Rules of Golf* 2.3.a.: The weight of the ball shall be not greater than 1.620 ounces avoirdupois (45.93 gm) and the size not less than 1.680 inches (42.67 mm) in diameter. . . . Note: the Rules of the Royal and Ancient Golf Club of St. Andrews, Scotland, provide that the weight of the ball shall not be greater than 1.620 ounces avoirdupois (45.93 gm) and the size not less than 1.620 inches (41.15 mm) in diameter.

2 A ball as played; a shot.

1858 *Unidentified newspaper clipping* (in Allan Robertson's album at the R. & A.): We question if he was ever known to drive a wild ball.

1907 Edward Blackwell (in Leach *Great Golfers in the Making* 132): I am frequently questioned as to how I get such long balls.

1950 Dai Rees *Golf My Way* 43: You want to ask me why Colonel Fitzpark, whose hands never go higher than his shoulders in the follow-through, always hits a straight ball.

1965 *Paul Hahn Shows You How to Play Trouble Shots* 46: It is a proved fact that the more upright the swing, the easier it is to hit a straight ball.

ballmaker or **ball-maker** *n.* A maker of golf balls.

1761 *Records of the Honourable Company of Golfers* (March 7) (in Clark *Golf: A Royal & Ancient Game* 1875, 50): The Captain and his Councill do appoint that Mr. Patrick Robertson, Jeweller and Goldsmith in Edinburgh, one of their number, shall in all time coming be Ball-maker to the Honourable Society of Golfers.

1823 James Grierson *Delineations of St. Andrews* 223: The employment is accounted unhealthy, and many of the ball-makers have been observed to fall sacrifice to consumption.

1890 Tom Morris (in *Badminton Golf* 431): I was made 'prentice to Allan as a ba'-maker at eighteen, and wrocht wi' him eleven years.

1968 J.S. Martin *The Curious History of the Golf Ball* 109: . . . enabled it to zoom Dunlop from near obscurity to front rank as a ball-maker.

ball-washer *n.* A device, installed on a golf course, for washing balls.

1929 Advertisement *Golf Illustrated* (May) 16: The golfer's reaction to the new Roterkleen ball washer has been most flattering.

1971 Tommy Bolt *The Hole Truth* 16: "Oh, those cold mornings when we also-rans would have to break the ice in the ball-washers."

banana ball. *Slang.* An extreme slice.

1962 Sam Snead *The Education of a Golfer*

7: So he had this banana-ball slice that sometimes sailed over two fairways.

1978 Ernie Vossler *Golf Magazine* (May) 68: . . . there are different degrees of slice—from the touring pro's skillfully controlled fade to the hapless hacker's banana ball.

bank shot. A shot played from close to a green with a steep bank confronting the player, in which the ball is played so as to pitch on the face of the bank and go over it, either running or on the bounce.

1922 Seymour Dunn *Fundamentals of Golf* (repr. 1977) 232: To pitch a ball onto the green and have it stop at the hole would be extremely doubtful, therefore the wise thing to do would be to bank the ball against the slope and thus have it run up the bank onto the green with just enough speed so that it will trickle down to the hole. The *bank* shot is an extremely useful shot under certain conditions.

1977 George Peper *Scrambling Golf* 115: Admittedly, the bank shot (sometimes called the "bump" shot) has its risks.

bap-headed *adj.* [Origin: see 1897 quotation.] (Of the head of a wooden club, late 19th and early 20th centuries) markedly round and flattish in shape, compared with the long-nosed woods of earlier times.

1897 Horace Hutchinson *Country Life* (Jan. 30) 141: It was one of those singular,

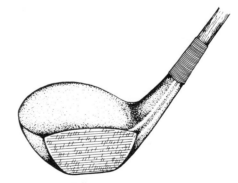

bap-headed
George Richard "bap" spoon, 1924

round-headed things that are having a considerable vogue just now—"bapp" headed clubs they are called, the "bapp" being the soft and altogether delicious breakfast roll that you get in Scotland.
1933 John Ressich *Thir Braw Days* 40: A bap-heided play-club, a sand-iron and a cleek ye micht shave wi' . . .

barranca n. [*Origin*: from Spanish *barranca*="gulley, ravine."] A typically rocky gulley or watercourse, incorporated as a hazard on golf courses in Spanish-speaking places.

1897 Horace Hutchinson *Country Life* (May 15) 525: [Links at Las Palmas, Canary Islands] . . . the surface is a bare crumbly clay, with stones interspersed among it, and intersected by dry barrancas or water-courses.
1927 Joseph Blake *Golf Illustrated* (Jan.) 26: Interesting California courses . . . What one takes to be a hazard is called a *barranca*.
1962 Sam Snead *The Education of a Golfer* 154: When did you last see a golfer hitting balls out of bushes and barrancas when he didn't have to?

baseball grip. A style of gripping the club in which the hands abut without overlap or interlock.

[**1906** Arthur Pottow *Illustrated Outdoor News* (Dec.) 183: His grip is on the order, broadly speaking, of a baseball or cricket grip.]
1969 Paul D. Peery *Billy Casper: Winner* 34: Heaney saw that Billy used a "baseball grip" in hitting the ball. And he coached the boy to change to the Vardon grip.
1976 J.C. Jessop *Golf* 19: There are three main grips in golf. . . . Thirdly, there is the "baseball grip," which has helped Dai Rees to remain a force in British golf when he was well past fifty years of age.

bend v. & n. **1** v.trans. To make (a shot) curve by using sidespin.

1977 Tom Kelly letter to *Golf Magazine* (Aug.) 88: Pros tell me they see nothing

wrong with my swing. I have no problem bending shots.

2 v.intrans. (Of a shot) to curve from sidespin.

1977 George Peper *Scrambling Golf* 71: They all know how to make a golf ball bend. Every pro on the P.G.A. tour can fade, slice, hook, and draw the ball intentionally.

3 n. Curve on a shot imparted by sidespin.

1965 Bob Charles *Left-handed Golf* 91: . . . will also roll my wrists after impact to accentuate the degree of bend I want to put on the ball.

bent n. [*Origin*: Scottish, from Old Scottish *bent* or *bynt*="coarse grass, rough pasture."] **1** *Chiefly Scottish*. A clump or tuft of long coarse grass on a golf course.

1779 Hugo Arnot *History of Edinburgh* 360: It [golf] is commonly played on rugged, broken ground, covered with short grass, and bents, in the neighborhood of the sea-shore.
1812 *Regulations for the Game of Golf* (St. Andrews) (in Clapcott 1935, 46): XV. When a Ball is completely covered with fog, bent, whins, etc., so much thereof shall be set aside as that the Player shall have a full view of his Ball before he plays.
1890 A.J. Balfour *Badminton Golf* 425: But after a long and rather wild drive, player A lost his ball in the middle of some long bents.
1919 Robert K. Risk *Songs of the Links* 43:
When the course seemed wholly bunker,
    and the bents like healthy hay . . .

2 Any grass of the genus *Agrostis*, native to moist northern parts of Eurasia and North America, selectively bred in many varieties for use on golf courses. It is hardy and resilient and can be cut very short.

1930 Advertisement *Golf Year Book* iii: For the finest Turf, sow Bent Grass Seed of known Quality . . . South German Bent, Colonial Bent, Rhode Island Bent, Cocos Bent, Special Putting Green Bent, Superfine Fairway Formula (with Bent), Bent Stolons . . .
1977 Larry Dennis *Golf Digest* (July) 54:

. . . one who learned to play and putt the ball with a gentler stroke on Northern bent greens would have difficulty putting in Florida.

Bermuda n. [*Origin:* so named because introduced to the southern states of the U.S. from Bermuda.] A grass, *Cynodon dactylon*, native to southern Europe, widely introduced in warm parts of the world and used on golf courses where bent grass will not grow.

1907 Arthur Pottow *Recreation* (March) 415: The St. Lucie and Bermuda . . . can both be used on the fair and putting greens. The Bermuda is slightly the better.
1963 Bob Rosburg *The Putter Book* 53: Most of the courses in Southern California, the Southwest and South, including the Caribbean area, have Bermuda grass greens. Bermuda is a hot-weather grass. It has a wide, dark-colored blade and grows flat, affording a strong grain.

best ball. **1** The better score of two partners in a four-ball or best-ball match. [*Note:* while it contravenes the rules of formal usage to refer to the *best* of two entities, it has long been traditional in golf to refer to the *best ball* of two partners; but many now refer to this as the *better ball.*]

1889 Alexander Lawson *Letters on Golf* 39: One form of three-ball match may be excepted from this general condemnation, and that is when two slightly weak golfers play against a strong one, the latter playing the best of their balls. Golf is not grammatical, because it says *best,* not *better.*
1912 Harry Vardon *How to Play Golf:* It was in a match against the best ball of two very good golfers at Boston.
1933 John Ressich *Thir Braw Days* 39: Kelty had matched hissel' for five pun' against the best ba' o' the Macleishes.

2 The best score of three partners playing against one player in a best-ball match.

1971 Henry Longhurst *My Life and Soft Times* 80: An awful lesson had been learned, namely that the only difference between the better ball of two players and the best ball of three is the number of holes at which the one who plays worst on that day beats both of the other two. As in our case, the answer may well be nil.

best-ball n., or **best-ball match.** **1** A match between one player and a side consisting of two or three partners scoring with their best ball.

1976 *Rules of Golf* Definition 28: *Best-Ball:* A match in which one plays against the better ball of two or the best ball of three players.

2 A four-ball.

1976 Arthur Haley *The Money-changers* 104: The four were playing a best-ball match—Big George and Heyward against Austin and the Vice-President.

better ball. The better score of two partners in a four-ball or best-ball match.

1970 Tony Jacklin *Jacklin* 135: We were two down after five, but finally went round with a better ball of sixty-five to win on the last green.
1978 Alistair Cooke *Golf Journal* (Mar./ Apr.) 9: If my handicap tripled . . . I could beat the better ball of Nicklaus and Watson.

bird n. [*Origin:* def. 1 is from 19th-century U.S. slang *bird*="anyone or anything excellent or wonderful." The use by golfers of *bird* for a fine shot doubtless further implied that it "flew like a bird." This obsolete expression is the immediate origin of *birdie.* Def. 2 is a secondary formation, shortened from *birdie.*] **1** *Obsolete.* A long, impressive shot.

1911 *Maclean's Magazine* (Sept.) 205: Lanesborough followed with a 'bird' straight down the course.
1915 A.W. Tillinghast *The Spur* (in *Cobble Valley Golf Yarns* 168): "They were going across there like birds too."
1922 P.G. Wodehouse *Sundered Hearts* (in *The Clicking of Cuthbert* repr. 1956, 75):

"Good God!" cried Mortimer, astounded. It had been a bird of a shot.

2 A birdie.

1929 A.W. Tillinghast *Golf Illustrated* (June) 42: I believe the winning score will be three strokes higher over the American course, where bird figures will be less frequent.
1975 Mark McCormack *Golf Annual* 148: After birds on 4 and 5 he ran into trouble again.
1978 Neil Singelais *Boston Globe* (July 29) 19: ... he ran into bogeys at the 11th and 17th, but balanced those off with birds at the 12th and 16th.

birdie *n. & v.* [*Origin*: U.S., from *bird* (def. 1), very possibly coined as described in the quotation of 1936 below.]
1 *n.* A score of one under par for a hole.

1913 Bernard Darwin *Country Life* (Sept. 20) 401: It takes a day or two for the English onlooker [in the U.S.] to understand that ... a "birdie" is a hole done in a stroke under par.
1915 A.W. Tillinghast *The Home Hole* (in *Cobble Valley Golf Yarns* 53): "Got away to a rotten start, but finished strong, even 4's for the last five, and I pinched a birdie on the home hole."
1926 *Golf Illustrated* (Sept.) 22: A birdie 3 on the 15th put Hagen ahead.
1936 H.B. Martin *Fifty Years of American Golf* 94: The slang word 'birdie' originated in 1899 ... Ab Smith tells the story: "... my ball ... came to rest within six inches of the cup. I said 'that was a bird of a shot.... I suggest that when one of us plays a hole in one under par he receives double compensation.' The other two agreed and we began right away, just as soon as the next one came, to call it a 'birdie.'"
1969 Tom Scott & Geoffrey Cousins *The Golf Immortals* 149: If you hit the green in the regulation number of strokes, you aim to hole the first putt for a birdie.
1977 Mark Mulvoy *Golf Digest* (Aug.) 59: On those rare occasions when he kept the ball in safe play on a hole, he usually made birdie.

2 *v.trans., present participle* **birdieing,** *sometimes* **birdying.** To play (a hole) in one under par.

1956 Herbert Warren Wind *The Story of American Golf* 545: On the 18th tee, just as Fleck had been faced with birdieing that hole the day before to gain his tie with Hogan, so now was Hogan faced with birdieing it to tie Fleck.
1970 Tony Jacklin *Jacklin* 132: An unhappy morning for Britain ended with Sanders and Dickinson birdieing the fourteenth and fifteenth.

3 birdie in *phr.v.* To hole out for a birdie.

1962 Sam Snead *The Education of a Golfer* 34: ... on the clubhouse hole he birdied in from 20 feet.

birdieable *adj.* Susceptible of being birdied.

1969 Jack Nicklaus *The Greatest Game of All* 225: All I needed was a birdie and a par. The seventeenth—why, that was a very birdieable hole.

bird's-nest *n., attributive.* (Of a lie) deeply cupped in grass.

1971 Henry Longhurst *My Life and Soft Times* 120: I drove our ball into a bird's-nest lie in the rough.

bisque [bisk] *n.* [*Origin:* borrowed from court tennis, in which *bisque* is recorded from the 17th century meaning a handicap point which may be claimed at any time during the set; from French *bisque* =same meaning; further origin unknown.] A handicap stroke in match play that may be taken at any hole nominated by the player who receives it (not used in standard handicapping).

1890 Horace Hutchinson *Badminton Golf* 269: But the bisque is a point which may be played at any moment.
1915 Harry Vardon, quoted in Alexander H. Revell *Pro & Con of Golf* 128: "There is much to be said for bisques as a form of handicapping."
1928 Richard A. Jones Jr. *Golf Illustrated*

(Sept.) 25: Glenna, this year, needed only 5 bisques to defeat Sweetser 3 and 2.

1974 *The Golfer's Handbook* 113: It is a sound principle to take bisques early in the game.

bite *v. & n.* **1** *v.intrans.* (Of a pitched ball) to land on the ground with backspin and stop dead or nearly so.

1890 Horace Hutchinson *Badminton Golf* 66: This ["cut"] imparts a twist to the ball which causes it to break to the right and bite close into the ground, instead of running freely, when it pitches.
1965 Bob Charles *Left-handed Golf* 54: . . . hitting it crisply to produce a lot of backspin. I would pitch this shot right up to the hole, knowing it would bite very quickly.
1970 Dick Schaap *The Masters* 204: Billy Casper takes a wedge and lofts his ball straight toward the flag. "Bite, bite, bite," his son shouts. The ball bites, and dies six feet from the cup.

2 *n.* Impact of a pitched ball with backspin, causing it to stop dead or nearly so.

1928 A. Linde Fowler *Golf Illustrated* (Sept.) 16: . . . the fine grass means that there is less for the ball to sink into before it strikes the soil at the finish of the approach and, consequently, not so much opportunity to get the "bite" of the backspin.
1948 Ben Hogan *Power Golf* xv: . . . it is almost impossible for the 85–90 shooters to hit the green with a wood shot and still hold the ball on it. Whereas, we can put plenty of bite on the ball with our short irons and it stays on the green almost where we want it.

blade *n. & v.* **1** *n.* The hitting part of an iron clubhead, not including the hosel.

1895 W. Dalrymple *Handbook to Golf* 70: [Willie Park's lofter]. . . as the blade is concave, it is clear you must play with very great accuracy.
1911 James Braid *Advanced Golf* 36: Long and fairly narrow blades, such as those of cleeks and mid-irons . . .
1953 Bobby Locke *Bobby Locke on Golf* (in Wind *The Complete Golfer* 1954, 269):

Throughout the swing, the putter blade stays square to the hole.
1977 Advertisement *Golf Magazine* (June) 26: The blades are compact with straight-set hosels.

2 *v.trans.* To hit (the ball) on the leading edge of the blade of an iron club.

1978 Oscar Fraley *Golf Magazine* (Oct.) 28: That's where his favorite shot became his worst. "I bladed it," he grunts at the memory, "and left it in the rough."

blade putter. A putter having an iron head with blade and neck of the same basic form as those of the standard numbered irons.

1962 Sam Snead *The Education of a Golfer* 123: I complained that a center-shafted putter, such as I used then, was illegal in English championships and that I hated to switch to a blade putter.
1977 *New York Times* (June 20) 36: Green crouched over the ball with the 55-year-old hickory-shafted blade putter that he obtained in a swap with a high-school buddy.

blade putter

blast *v. & n.* **1** *v.trans. & intrans.* To play (the ball) from sand, now normally with a wedge, hitting the sand behind and under the ball; play an explosion shot.

1927 Robert T. Jones, Jr. & O.B. Keeler *Down the Fairway* 217: To blast, I stand normally . . . and hit hard into the sand.
1952 Henry Cotton *History of Golf in Britain:* Even from a very teed-up lie in sand, the modern professional will blast the ball on to the green.
1970 Dick Schaap *The Masters* 188: Then Billy Casper, who is considered more skilled at putting and chipping than sand play, blasts to within four feet of the pin.

2 blast out *phr. v.* To blast from a bunker.

1978 Dave Anderson *New York Times* (June 18): . . . hit another 9-iron into a bunker . . . He blasted out . . .

3 *n.* An explosion shot.

1971 Tommy Bolt *The Hole Truth* 120: I was fortunate with my blast. The ball cleared the lip and fell softly on the green.

4 *n.* A powerful drive.

1975 Mark McCormack *Golf Annual* 152: Even a blast of 300 yards from the tee . . .

blaster *n.* **1** A sand wedge.

1937 Henry Longhurst *Golf* 198: The blaster gives no margin for error above the ball, but an almost infinite margin below it.
1960 Rex Lardner *Out of the Bunker and into the Trees* 147: I bent my blaster into a sharp V and hurled it end over end into the branches.

2 A driver.

1962 Sam Snead *The Education of a Golfer* 57: . . . the Picard driver . . . Most of my major titles have been won with that big blaster.

blind *adj.* (Of a hole, green, or hazard) hidden from the player by intervening ground; (of a shot) played toward an objective so hidden.

1896 *Golfer's & Angler's Guide* 149: . . . if the second is badly topped it may land in a blind bunker.
1913 Bernard Darwin *Country Life* (Oct. 11) 505: . . . we have become too fiercely prejudiced against blind shots. Mr. [Charles B.] Macdonald has designed two or three blind holes.
1931 T. Simpson *The Game of Golf* 181: . . . it is one of the best blind holes in the country.
1969 Jack Nicklaus *The Greatest Game of All* 92: Royal St. George's is a rather old-fashioned kind of course with many blind tee-shots.

block *v.trans.* To prevent or delay rotation of the wrists during a swing, so that the clubface does not close to square at impact, causing the ball to be sliced; play (a stroke or shot) in this manner.

1975 Mark McCormack *Golf Annual* 204: He blocked his drive . . .
1979 *Golf Monthly* (March) 54: . . . losing out mainly because of one disastrous blocked-shot (his bete noir) with a fairway wood.

blow *v.intrans.* To suffer a sudden collapse of good play, typically when under pressure; now often used with *to* (indicating the resulting score).

1915 A.W. Tillinghast *Once to Every Man* (in *Cobble Valley Golf Yarns* 106): "This damned fool is playing golf that nobody could beat. . . . Maybe he'll blow going back."
1962 Sam Snead *The Education of a Golfer* 97: The minute you blow, a charge seems to go through your opponent and he begins to play better golf.
1962 Paul D. Peery *Billy Casper: Winner* 73: But Jacobs blew to three bogeys on the first six holes and never recovered.
1975 Mark McCormack *Golf Annual* 73: Schlee blew to a 75 that dropped him back to a tie for sixth place.
1977 *Golf Magazine* (Aug.) 18: It takes a lot of nerve to write that a touring pro "blew" to 74 when you take that many strokes for 9 holes.

blow up *phr.v. &* **blowup** *n.* **1** *phr.v.* To suffer a sudden collapse of good play, typically when under pressure.

1915 A.W. Tillinghast *The Home Hole* (in *Cobble Valley Golf Yarns* 53): "I tell you he had some card up to the eighteenth, and it was pathetic to see him slashing around when he blew up."
1927 Robert T. Jones, Jr. & O.B. Keeler *Down the Fairway* 69: I've lost many a tough match since then, . . . more than one because I simply blew up under pressure.
1977 Johnny Miller *Golf Magazine* (Aug.) 73: There are lots of players on the Tour who spill over the red line when they're playing well. They come down to the wire and blow up.

2 *n.* A sudden collapse of good play, typically when the player is under pressure.

1975 Henry Cotton *History of Golf* 113: Coming home I began with three 5's and had three long holes to come. The crowd anticipated the most appalling 'blow-up' in championship golf.
1977 *New York Times* (June 25) 15: The biggest blowup was by Lietzke, who shot an 80.

bogey *n. & v.* [Origin: As early as the 1880s, at some courses in England, a standard score in strokes was being assigned to each hole as the target score which a good amateur ought to be able to make; this was on an informal and unofficial basis, and was not systematically applied. In 1890 or 1891 Major Charles Wellman, playing at Great Yarmouth in Norfolk (England), is said to have exclaimed that the standard score of the course was "a regular Bogey Man," referring to the current music-hall catch-song "Hush, hush, hush, Here comes the Bogey Man, . . . He'll catch you if he can." Dr. Thomas Browne of the Royal Navy, secretary of the Great Yarmouth club, thereupon adopted the name *Bogey* as a personification of the demon golfer who played every hole in the standard score. He was later playing at the United Services Club at Alverstoke in Hampshire (the members of which were all army or navy officers), and introduced his imaginary player. Here Captain S.

Vidal of the Royal Engineers insisted that such a player must obviously be a commanding officer, and so *Bogey* became *Colonel Bogey*. For subsequent developments, see Note at def. 3 below.]
1 *proper noun* **(Colonel) Bogey** An imaginary player of high amateur standard, held to play every hole of a given course in the standard stroke score, and regarded as the opponent of players in "Bogey competitions."

1892 *Golf* magazine (Feb. 12) 348: "COLONEL BOGEY." This is a personage whom many golfers have recently had the pleasure of playing. He is a gentleman of uncertain pedigree, and no one knows exactly by what steps he graded into his self-styled military rank. As far, however, as one can trace his lineage, it would seem that the parentage of this estimable antagonist is due to the ingenious and versatile golfers of the United Services on the banks of the Solent.
1895 Horace Hutchinson *Badminton Golf* 281: The score of Colonel Bogey, as settled by the committee of the club, is usually not a prohibitive score, so to speak—not an impossible score. Rather it is such a score as may be made by the ordinary scratch player, playing not ideally well, but without a single big mistake.
1919 Robert K. Risk *Songs of the Links* 37:
We call him Colonel Bogey; 'tis the way
Of mankind to invent a kindlier name,
A jesting phrase for the arch-enemy.

2 Bogey competition, Bogey play, etc. A form of scoring in which a field of competitors play against the Bogey score of the course, scoring as in match play, the winner being the player who does best against Bogey. (It was recognized by the R. & A. in 1910 and remained popular for a few years, but for tournaments was abandoned in favor of stroke play.)

1892 *Golf* magazine (July 29) 334: A "Bogey" tournament was played on Saturday the 16th . . .
1897 Price Collier *The Outing* (Nov.) 197: A Bogie Handicap competition was played later at Tuxedo. "Colonel Bogie" was credited 1st hole, 5; 2nd hole, 3 . . .
1954 George Houghton *The Truth About*

Golf Addicts 21: That year there was a record entry. Medal competition in the morning, and Four-ball against Bogey in the afternoon.
1976 *Rules of Golf* 39.1: A bogey, par or Stableford competition is a form of stroke competition in which play is against a fixed score at each hole of the stipulated round or rounds.

3 *n.* A standard score in strokes assigned to each hole, and to a round, of a given course. [*Note:* bogey, originating as the standard of play of a good amateur, was always a little more lenient than the slightly older *par,* which became the standard for professionals and for championship-level amateurs. Many courses assigned both par and bogey; for most holes they were the same figure, but for a few holes bogey was one stroke higher than par. Professionals and low-handicap amateurs, especially in the United States, thus came to regard a bogey score as a failure to achieve par, while many amateurs, especially in Britain, preferred to keep bogey as an attainable standard of good play.]

1894 *Baily's Magazine* (Apr.) 283: The "Bogey" or scratch score of the Furzedown course is 80.
1899 Walter Camp & Lilian Brooks *Drives and Puts* 83: Lucy and her partner made the seventeenth hole in four, which was one better than bogie.
1908 Arnold Haultain *The Mystery of Golf* (repr. 1965) 95: . . . men high up in the handicap have always Bogey; scratch men can compete with par.
1911 James Braid *Advanced Golf* 250: The difference between par and bogey is, of course, that the former represents perfect play and the other stands for good play, with a little margin here and there.
1932 Frank Reynolds *The Frank Reynolds Golf Book* 67: [Caption to cartoon]: "No, darling, not in the study. Your father went round in bogey today and wants to have a nice long think about it."
1961 John Stobbs *Tackle Golf* (repr. 1977) 15: . . . your first good drive, or bogey—or even a hole in one—will whet your appetite for more and greater trial and error.
1975 Robert Browning *History of Golf* 27:

To the English handicap golfer, accustomed to preen himself on the number of 'bogeys' he achieves in the course of his round, the American use of the word naturally appears the rankest blasphemy.

4 *n., plural* **bogeys.** A score of one stroke over par for a hole.

1954 Robert Trent Jones (in Wind *The Complete Golfer* 302): One must really see Pine Valley to appreciate it. . . . Thrill with one's pars, be satisfied with a "bogey," and continue on far from downcast after a "double bogey."
1970 Tony Jacklin *Jacklin* 27: This time I hit nine fairways, had twenty-nine putts, four birdies and two bogies.
1977 *New York Times* (June 11) 14: . . . said she was pleased with her 71 today, despite a seesaw round of five birdies and four bogeys.

5 *v.trans. & intrans., past* **bogeyed.** To play (a hole) in one stroke over par.

1948 Ben Hogan *Power Golf* 57: . . . after he drove into the rough he bogeyed the hole and lost his advantage.
1975 Mark McCormack *Golf Annual* 17: Irwin bogied 5 with three putts.
1977 *New York Times* (June 13) 43: Player hooked his approach, missed the green and bogeyed.

bolt *v.trans.* To hole out (a shot or putt) with a hard, fast shot; to putt out (the hole) with such a stroke.

1853 *Unidentified newspaper clipping* (in Allan Robertson's album at the R. & A. 44): . . . but Mr. Sharp deducted 3 at the high hole by bolting a click shot at 2, while Mr. Fairlie got in at 5 only.
1895 "Calamo Currente" *Half Hours with an Old Golfer* 72: Now Sanders putts, and bolts the hole instead. . . . [*Footnote:*] To bolt the hole is to get it at a good pace with deadly aim.
1911 James Braid *Advanced Golf* 168: What prevents most players from having the courage to bolt these short putts . . .
1930 Bernard Darwin *Second Shots* 47: . . . he also halved the last by bolting a difficult corkscrewy putt.

borrow *v. & n.* [*Origins:* Scottish; there is a similar use of the word in curling="the allowance made for unevenness of ice, other stones to be circumvented, etc." (Sc.N.D.); this and the golfing usage might be a specialized application of the common word *borrow*="take, something with the intention of returning it"; if not, further origin unknown.]

1 *v.intrans.* In putting across a slope, to compensate for the slope by aiming somewhat uphill.

1858 *Unidentified newspaper clipping* (in Allan Robertson's album at the R. & A. 88): Jones also takes his putter, and carefully surveying the 'lie' of the ground, that he may 'borrow' if it be sloping, plays . . .
1890 Lord Wellwood *Badminton Golf* 43: There is an awkward side slope between your ball and the hole, and you must either borrow or put a spin on the ball.
1931 T. Simpson *The Game of Golf* 188: If there are undulations on the green that necessitate "borrowing"—there may be, for instance, a sharp slope from right to left—would anyone complain because he had to aim either to the right or to the left of the hole?

2 *v.trans.* In putting across a slope, to take (compensating direction, ground, or roll) from the slope.

1890 *Baily's Magazine* (May) 310: Once when he followed his ball, as it borrowed a little from the side of the undulating ground, and dribbled gently down, down, down into the hole . . .
1912 Harry Vardon *How to Play Golf* n.p.: I know that I can generally putt better when I have to "borrow" some ground to allow for a slope than when the stroke is perfectly straightforward.
1963 Bob Rosburg *The Putter Book* 58: The downhiller is more susceptible to break because it necessarily is stroked gently and travels slowly most of the way to the hole. So plan to "borrow" a bit more roll.

3 *n.* The degree of uphill compensation required for a putt across a slope.

1862 Robert Chambers *A Few Rambling Remarks on Golf* 25: You observe possibly that it slopes a little; in that case a 'borrow' is required up the slant, and that borrow you must make.
1913 Bernard Darwin *Country Life* (Nov. 29) 759: . . . the player who does not put his approach shots very near the hole will be constantly calculating the "borrow" of entertaining undulations.
1962 Sam Snead *The Education of a Golfer* 140: I needed a 12-foot sidehill putt across a left-to-right slope for a birdie deuce. It was a question of how much "borrow" I needed to compensate for the curve, or break, of the ball.

bramble *n.* [*Origin:* from *bramble*= blackberry.] One of the small molded bumps on the surface of some makes of golf ball of the late gutta-percha and early rubber-core periods, intended to give aerodynamic properties similar to those given by dimples.

1902 Horace Hutchinson *Country Life* (Nov. 22) 648: The [Haskell] balls were not as well made at that time as they have since become; for one thing they had not the "bramble" marking.
1916 P.A. Vaile *The New Golf* 233: Well, the pimple, or bramble, has not yet become obsolete, but before many years have gone by we shall find it only in museums and collections.
1968 J.S. Martin *The Curious History of the Golf Ball* 41: Agrippa was the first ball to be given "brambles," bumps like a blackberry's all over it instead of grooves.

brassie or **brassy** *adj. & n.* **1** *adj.* Obsolete. Fitted with a brass sole plate. Applied to various lofted wooden clubs in the 1880s and 1890s.

1881 Robert Forgan *The Golfer's Handbook* 11: The "Brassy Spoon" is a recent invention, and bids fair to be a useful one. Being furnished with a "brass-sole," it is stronger than an ordinary spoon, and may, therefore, be employed in more difficult ground where the Cleek would otherwise be necessary.
1893 J. Stuart Balfour *Golf* (*Spalding's Athletic Library*) 7: WOOD CLUBS . . . Brassy Niblick. Brassy Spoon. Brassy Bulger. *ibid.* 9:

brassie

William Park, c. 1895

Some players have all their [wood] clubs soled in this manner.

2 *n.* A wooden club lofted somewhat more than the driver and less than the spoon, and having a brass sole plate.

1890 Horace Hutchinson *Badminton Golf* 60: But in place of the numerous spoons of a nearly bygone age there has come into very general use a club that is named the 'brassy.' This weapon is shod, or soled, with brass, whereby its wielder is enabled to play off roads and hard lies without injury to the head.

1915 Alexander H. Revell *Pro & Con of Golf* 16: The brassie is a near-driver.

1937 Abe Mitchell *Essentials of Golf* 80: Many players use their brassie off the tee.

3 *n.* Alternate name for the number two wood.

1948 Ben Hogan *Power Golf* 56: Snead, like yours truly, elected to use a brassie off the tee. . . . The brassie has more loft than a driver. It gives you more height.

1967 George Plimpton *The Bogey Man* 119: Brassie and spoon for the two and three woods are fast disappearing.

1970 Dick Schaap *The Masters* 195: "We live about two good brassie shots away from each other," Casper says.

break[1] *v.trans.* To make less than (a specified score).

1915 A.W. Tillinghast *Putting It Over Matthew* (in *Cobble Valley Golf Yarns* 116): Fi-

nally he succeeded in breaking 100 for the double round of the nine holes.

1929 *Golf Illustrated* (May) 21: Everyone seems to want to break 90. The old figure was 100.

1962 Richard Armour *Golf Is a Four-letter Word* 65: I married, had children, and once in a while broke 90.

1970 Dick Schaap *The Masters* 96: For four straight years, Casper has broken par in the first round of the Masters.

break[2] *v.* **1** *v.intrans.* (Of the wrists) to bend back during the swing.

1931 Joyce & Roger Wethered *The Game of Golf* 46: Allow the wrist to break and the strength of the connection is ruined.

1978 Shelby Futch *Golf Magazine* (Oct.) 54: You should attempt to keep the clubface as square as possible at all times, allowing your wrists to break naturally on the longer shots.

2 *v.trans.* To bend (the wrists) back during the swing.

1941 Patty Berg *Golf* 16: So much has been written about "cocking the wrists" that I believe some players are confused as to the real implication of the term. I like to think of this action as a "breaking" or bending of the hands backward to aid hitting potential.

1969 Tom Weiskopf *Go For the Flag* 50: If you study the four pictures, you can see I hardly break my wrists at all.

break[3] *v. & n.* **1** *v.intrans.* To bounce or roll sharply to left or right.

1946 Frank Moran *Golfers' Gallery* 7: But on arriving beside us at the green the ball, instead of running to the right, broke rather badly to the left.

1970 Tony Jacklin *Jacklin* 45: I watched the putt do what it always threatened to do, break quickly near the hole and finish on the right.

2 *n.* Sideways slope on a putting green.

1977 Frank Hannigan *Reader's Digest* (July) 149: It was and is a vicious green. Jones was above the hole and there was a big left-to-right break.

break-club n.   *Obsolete*. An object or obstruction that might break a club.

1744   *Articles & Laws in Playing at Golf* (St. Andrews) (in Clapcott 1935, 21):   4. You are not to remove Stones, Bones, or any Break-club for the sake of playing your Ball, except upon the fair Green.
1824   *Rules of the Thistle Golf Club* 47:   IV. You are not to remove stones, bones, or any break-club, in order to play your ball.
1890   *Badminton Golf* 445:   Break-club.— An obstacle lying near a ball of such a nature as might break a club when striking at the ball.

British ball.   The golf ball as specified by the Royal and Ancient Golf Club of St. Andrews, now used chiefly for amateur play, having a diameter not less than 1.620 inches and a weight not more than 1.620 ounces.

1969   Jack Nicklaus *The Greatest Game of All* 83:   . . . the smaller British ball can be hit appreciably farther than ours.

brogue n.   [*Origin*: Scottish, from Old Scottish *brog*="spike."]   A tool, consisting of an iron prong set in a wooden crosspiece, that was used for ramming boiled feathers into the leather cover of a featherie golf ball.

1743   Thomas Mathison *The Goff* 10:
Crowds urging crowds the forceful
   Brogue impels,
The feathers harden and the Leather
   swells.
1975   Henry Cotton *History of Golf* 19:   Accumulated feather dust in the lungs and the pressure of the 'brogue' on the craftsmen's chests caused havoc with respiratory systems.

bulger n.   A wooden club, especially a driver, with a slightly convex face.

[**1890**   Horace Hutchinson *Badminton Golf* 64:   Henry Lamb . . . His novel driving club, in all other respects similar to others, has a

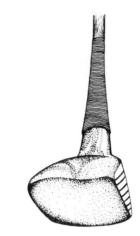

bulger
driver, c. 1885

face which, instead of being a flat surface, bulges out at the centre.]
1907 *Army & Navy Stores Catalogue* 997: Bulgers . . . Brassey Bulgers . . . Bulger Spoon . . . Driver—D A Model, with slightly Bulger Face.
1929   *Spalding's Athletic Library* n.p.: Model 1000. Driver, Brassie or Spoon . . . medium lie, bulger face.

bunker n. & v.   [*Origin*: Scottish, from *bunker*="chest or box," hence also "small deep sandpit in linksland," from Old Scottish *bonker* or *bunker*="chest or box," probably from Scandinavian.]
1   n. A sandpit, or a flattish area of sand, often edged with embankments, on a golf course, defined as a hazard; occurring naturally on old linksland courses, later generally constructed artifically.

1812   *Regulations for the Game of Golf* (St. Andrews) (in Clapcott 1935) 44:   Stones, Bones, or any break-club within a club-length of the Ball may be removed when the Ball lies on grass, but nothing can be removed if it lie on Sand or in a bunker.
1848   William Graham *In Praise of Gutta Percha* (in Clark *Golf: A Royal & Ancient Game* 1875, 204):
   They whirred, and fuffed, and dooked,
      and shied,
   And sklenkit into bunkers.

1857 H.B. Farnie *The Golfer's Manual* 13: The surface is dotted over at frequent intervals with sandy holes, technically called bunkers, from two to six feet deep, of irregular forms and sizes.

1893 John Thomson *The Caddie* (in *Golfing Poems & Songs* 3):

> I can hand the richt club, and gie the richt line,
> And ken ilka whin, cup, and bunker.

1915 Alexander H. Revell *Pro & Con of Golf* 18: The sand in the ordinary bunker today is not kept as level as formerly.

1931 T. Simpson *The Game of Golf* 18: All bunkers should have a rough, broken, uneven edge which gives the effect of coast erosion.

1976 *Rules of Golf* Definition 14.a: A "bunker" is an area of bare ground, often a depression, which is usually covered with sand.

1977 Gordon S. White *New York Times* (June 22): His 2-iron shot went over the green into a bunker.

2 *n.* Obsolete. Any hazard (def. 1).

1893 *Rules of Golf* (in Clark *Golf: A Royal & Ancient Game* repr. 1975, 295): 15. A "hazard" shall be any bunker of whatever nature:—water, sand, loose earth, mole hills, paths, roads or railways, whins, bushes, rabbit scrapes, fences, ditches . . .

1895 James P. Lee *Golf in America* 174: Bunker—A term originally confined, almost exclusively, to a sandpit. Its use is now extended to almost any kind of hazard.

1899 *Golf Illustrated* (Aug. 11) 245: The following is an extract from an article in *The American* . . . "Between the teeing ground and the 'putting green' there are often ponds, trees or walls of earth (bunkers) made to catch balls played on top instead of being struck fairly, or bared places of sand caused by the sod being dug up, which are called 'hazards' . . ."

1929 *Spalding's Athletic Library* 120: Bunker—Generally a rough, hazardous, elevated mound, usually artificial.

1936 Willie Dunn (in H.B. Martin *Fifty Years of American Golf* 34): The place was dotted with Indian burial mounds, and we left some of them intact as bunkers in front of greens.

3 *v.intrans.* Obsolete? To play into a bunker.

1852 *Unidentified newspaper clipping* (in Allan Robertson's album at the R. & A. 52): Driving off at the succeeding one, Dunnie bunkered in the Principal's Nose.

1891 *Golf* magazine (Sept. 18) 13: Approaching the third Sayers bunkered . . .

4 *v.trans.* To play (oneself, or a shot) into a bunker.

1899 *Golf Illustrated* (June 16) 10: . . . he sliced to the right in his drive, bunkered his approach and required six.

1970 Tony Jacklin *Jacklin* 23: . . . I parred the next two, both times bunkering my second shots.

1975 Mark McCormack *Golf Annual* 15: And on 18 he bunkered himself in two, came out and missed his putt.

5 bunkered *adj.* Trapped in a bunker.

1833 George Fullerton Carnegie *The Golfiad* (in *Poems On Golf* 1867, 24):

> Bang goes my ball—it's bunker'd, by the pow'rs.

1897 *Country Life* (May 15) 512: But at the short hole he got bunkered.

1912 Harry Vardon *How to Play Golf* 111: My advice to the bunkered player is—"Don't be greedy; be content to get out."

1946 Frank Moran *Golfers' Gallery* 25: . . . he was bunkered at the thirteenth hole.

1977 John S. Radosta *New York Times* (June 15) A18: Then he slipped to one over at 17, where he was bunkered.

buzzard *n.* [Origin: continuation of the metaphor of *birdie* and *eagle*.] A score of two strokes over par for a hole.

1927 Robert T. Jones, Jr. & W.B. Keeler *Down the Fairway*: And Old Man Par is a patient soul, who never shoots a birdie and never incurs a buzzard.

bye *n.* In match play, the hole or holes remaining if the match is won before the eighteenth hole. **—bye hole.** A hole in the bye.

1892 Andrew Lang et al. *Golfing Papers* 43: . . . lost by six and four on the second round, but he was still able to win the whole four holes of the bye.

1915 A.W. Tillinghast *From the Shoulder* (in *Cobble Valley Golf Yarns* 179): "You may recollect, Volmer, that we haven't played the bye-hole yet."

1929 *Spalding's Athletic Library* 120: *Bye* —any hole or holes that remain after the match is finished. They are played for singly, unless the sides agree to make another match of it.

1957 George Houghton *The Truth About Golf Addicts* 34: For the bye he gave me a stroke a hole and won comfortably.

1976 *Webster's Sports Dictionary* 63: If one contestant has a lead greater than the number of holes left, these bye holes are not played.

C

caddie or **caddy** n. & v. [*Origin:* Scottish, from *caddie* or *cadie* (18th century) = "messenger, errand-boy," from Old Scottish *caddie*, *cadie*, or *caudie* = "army cadet," from French *cadet* = "younger son, army cadet." Several points in this etymology require elucidation. (1) French *cadet:* in the 17th century it was the custom in France for younger sons of noble families to serve in the army as officer-apprentices without commissions; hence *cadet* = "younger son" came to mean also "army cadet," and the word was so borrowed into most European languages. (2) In Old Scottish (17th century) the word became *caudie*, *cadie*, or *caddie*, continuing to mean "cadet, young gentleman serving with an army." (3) In the 18th century there were in Edinburgh and other Scottish towns certain odd-job men and messengers, plying the streets for public hire, who had formed themselves into guilds or societies, apparently with rules, captains, and a convivial life mimicking those of the gentlemen's clubs that were being formed in the same period. For an interesting description, see Smollett *Humphrey Clinker* (1771, repr. 1902, 237–39). The members of these societies, or corporations, of freelance servants, called themselves *caddies*. The precise reason for the name remains obscure; probably many of them were old soldiers, and it may be that they jocularly styled themselves *caddies* meaning "gentlemen freelancers, noncommissioned officers," in distinction from regularly employed private servants. The word thus came to be applied to any man or boy available for hire for odd jobs. (4) Gentlemen golfers had no doubt long employed servants to carry their clubs and assist in other ways. In the late 18th century the golfing societies and clubs began to hire *caddies* for this purpose (see quotations below), and hence the word was perpetuated in the world of golf. (5) The often-repeated story that Mary Queen of Scots introduced the caddie to Scotland is unfounded. She left Scotland forever in 1568 and died in 1587, and *caddie* = "servant" does not appear until the 18th century.]

[*Note on spelling:* the spelling *caddie* is in accordance with traditional Scottish usage, and it remains the strongly preferred form in both British and American golfing writings, including the official publications of the R. & A. and the U.S.G.A. But the spelling *caddy* is also a perfectly correct Scottish form and continues to be used by a respectable minority of golfers.]

1 *n.* A person who carries clubs for a golfer, gives other assistance, and may under the Rules give advice about the game. (A caddie may be a professional employee, a young person working for pocket money, or a friend of a golfer caddying without remuneration.)

1773 *Regulations of the Society of Golfers* (Bruntsfield) (in Clapcott 1935, 23): In order to preserve the holes, no Golfer or Cadie shall be allowed to make any Tee within ten yards of the hole.

1783 *Records of the Honourable Company of Golfers* Nov. 22 (in Clark *Golf: A Royal & Ancient Game* 1875, 55): The Company having collected a small sum for David Lindsay, an old ball-maker and cadie, now very infirm . . .

1823 James Grierson *Delineations of St. Andrews* 224: These persons [ballmakers] are generally great judges of the game of golf, and expert at playing it: and are ready, for a trifling consideration, under the name of *cadies*, to attend any gentleman who chuses to take the amusement.

1858 Delabere P. Blain *Encyclopaedia of Rural Sports* 116: . . . the attendant cad or caddy.

1890 Horace Hutchinson *Badminton Golf* 288: It is your caddie's business to find out how far you can drive with each club.

1915 Alexander H. Revell *Pro & Con of Golf* 58: An army of caddies is employed [in the U.S.], perhaps two hundred thousand . . .

1926 *Golf Illustrated* (Sept.) 11: It has been estimated that two million players invest $80,000,000 annually in caddie service.

1968 Buddy Hackett *The Truth About Golf* 61: Caddies are a dying breed. They are getting scarcer and scarcer while electric carts are getting more and more prevalent.

1970 Tony Jacklin *Jacklin* 48: Willie Hilton, my caddy . . .

1973 *Bartlett's World Golf Encyclopaedia* 272: An interesting feature at Fuji are the excellently trained female caddies, some of the best in the world.

1977 Dave Hill *Teed Off* 49: I learned to love the game as a caddie, and for that reason I'll always feel a strong empathy for the touring caddies.

2 *v.intrans.* To act or work as a caddie.

1892 R. Whyte Gibson (in Andrew Lang *Golfing Papers* 87): Some of the youths of the unique city [St. Andrews] recruit their strength by caddying for a few years.

1908 Arnold Haultain *The Mystery of Golf* (repr. 1965) 113: Willie Dobson learned golf by caddying for a St. Andrews golfer.

1921 Andrew Kirkaldy *Fifty Years of Golf* 15: I was in my fifteenth year, playing golf for a living or caddying when games were hard to get.

1932 Francis Ouimet *A Game of Golf*: Soon I was old enough to caddy.

1964 Tony Lema *Golfer's Gold* 35: I began to caddy when I was twelve.

1977 Oscar Fraley *Golf Magazine* (June) 84: Bob Allan, who totes for Carol Mann, insists he would sooner caddie for a female pro because the male pros are more inclined to blow off steam.

caddie bag or **caddy bag.** A golf bag.

1893 *Spalding's Athletic Library* (May) 33: CADDY BAGS For Carrying Golf Clubs. No. 1 Heavy Tan Waterproof Canvas, Sling-strap, and Leather Bottom and Handle. Each, $4.00.

1915 Alexander H. Revell *Pro & Con of Golf* 29: It is and has been something of a fad among many young golfers to carry from nine to twelve clubs in a big hooded caddie bag, which still has room for a sweater, a pair of shoes, perhaps a suit of underwear, and often a change of linen.

1975 Geoffrey Cousins *Golf in Britain* 4: Caddie bags were not introduced until about 1880.

caddie-car *n.* A golf cart.

1957 George Houghton *The Truth About Golf Addicts* 45: Addicts, like ants, crawl about in tight circles, dragging their caddie-cars as the wee beasties drag their eggs.

1962 *R. & A. Decision on the Rules* (in The *Golfer's Handbook* 1974, 910): In a stroke tournament, A with caddie was playing with his fellow-competitor B, pulling a caddie-car . . .

2 A golf car.

1975 Geoffrey Cousins *Golf in Britain* 103: In the United States the hand type [of trolley] was succeeded by the sophisticated electric caddie-car. . . . This machine is rare in Britain, and when seen is almost always in use by golfers handicapped by age or disability.

caddie cart. A golf cart.

1949 Fred Beck & O.K. Barnes *Seventy-three Years In a Sand Trap* 83: It's no wonder the caddie cart came upon the golf scene. **1979** *Public Notice* at the Old Course, St. Andrews: CADDY CARTS ARE NOT ALLOWED.

caddie master or **caddy master.** An employee of a golf club or course who manages caddies.

1907 Alexander Herd (in Leach, *Great Golfers in the Making* 120): . . . I moved on to Blundellsands [c 1891], where I was a combination of professional and caddie-master— just the kind of job I did not like, particularly the caddie-master. **1915** A.W. Tillinghast *Putting It Over Matthew* (in *Cobble Valley Golf Yarns* 121): Early next morning I was at the club and I passed the word all along the line, beginning with the caddie master . . . **1926** *Golf Illustrated* (Sept.) 11: Charles A. Gordon established schools for both caddie-masters and caddies at Detroit. **1970** Dick Schaap *The Masters* 36: At Augusta, the caddies do not get to pick their golfers. They are assigned by the caddymaster.

Calamity Jane. A putter modeled on *Calamity Jane*, a hickory-shafted blade putter used by Robert T. Jones, Jr.

1950 Gene Sarazen *28 Holes in 100 Strokes* (in Wind *The Complete Golfer* 1954, 189): The one club in my bag I was playing with decisiveness was my putter, a Calamity Jane model.

can n. & v. *Slang, chiefly U.S.* **1** n. The hole.

1962 Sam Snead *The Education of a Golfer* 139: "The only difference in Snead," said Jimmy [Demaret], "is that he's gettin' humpbacked from pickin' balls out of the can."

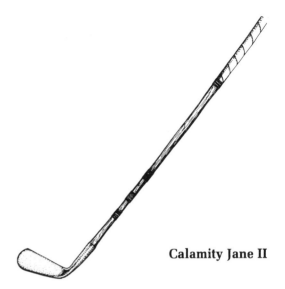

Calamity Jane II

2 *v.trans.* To hole (a ball or putt).

1974 Howard Liss *The Masters* 33: On the third hole he tried a 40-foot putt and canned it.

car n., or **golf car.** A four-wheeled electrically powered vehicle on which golfers drive around courses.

1976 *Bartlett's World Golf Encyclopaedia* 376: The golf car came on the scene about 1960 and since then has grown to be an integral part of the scene. **1977** Art Spander *Golf Digest* (Aug.) 15: Golf cars have become a necessary evil in the second half of the 20th century—in the U.S. Yet, hardly anyone rides in golf cars in Great Britain and Europe. **1977** Robert L. Balfour, letter to *Golf Digest* (Dec.) 7: The number of cars has increased from 80,000 in 1963 to 440,000 today.

card n. & v. **1** n., also **scorecard.** A card on which scores are recorded in stroke play.

1824 *Rules of the Thistle Golf Club* 45: On comparing these cards, he who shall be found to have made the ten holes in the fewest strokes, to be declared the gainer of the Medal. **1976** *Rules of Golf* 38.1: On completion of the round the marker shall sign the card and hand it to the competitor.

2 *n.* A stroke score recorded on a card.

1899 Price Collier *The Outing* (Jan.) 424: Even the professionals who took part in the open tournament handed in cards far better than these.
1946 Frank Moran *Golfers' Gallery* 19: Jones jumped right off in the Championship race with a card of 68.

3 *v.trans.* To make and record (a stroke score).

1928 Lucille McAllister *Golf Illustrated* (July) 24: Miss Orcutt carded an 84.
1977 *New York Times* (May 20) A23: Jim Albus . . . carded a five-under-par 65 today at Garden City Country Club.

car path or **cart path.** *Chiefly U.S.* A hard-paved road or track on a golf course for golf cars.

1977 Art Spander *Golf Digest* (Aug.) 15: Car paths at Pebble Beach? . . . I'd like to plough up all the car paths and destroy all the golf cars.
1978 Gordon S. White *New York Times* (Aug. 5) 13: . . . Miss Daniel's high drive bounced on a paved cart path and the ball flew away into heavy trees.

carpet *n.* *Slang, chiefly U.S.* **1** The fairway.

1929 A.W. Tillinghast *Golf Illustrated* (June) 43: As usual off the carpet on either side will find fairly exacting rough but not poisonous.

2 The putting green.

1956 Herbert Warren Wind *The Story of American Golf* 163: . . . punching a recovery shot through the brambles and onto the carpet.
1963 Bob Rosburg *The Putter Book* 157: If you're a pretty fair putter right now, and already averaging about 33 strokes on the carpets . . .

carry[1] *v.intrans.* To carry clubs; serve as a caddie.

1890 A.J. Balfour *Badminton Golf* 428: . . . that Long Willie was a most invaluable caddie, that he could drive ever so much further when he had Long Willie to carry for him.
1907 Robert Ferguson (in Leach *Great Golfers in the Making* 188): In later years I had the honour of carrying to most of the prominent players who came to Musselburgh.
1933 John Ressich *Thir Braw Days* 33: It cam' oot efter, that they'd been tryin' tae get some o' the lads tae cairry for them.
1936 H.B. Martin *Fifty Years of American Golf* 228: [Joe Horgan] received a tip of $250 that year, as he had also carried for Dexter Cummings . . . when he won the intercollegiate championship.

carry[2] *v. & n.* **1** *v.trans.* To play clear over (a hazard or obstacle).

1890 H.S.C. Everard *Badminton Golf* 335: . . . long drivers now frequently carry the whole lot of bunkers.
1899 Willie Tucker *The Outing* (Aug.) 523: Holabird took his brassey for his second and made a beautiful shot of 170, carrying the bunker onto the green.
1908 W.W. Tulloch *Life of Tom Morris* 10: With what wile and cunning he would, of purpose, heel or draw a ball with the object of getting round a hazard, which he thought it too great a risk to attempt to carry.
1921 Andrew Kirkaldy *Fifty Years of Golf* 38: He carried the road against a wind from the back tee at the last hole.
1962 Sam Snead *The Education of a Golfer* 33: It was a hazard nobody had ever carried, though a lot had tried.

2 *n.* Clear flight of a ball before pitching.

1895 "Calamo Currente" *Half Hours with an Old Golfer* 70: "It's a' carry an' ye mauna rin . . ."
1910 Walter J. Travis *The American Golfer* (Mar.): In a direct line to the hole it meant a carry of 180 yards to clear the "Sahara."
1950 Anthony F. Merrill *The Golf Course Guide* 121: The 130-yd. Second is a full carry over salt water.
1977 Johnny Miller *Golf Magazine* (July) 42: . . . 222 yards of pure carry to a plateau green that is flanked with cavernous traps.

cart
The Play Day cart, 1979

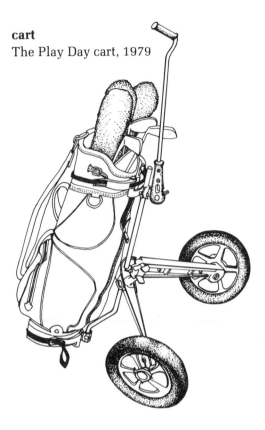

cart n., or **golf cart.** **1** A two-wheeled trolley on which a golf bag can be fitted and pulled around a course. Some are electrically powered.

1976 *Bartlett's World Golf Encyclopaedia* 378: Carts are those two-wheeled carriers with handle which you use to pull your bag around the course instead of lugging it on your shoulder.
1977 Advertisement *Golf Illustrated* (Summer) 7: Bag Boy puts the walking back in golf. . . . The toughest golf cart you can buy.

2 A golf car.

1968 Buddy Hackett *The Truth About Golf* 26: You can even cut the walking and take a cart if you want.
1971 Tommy Bolt *The Hole Truth* 129: How does it feel to ride in an electric cart? I have never used one in my life. I never will.
1978 Frank Tatum *Golf Magazine* (Oct.) 85: Golf carts are an intrusion into the environment of the game.

cart path. See **car path.**

casual water. Standing water on the course that is not part of a water hazard, and from which unpenalized relief is allowed under the rules.

1890 Horace Hutchinson *Badminton Golf* 250: . . . it often happens that after a shower of rain there will be left what is termed 'casual water' on the links—puddles of rainwater not contemplated in the rules.
1929 W.H. Faust *Golf Illustrated* (Apr.) 25: Casual water in a hazard is not the same thing as casual water on the fairway or green.
1976 *Rules of Golf* Definition 8: "Casual water" is any temporary accumulation of water which is visible before or after the player takes his stance and which is not a hazard of itself or is not in a water hazard.

center-shafted [U.S.] or **centre-shafted** [Brit.] *adj.* (Of a club) having the shaft joined to the head some distance in from the back of the heel, a feature that is banned by the rules except for putters (and was banned for putters also by the R. & A. from 1909 to 1952).

1907 *Army & Navy Stores Catalogue* 1000: Mill's Centre Shafted Putter . . . American pattern, as used by Mr. W.J. Travis.
1916 P.A. Vaile *The New Golf* 225: In the "Vaile" putter I have carried the center-shafted principle to the full length.

center-shafted
brass-headed P.G.A. model

1936 H.B. Martin *Fifty Years of American Golf* 128: ...it came under the head of center-shafted clubs, a menace that threatened the art of club-making for a while.

1953 Ben Hogan *Saturday Evening Post* (Oct. 17): ...the British agreed to permit use of the center-shafted putter after having banned it for many years.

charge *v. & n.* **1** *v.trans.* To play (a putt), or putt for (the hole), with a boldly or recklessly strong stroke.

1962 Sam Snead *The Education of a Golfer* 116: He had about an 18-foot putt, me a 25-footer. Hogan didn't like the looks of his putt. Seeing that, I decided to "charge" the cup—play it boldly and add pressure, if possible.

1969 Tom Scott & Geoffrey Cousins *The Golf Immortals* 152: Locke had a putt of no more than a foot to square the match. He "charged it," to use an old golfing expression —and missed.

1977 *Woman Golfer* (Nov.) 28: She charged a 25-footer and it ran two feet past the hole.

2 *v.trans.* To play (a course) aggressively and successfully.

1977 *New York Times* (July 8) A13: ... posted six-under-par 65's...The three charged the 6,620-yard, par-71 Oakwood Country Club course ...

3 *n.* A dramatic surge of superior play, especially by a player who has been trailing.

1970 Tony Jacklin *Jacklin* 114: There are players like Palmer who like to make a charge from behind but I like to lead.

1978 Dick Osgood *Springfield (Mass.) Republican* (Aug. 13) D1: Mahaffey, who made his charge with four straight birdies ...

4 *v.intrans.* To put on a dramatic surge of superior play, especially from a trailing position.

1962 Sam Snead *The Education of a Golfer* 48: Most of my wins have come from charging up from behind—by never quitting.

1970 Dick Schaap *The Masters* 209: Pumped up, and charging, Gene Littler rifles a two-iron to the fifteenth green.

1977 Gordon S. White, Jr. *New York Times*

(July 25) 14: JoAnne Carner, the defending champion, seemed ready to charge as she posted a birdie at the third hole. But she fell victim to two bogeys.

chili-dip *or* **chilly-dip** *v.intrans.* *U.S. slang.* [Origin; possibly refers to the feeble scooping motion of picking up some *chili dip* (Mexican or southwestern hors d'oeuvre) on a piece of taco.] To mishit (a shot) by hitting the ground before the ball, producing a very weak lofted shot.

1967 George Plimpton *The Bogey Man* 118: I asked about "chilly-dipping," just to be certain, and they said it meant a flub.

1977 Dave Hill & Nick Seitz *Teed Off* 43: If you miss a green and have to pitch the ball from a tight lie you always have to worry about catching the ball thin and sculling it or chili-dipping it short.

chip *n. & v.* **1** *n.,* *also* **chip shot.** A short, moderately lofted approach shot with little backspin.

1913 Henry Leach (in H. B. Martin *Golf Yarns* 59): "I absurdly fluffed a little chip onto the green from the woolly grass along the side with a niblick."

1931 Roger Wethered *The Game of Golf* 72: But the chip shot, as a distinct species of shot in itself, never quite reached its present prominence until Walter Hagen illustrated the merit of good approaching.

1969 Tom Weiskopf *Go For the Flag* 52: A chip is a low shot that runs on the green toward the hole.

2 *v.intrans. & trans.* To hit a chip shot.

1910 Jerome D. Travers & Grantland Rice *The Winning Shot* 23: But he chipped up dead within a foot of the cup.

1928 Roland Hancock *Golf Illustrated* (Aug.) 16: I chipped through the trees out to the fairway.

1976 J. C. Jessop *Golf* 58: ...the ball is "chipped" or pitched on to the green with just sufficient run to reach the hole.

1977 Hubert Green *Golf Magazine* (July) 36: I chip essentially the same way I hit full shots.

chip-and-run n. & v. **1** n., or **chip-and-run shot.** A chip shot, including its run after landing.

1962 Sam Snead *The Education of a Golfer* 210: When chipping within a few unobstructed feet of the putting surface, with a roll-up to the cup wanted (the chip-and-run shot)—the 5- or 6-iron.

2 *v.intrans.* To make a chip-and-run shot.

1977 *New York Times* (Sept. 3) 11: "I can chip-and-run pretty good," he said.

chip in *phr.v.* & **chip-in** n. **1** *phr.v.* To hole out with a chip shot.

1977 *New York Post* (June 10) 85: He one-putted 10 times, once chipped in for an eagle three . . .

2 n. A chip shot that holes out.

1977 *New York Times* (Sept. 24) 12: Miss Austin had six birdies—including a 60-foot chip-in.

chipper n. **1** A club used for chip shots.

1957 George Houghton *The Truth About Golf Addicts* 108: Many addicts, realizing the truth in my foregoing remarks, carry a special club which they affectionately call their 'chipper,' usually an ancient mashie— the shaft has been shortened—and with this faithful friend the proficient addict plays an easy half shot up to the hole.
1977 George Peper *Scrambling Golf* 110: The mid and short irons (and all those "chipper" clubs sold today) . . .

2 A player rated as to his or her chipping abilities.

1978 Shelby Futch *Golf Magazine* (Oct.) 54: You must be a good chipper if you are to break 85.

choke[1] v. [Origin: borrowed from baseball.] *chiefly U.S.* **1** *v.trans.* To shorten the swinging length of (a club) by gripping it farther down than usual.

chipper
c. 1935

1950 Sam Snead *How to Hit a Golf Ball* 18: You probably will find you need to choke the club slightly, but don't fall into the mistake of the baseball swing.

2 choke down on *phr.v.* Same as def. 1.

1962 Sam Snead *The Education of a Golfer* 160: I choked down on the club, to make sure I stayed down to the ball throughout the swing.
1970 Tony Jacklin *Jacklin* 22: . . . from the rough I choked down on a somewhat lucky seven iron and the ball finished only two feet away.
1977 Davis Love *Golf Digest* (July) 47: So you must stand closer to the ball, bend more at the waist and choke down on the club.

3 choke up on *phr.v.* Same as def. 1.

1963 Arnold Palmer *My Game and Yours* 81: I used a 5-iron, choking up on it, punched the ball out through the trees . . .
1977 George Peper *Scrambling Golf* 38: Begin by addressing the ball at its own height, whether it's an inch or a foot off the ground. This means choking up on your club.

choke[2] v. & n. [Origin: in general U.S. sports usage, including baseball, basketball, tennis, from about the 1940s; refers to the psychosomatic drying up of saliva and inability to swallow, sometimes leading to actual throat spasms.] *U.S.* **1** *v.intrans.* To suffer an onset of nervousness while playing.

1970 Dick Schaap *The Masters* 94: Chi Chi Rodriguez . . . admits that, despite his antics

and his wisecracks, he was nervous on the course. "If this was any other tournament but the Masters," says Chi Chi, "I'd have shot a 66. But I was choking out there."
1975 Dan Jenkins *Dead Solid Perfect* 215: I think I'm choking on the Open lead.

2 *n.* An onset of nervousness during play.

1967 Dave Marr in George Plimpton *The Bogey Man* 194: "Sometimes a particular hole will cause a choke—a choke hole.... Like the 18th at Cypress. It's like walking into a certain room in a big dark house when you were a kid—you get this fear that hits you."
1977 Dave Hill & Nick Seitz *Teed Off* 53: We even kid about "Chester Choke" grabbing me under pressure.

cleek *n.* [*Origin:* Scottish, from *cleek* = "hook, crook, walking stick with a hook," from Old Scottish *cleke, cleik,* or *cleek* = "metal hook"; related to *clutch.* (In the 19th century it was sometimes also spelled *click,* and so associated with the sound of the impact of club on ball; but this was not the origin of the word.)]
1 Any of numerous narrow-bladed iron clubs, variously adapted and used for playing long shots through the green, for playing from sand and rough, for approaching, and for putting. The basic characteristics of cleeks were that they were narrow-bladed and relatively light.

1842 *Chambers' Edinburgh Journal* (Oct. 8) 298: For this he takes a short club not yet adverted to, called the *cleek,* the striking part of which consists of a thick slip of smooth iron, with its face inclined at an angle of forty-five degrees backward.
1851 *Unidentified newspaper clipping* (in Allan Robertson's album at the R. & A. 40): ... the ball rolling back among sand, out of which he played it with his click into *hell* [bunker].
1857 H.B. Farnie *The Golfer's Manual* 20: The cleek or click, deriving its name either from an old Scotch word signifying "hook," or from the sharp clicking sound produced in making the stroke, is also an iron club, but lighter than either of the others. It is used chiefly for driving the ball out of rough

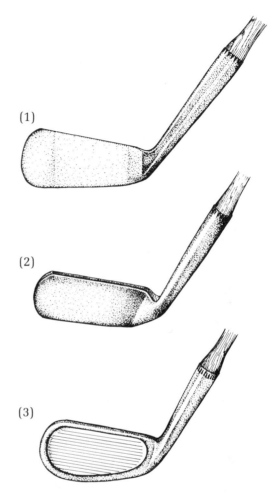

(1)

(2)

(3)

cleek
(1) ordinary cleek, c. 1875
(2) putting cleek, R.W. Kirk, Liverpool (1845–86)
(3) "Cran" cleek with wood face inset, 1897

ground when elevation is not such an object, and when no impediments surround and obstruct the *lie* which would demand an heavier club.
1858 *Unidentified newspaper clipping* (in Allan Robertson's album at the R. & A. 88): ... but he is 'good at the cleek,' so he takes that little straight-faced iron-headed tool, and, by a beautifully played shot, and admi-

rable strength, 'lofts' his ball over the bunker.
1867 "R.C." *The Second or Cartgate Hole* in
Poems on Golf 49:

But see, one glorious cleek-stroke from
 the sand
Sends Tyro home . . .

1875 Robert Clark *Golf, A Royal & Ancient
Game* 270: He [Allan Robertson] it was that
introduced the deadly use of the cleek in
playing up to the hole. [Before 1848 it was
the baffing spoon or short spoon.] But Allan
employed the cleek to jerk up his ball.

1881 Robert Forgan *The Golfer's Handbook*
14: There are three varieties of clubs known
by this rather expressive name. 1. The ordinary "Cleek" is ubiquitously useful. In very
bad lies throughout the green, in cups and
ruts, in open whins and sand, wherever the
player desires to extricate his ball and get distance at the same time. . . . The handle is
much shorter than that of the Driver . . . the
head . . . is sloped in the face like a Spoon to
enable it to elevate the ball. 2. The "Driving
Cleek" differs from the ordinary Cleek chiefly
in respect of the handle, which is somewhat
longer. . . . Many players employ this club for
the three-quarters stroke, finding it more
steady and reliable than the Middle Spoon.
. . . 3. The "Putting Cleek" is a club which
few good players use, and is only mentioned
here to be condemned. Its head is almost perpendicular in the face, but in all other respects it resembles the Driving Cleek.

1890 Horace Hutchinson *Badminton Golf*
64: There are long cleeks and short cleeks,
driving cleeks, lofting cleeks, and putting
cleeks.

1903 Harold Hilton *The Outing* (April) 125:
The driving mashie superseded the cleek.
. . . Certainly the cleek still survives, but its
outward appearance is little in keeping with
the weapon of old, as its head is short, and its
face narrow.

1907 *Army & Navy Stores Catalogue* 998:
Special Approaching Cleek or "Jigger" . . .
CLEEKS. Ordinary Driving Cleek . . . Bev-
elled Edged Driving Cleek . . . Plaid-Backed
Putting Cleek . . . Concentrated Driving Cleek
. . . Round-backed Cleek . . . Diamond-backed
Cleek.

1915 Alexander H. Revell *Pro & Con of Golf*
15: If the shot is one that calls for accuracy
in direction, I prefer to use the cleek or driving iron rather than the brassie.

1916 P.A. Vaile *The New Golf* 313:

"Cleek" is a word nearly as holy as "Golf." It
sounds almost like blasphemy to say it but
the cleek is moribund. . . . Dealers in America
cannot now sell them. Soon the shallow-
faced club will be dead here and later in other
golfing lands. It is a difficult and dangerous
club.

1928 A.T. Packard *Golf Illustrated* (Nov.)
17: The diameter of the hitting spot length-
wise of the face on the cleek remains so narrow as to class the club as one for experts; too
difficult for the average player. And right
there is the reason why the very name of the
cleek is becoming a memory.

2 Alternate name for the number one
iron.

1972 *Encyclopaedia Britannica* 10:557:
Irons—Number One (Driving iron or
cleek) . . .

3 A lofted wooden club, similar to the
spoon but shallower-faced.

1912 Harry Vardon *How to Play Golf* 85:
Of late there has come into vogue a club
called the wooden cleek, which is helpful to
the bad golfer because it has a deeper and
broader face than the iron-headed cleek.

1931 Bernard Darwin *The Game of Golf*
139: . . . the middle-aged golfer should
make a friend of the spoon or the wooden
cleek.

4 Alternate name for the number four
wood.

1977 George Peper *Scrambling Golf* 31:
With favorable lies and wide-open holes the
golfer with average power can use the 4-wood
for shots of anywhere from 175 yards up—
which makes the old cleek a pretty versatile
club.

cleekmaker n. A hand-maker of iron
clubs.

1979 Ian T. Henderson & David I. Stirk *Golf
in the Making* 169: By tradition the iron
clubmakers are called cleekmakers.

click n. & v. **1** n. The sound and the satisfying sensation of a hard and resilient
golf ball well hit.

1897 "Albion" *The Outing* (June) 249: East, West, North and South the click of the golfer's club and the sound of the air-cleaving ball may be heard.

1901 Horace Hutchinson *Country Life* (Nov. 2) 552: [Trying out the first Haskell rubber-cores] One misses the sharp click of the "gutty" ball on the club.

1905 Mr. Justice Buckley (in Henderson & Stirk *Golf in the Making* 59): . . . he could not sell it [an early rubber-wound ball] commercially; it had no click, and, according to the sentiment of the day, golf without a click was not golf, but a waste of time.

1919 Robert K. Risk *Songs of the Links* 16:
Can't you hear the click of your putt,
    dear lass,
That tells you have struck it true?

1926 Advertisement *Golf Illustrated* (June) 57: A sweet sounding CLICK and like a rifle bullet it's off into the blue.

1941 Patty Berg *Golf* 36: There is a certain "click" associated with a well-hit iron shot that will come to be music to your ears.

1975 Henry Cotton *History of Golf* 214: [the new solid ball] gives a most satisfying click off the club face, which all golfers enjoy, particularly on the putting green.

club

(1) three-wood, Ben Hogan, 1979
(2) four-iron, Walter Hagen, 1979

2 *v.intrans.* To come suddenly into top form.

1936 H.B. Martin *Fifty Years of American Golf* 208: The next two starts availed her nothing, despite some excellent and even sensational golf, but in 1922 her game began to click.

1964 Tony Lema *Golfer's Gold* 163: By this time I had begun to click on the tour. In 1962 I had . . . made a total of $48,000.

club *n. & v.* **1** *n.*, or **golf club.** Any of the various implements used in golf to strike the ball, consisting essentially of a thin shaft with a grip for holding it and a clubhead of wood or iron.

1503–4 *Accounts of the Lords High Treasurers of Scotland* (Feb. 3): Item to golf Clubbis and Ballis to the King that he playit with . . . xlij *s.* [= 42 shillings].

1638 Henry Adamson *The Muses' Threnodie* (in *Badminton Golf* 1890, 21):
And ye, my clubs, you must no more
    prepare
To make your balls fly whistling in the
    air.

(1)

(2)

1743 Thomas Mathison *The Goff* 21:
His trusty club *Pygmalion* dauntless
    plies;
The ball ambitious cleaves the lofty
    skies.
1779 Hugo Arnot *History of Edinburgh*
361: This they strike with a slender and
elastic club, of about four feet long, crooked
in the head, and having lead run into it, to
make it heavy.
1872 John Henry Walsh *British Rural Sports*
636: Every golfer has a variety of clubs dif-
ferently formed, and adapted for playing in
different situations of the ball, and in different stages of the game.
1915 Alexander H. Revell *Pro & Con of Golf*
5: As to the five clubs I have mentioned, the
cost of them will be about ten dollars.
1975 Henry Cotton *History of Golf* 20: The
oldest known set of clubs (probably early seventeenth century) can be seen in the clubhouse at Troon.
1976 *Rules of Golf* 2.a.: The golf club shall
be composed of a shaft and a head, and all of
the various parts shall be fixed so that the
club is one unit.... The club shall not be
substantially different from the traditional
and customary form and make, and shall con-
form with the regulations governing the design of clubs at Appendix II.

2 *n.* *Obsolete.* A wooden club.

1850 *Unidentified newspaper clipping* (in
Allan Robertson's album at the R. & A. 39):
... a number of the young lads, who cannot
use properly the ordinary club, using an iron
one, and thus inflicting a cut on the green at
every stroke.
1887 Sir Walter Simpson *The Art of Golf*
10: D. can drive as far with a cleek as common men with a club.
1908 Tom Morris (in W.W. Tulloch *Life of
Tom Morris* 11): "An awfu' player, Allan
[Robertson], the cunningest bit body of a
player that ever handled club, cleek, or
putter."

3 *n.* Hitting power or distance, reckoned by the numbered clubs of the standard modern set.

1953 Ben Hogan *Saturday Evening Post*
(Oct. 17): If I picked a No. 5 iron, for example, and the shot was short, I might comment
that I should have taken more club.
1969 Jack Nicklaus *The Greatest Game of*

All 226: I settled on a 5-iron. ... I made my
allowance more or less this way: one club less
for the small ball; one and a half clubs less for
the following wind; one club less for the run
on the ground ... ; and a half a club less for
the extra distance you get when you're
charged up.

4 *v.trans.* (Of a caddie) to select a particular club for (a player).

1962 Sam Snead *The Education of a Golfer*
124: The next hole he clubbed me with a 5-
iron.

clubface. See **face**[1].

clubhead. See **head.**

club-length *n., formerly* **club's length.**
The length of a club, used traditionally
as a measure of distance on the course
for various purposes.

1743 Thomas Mathison *The Goff* 21:
Answ'ring its master's just designs, it
    hastes,
And from the hole scarce twice two
    clubs' length rests.
1744 *Articles & Laws in Playing at Golf* 1:
You must Tee your Ball, within a Club's
length of the Hole.
1950 Dai Rees *Golf My Way* 15: ... the left
knee should be rather less than a clublength
behind the ball.
1976 *Rules of Golf* Definition 33: The
"teeing ground" ... is a rectangular area two
club-lengths in depth. ... Rule 21.3.b.: ...
the ball shall be placed ... not more than two
club-lengths from the original lie.

clubmaker *n.* A maker of golf clubs.

1603 James VI *Letter* (April 4) (in J.C. Irons
Leith and Its Antiquities 1897, 402): William Mayne bower, burgess of Edinburgh ...
[to be] during all the days of his lyf-time,
master fledger, bower, club-maker, and spier-
maker to his Hieness.
1735 Anon *Letter* (in Henderson & Stirk
Golf in the Making 1979, 93): Will you take

the trouble any forenoon or afternoon you are at leisure to take a walk to Bruntisfield Links and call at Andrew Bailey's clubmaker.
1833 George Fullerton Carnegie *The First Hole At St. Andrews* in *Golfiana* 11:
Here, Mr. Philp, club-maker, is as great
    As Philip—as any Minister of State!
1897 Price Collier *The Outing* (April) 98: . . . we could supply our own professionals and clubmakers, instead of importing them.
1907 Willie Auchterlonie (in Leach *Great Golfers in the Making* 222): . . . I went to work with Messrs. Forgan & Son here, and I served my apprenticeship of four years as a clubmaker with them.
1911 James Braid *Advanced Golf* 292: Because of my being a clubmaker, I was now, of course, a professional.
1919 Robert K. Risk *Songs of the Links* 13:
Myself when young did eagerly frequent
Club-makers' shops, and heard great argument
Of Grip and Stance and Swing . . .
1936 H.B. Martin *Fifty Years of American Golf* 185: In 1906 the author recalls a clubmaker who had turned out two fine looking woods, a driver and a brassie, and insisted that he should have $2 each instead of the old special price of $1.75.
1977 *New York Times* (Aug. 10) A16: . . . one of the three men in Texas and 40 in the nation who consider themselves master clubmakers.

clubshaft. *See* **shaft.**

cock *v. & n.* **1** *v.trans. & intrans.* To bend (the wrists) backward in the backswing.

1934 Anon. *From 102 to 82* 18: At top of swing left arm straight with wrists cocked back.
1946 Percy Boomer *On Learning Golf* 85: "Do I have to 'cock my wrists' on the back swing?" "No, you do not! The wrists cock themselves."
1969 Jack Nicklaus *The Greatest Game of All* 257: On the backswing you don't restrain your wrists from cocking; but you don't make a definite move to cock them.

2 *n.* The bending of the wrists backward in the backswing.

1947 Jim Dante & Leo Diegel *The Nine Bad Shots of Golf* 28: This bending is called a "break" or a "cock."
1978 Shelby Futch *Golf Magazine* (Oct.) 55: There is very little if any wrist cock.

collar *n.* Apron.

1978 Denis J. Harington *Golf Score* (Oct./Nov.) 53: . . . caught a bunker short of the green and became buried near the front collar.

come back *phr.v.* To play a putt after having putted past the hole.

1928 A. Linde Fowler *Golf Illustrated* (Oct.) 40: . . . he missed the putt coming back and lost the hole.
1969 Paul D. Peery *Billy Casper, Winner* 63: He shot past the hole, and had trouble when he came back.

come out *phr.v.* To play out of a bunker.

1977 *New York Times* (Aug. 12) A19: . . . he came out of a bunker to 35 feet from the hole.

common club. *Obsolete.* Driver (def. 1).

1790 *Hoyle's Games* 288: . . . there are six Sorts used by good players; namely, the Common Club, used when the ball lies on good ground . . .
1823 James Grierson *Delineations of St. Andrews:* A set consists of four at least, viz. the common or play club . . .

compression *n.* The degree of resilience of a golf ball.

1929 *Spalding's Athletic Library* n.p.: An extremely tight-wound center is known as a high-power, or high compression, center.
1977 Dave Hill & Nick Seitz *Teed Off* 185: Essentially the ball's compression is its hardness. The higher the compression, the harder the ball—the less it will compress. The usual compressions are 80, 90, and 100. I play a high compression ball. . . . Most average

players would be better off with a low compression ball.

concede v.trans. To grant one's opponent (a match, hole, or final putt) that has not been completed; especially, to grant (a short putt) to have been made without physically being holed out.

1890 Horace Hutchinson *Badminton Golf* 253: . . . it may put him in a dilemma between conceding you a stroke which he does not consider an absolute certainty . . .
1915 Tom Ball (in Revell *Pro & Con of Golf* 74): ". . . if you happen to oppose a man who agree with the recommendation in the rules that players should not concede putts to their rivals."
1931 Henry Cotton *Golf* 67: A good deal of recrimination would be saved if every young player made up his mind that he would not concede any putts at all.
1961 R. & A. *Decisions on the Rules* (in *The Golfer's Handbook* 912): A player is entitled to concede a hole or match at any time.
1976 *Rules of Golf* 35.2.d.: If the opponent's next stroke has not been conceded, the opponent shall play without delay in correct order.

cop n., *also* **cop bunker**. [*Origin:* from English dialect *cop* = "hillock, top of a hill."] *Obsolete.* A knoll or bank regarded as a hazard or obstacle.

1887 Sir Walter Simpson *The Art of Golf* 20: Walls, roads, ditches and cops serve as hazards on the course, but these are not recognized as so desirable as bunkers.
1898 John Reid *The Outing* (July) 401: There is nothing on the way to penalize bad play excepting some rough cops about forty yards from the tee.
1902 *Golf Illustrated* (Aug.) 148: The green is guarded on three sides by a bunker and cop . . .
1914 J.H. Taylor *Country Life* (Jan. 17) 103: . . . it got into the narrow cop bunker that runs parallel to the course.
1926 Percy Fridenberg *Golf Illustrated* (Dec.) 14: . . . a ball sitting almost teed up in front of a looming cop bunker.

couple n. Two players playing together in a stroke competition.

1869 Charles MacArthur *The Golfer's Annual* (1869–70) 118: Thirty couples started to compete for the Silver Cross and the Bombay Medal.
1890 Horace Hutchinson *Badminton Golf* 261: It is not the slightest use passing one couple, to be immediately kept back as badly as ever by the couple again in front.
1911 James Braid *Advanced Golf* 306: . . . it would not generally be regarded as in a man's favour that he was drawn to play as one of the last couples going out.
1926 Lucille MacAllister *Golf Illustrated* (Sept.) 29: There was a large entry of about seventy-five couples.
1946 Frank Moran *Golfers' Gallery* 47: He was one of the second couple off the tee.
1974 *The Golfer's Handbook* 87. In stroke play, two players competing together are a "COUPLE."

course n. **1** *also* **driving course.** *Obsolete.* The area of an old natural links where the grass was relatively short and free of whins and hazards; the part corresponding to the modern fairway, or the sequence of fairways regarded as a continuous route or zone.

1823 James Grierson *Delineations of St. Andrews* 218: The track along which the players proceed is denominated the course, and may be either rectilinear, or a figure of any number of sides.
1829 *Rules* (St. Andrews) (in Clapcott 1935, 60): IV. . . . no other loose impediment, such as turf, bent, whins, or anything whatever can be removed on the driving course.
1857 H.B. Farnie *The Golfer's Manual* 13: Still the theatre of our scientific pastime is by no means a Bowling-green; the course proper alone has this appearance. On each side bristle all kinds of furzy horrors. . . . The course on a good Links is not wider, on an average, than thirty to sixty yards.
1868 George Robb *Manual of the Bruntsfield Links Allied Golfing Club* 7: . . . with the above surplus of, say, £20, we could afford to have . . . a golfing course of twenty yards wide round the whole Green cut with the scythe; thus making a pleasant Green for all, and affording an opportunity to good

players to show their skill by keeping on this course.

1887 Charles Chambers *Golfing* 92: Course, that portion of the Links on which the game ought to be played, generally bounded on either side by rough ground or other hazard.
1914 J.H. Taylor *Country Life* (Jan. 17) 103: . . . the narrow cop bunker that runs parallel to the course.

2 *or* **golf course.** A tract of land laid out for golf, now usually occupying from 50 to 300 acres, having fixed boundaries, and comprising nine or eighteen holes, or more.

1862 Robert Chambers *A Few Rambling Remarks on Golf* 32: St. Andrews has ever held the palm over all other golfing-courses, and maintains in consequence more professional men than any other.
1893 John Thomson *Glasgow* (in *Golfing Poems & Songs* 10):
Some think our course is easy, wi'
hazards nane ava' . . .
1901 *Country Life* (Mar. 30) 410: Mr. Norman Hunter's beating of Mr. S.H. Fry on his home course, mid-Surrey . . .
1952 Henry Cotton *History of Golf in Britain*: . . . in 1896 there were only sixty-one courses in Scotland and forty-six in England.
1976 *Rules of Golf* Definition 11: The "course" is the whole area within which play is permitted.
1977 Charles Price *Golf Magazine* (June) 36: By the records of the National Golf Foundation, there are 12,000 golf courses in the United States.

crack[1] *n. & adj.* First-class or champion (player).

1853 *Goulburn Herald* (July 6): Mr. R. is the brother of Mr. Allan Robertson, one of the crack if not the crack player in Scotland of that manly game—golf.
1891 *Golf* magazine (Feb. 20) 365: The latest improver of putting-cleeks is Mr. A.M. Ross, the well-known crack of the Edinburgh Burgess Club.
1908 W.W. Tulloch *Life of Tom Morris* 17: He is the friend of new and mighty cracks, who are worthily carrying on the traditions of

the game—Vardon and Taylor, Braid and Herd.
1921 Andrew Kirkaldy *Fifty Years of Golf* 120: . . . I have seen all the cracks and beaten most of them at odd times.
1946 Percy Boomer *On Learning Golf* 36: All crack players feel that they swing from in-to-out when driving.
1961 Eric Brown *Knave of Clubs* 50: If I was to be beaten, being beaten by this crack golfer would do me the world of good and I would surely learn a great deal from him.

crack[2] *v. intrans.* To suffer a sudden collapse of good play, typically under pressure.

1890 Horace Hutchinson *Badminton Golf* 218: The excitement grows constantly; they are passing through the crucial test. Then one or the other, in the expressive golfing parlance, 'cracks.' He plays badly, just because it is the moment at which he most wants to play his best.
1907 Harold Hilton *My Golfing Reminiscences* 70: It was the only time I ever played against Freddie Tait in which he may be said to have in any way cracked, and he certainly did crack when playing those last two holes.
1946 Frank Moran *Golfers' Gallery* 9: On his form up to that point it looked as if nobody else could take the title, but over those four holes Kirkwood cracked and including a 7 at the short seventeenth they actually averaged two over 5's.
1962 Sam Snead *The Education of a Golfer* 110: He had cracked, and one big reason for it was that after I knew the truth about him, my own tension disappeared and I began shooting my best offensive golf.
1977 *New York Times* (July 25) 13: Hollis Stacy, who failed to crack under pressure today, contrary to what many had expected, played a strong and steady game.

croquet *n. or attributive.* Used with reference to a putting stance astride the line of putt, or to a putter held to resemble a croquet mallet.

1963 Bob Rosburg *The Putter Book* 23: Bob Duden from Portland, Oregon, who more or less introduced the croquet putter . . .

1968 R. & A. Decisions on the Rules (in The Golfer's Handbook 1974, 998): The new Rule 35.1.L. prohibits a player from making a stroke on the putting green from a stance astride, or with either foot touching, the line of putt. It has been stated that this is intended to prohibit the croquet style of putting.
1977 Dave Hill & Nick Seitz Teed Off 137: . . . was a pretty fair player until croquet-style putting was outlawed.

cross-bunker n. A generally elongated bunker situated astride a fairway.

1913 Bernard Darwin Country Life (Mar. 22) 434: . . . one or two good, old-fashioned crossbunkers rearing their alarming heads in the middle of the fairway.
1961 John Stobbs Tackle Golf (repr. 1977) 121: You may be two down and scared stiff that you are going to top the next one into the cross-bunker; but for heaven's sake don't let him see it.

cross-handed adj. & adv. (Of a grip, as used by a right-handed player, especially in putting) holding the club with the left hand below the right; and the converse for a left-handed player.

1977 John S. Radosta New York Times (July 8) A13: . . . Hayes putted cross-handed. . . . As for cross-handed putting, Hayes considers it "the most natural way."

cross-hazard n. A hazard situated astride a fairway.

1911 Harry Vardon How to Play Golf 26: . . . the outstanding tendency has been to abandon cross-hazards and substitute bunkers and other agents of retribution on the wings.
1931 T. Simpson The Game of Golf 190: The cross-hazard is often another object of adverse criticism.

cup n. & v. **1** n. Obsolete. A small deep depression or hole on the course.

1862 Robert Chambers A Few Rambling Re-

marks on Golf 6: . . . the ball, which possibly lies in a small indentation or 'cup' in the turf, and so requires the long-spoon to drive it forth.
1881 Robert Forgan The Golfer's Handbook 59: Cup.—A small hole in the course, probably made by the stroke of some previous player.
1907 Army & Navy Stores Catalogue 1000: This club . . . will pick up the ball out of "cups" or "hanging lies."

2 n. The hole.

c1910 Jerome D. Travers & Grantland Rice The Winning Shot 20: He putted for his three and missed, the ball trickling eighteen inches beyond the cup.
1913 Bernard Darwin Country Life (Sept. 20) 401: It takes a day or two for the English onlooker [in the U.S.] to grow accustomed to hear a hole called a cup.
1919 Robert K. Risk Songs of the Links 55:
Golf means the long and leary putt that
   glides into the "cup" . . .
1963 Bob Rosburg The Putter Book 49: How to maneuver a ball that is 1.68 inches in diameter into a 4¼-inch cup.

3 v.trans. To hole (the ball or a putt).

1969 Paul D. Peery Billy Casper, Winner 92: . . . he cupped a 15-footer for another birdie.

cupped adj. (Of a ball) lying in a small deep depression or hole on the course; (of a lie) deep and enclosed.

1888 Chambers's Journal (May 26) 323: My ball lay cupped, for instance, on one occasion . . .
1898 Willie Tucker The Outing (Aug.) 440: The Brassey . . . should be used through the green if your lie is a little cupped.
1907 Tom Vardon in Leach Great Golfers in the Making 254: . . . when he had driven from the first tee and had obtained a cupped lie.
1931 Joyce & Roger Wethered The Game of Golf 54: . . . a perfectly accurate swing will pick a ball out of a cupped or heavy lie without any forcing or extra hitting.
1976 J.C. Jessop Golf 40: If the ball is "cupped" or lying very close, a No. 3 wood should be used.

cuppy *adj.* (Of a lie) deep and enclosed.

1890 Horace Hutchinson *Badminton Golf* 313: . . . but after all to a really first-class golfer a cuppy lie is not important.
1922 P.G. Wodehouse *Sundered Hearts* (in *The Clicking of Cuthbert* repr. 1956, 64): Mortimer, after a drive which surprised even himself, found his ball in a nasty cuppy lie.
1962 Sam Snead *The Education of a Golfer* 68: In any cuppy position, a driving iron, 2-iron, or 4-wood was my selection.

cut[1] *n. & v.* **1** *n.* Backspin, usually with slice.

1890 Horace Hutchinson *Badminton Golf* 66: Almost every professional gets his ball to stop comparatively dead . . . by means of putting cut upon it; which he does by drawing the club towards him, as its head comes to the ground, so that its face scrapes, instead of directly striking, the ball.
1895 "Calamo Currente" *Half Hours with an Old Golfer* 168: Cut. Under-cut is a back spin on a ball. Slice-cut is diagonal right and back spin.
1916 P.A. Vaile *The New Golf* 149: . . . for cut (except back-cut) is merely slice by another name.
1929 *Spalding's Athletic Library* 120: Cut —A reverse spin imparted to the ball which prevents roll.
1969 Jack Nicklaus *The Greatest Game of All* 22: . . . my irons were flying on a high trajectory with a touch of cut on them.

2 *n.,* or **cut shot** or **cut-up shot.** A short, high-trajectory shot with strong backspin and usually slice.

1899 Findlay S. Douglas *The Outing* (June) 224: . . . what is known as the "cut stroke." The object is to get the ball to carry a certain distance and drop dead.
1912 Harry Vardon *How to Play Golf* 113: When the ball is close to the face of the hazard, it is often possible to play a cut shot in just the same way as with the mashie.
1926 Francis Ouimet *Golf Illustrated* (Nov.) 45: . . . you can draw the blade of your club head slightly across the ball at the moment of impact, which produces the shot known to golfers as the "cut shot."
1927 Robert T. Jones, Jr. & O.B. Keeler *Down the Fairway* 184: The other type [of pitch shot] is known as the cut shot, in which the club comes on the ball from outside the line of flight, hitting more under the ball than down on it, and, as it is termed, "cutting the legs from under it." . . . J.H. Taylor has the reputation of a cut-shot artist with the mashie and other pitching clubs.
1950 Sam Snead *How to Hit a Golf Ball* 46: Playing from the rough or from a sand trap, the cut shot will help you hold the green once the ball hits it.
1971 Henry Longhurst *My Life and Soft Times* 41: . . . for much of the year it was muddy enough to require a cut-up shot to get the ball in the air at all.
1977 George Peper *Scrambling Golf* 105: The cut is probably the epitome of golfing finesse.

3 *v.trans.,* or **cut up** *phr.v.* To hit (the ball) in a cut shot.

1897 Price Collier *The Outing* (Nov.) 196: To play these shots the club-head must get underneath the ball, and both lift it and cut it, so that the ball has a rotary motion in the exact opposite direction to that in which it is going.
1921 Andrew Kirkaldy *Fifty Years of Golf* 128: The man has not been born who could pitch over that bunker, when the greens are baked, and cut the shot enough to keep the ball out of the road beyond the pin.
1931 Henry Cotton *Golf* 109: You can cut a ball up—that is, give it spin that results in greater elevation than it would otherwise have, so that it gets started on its way—more easily with a spoon than a brassie.

4 *v.trans.* To slice (the ball or a shot).

1946 Frank Moran *Golfers' Gallery* 84: At the fourteenth he cut his drive out of bounds.
1966 Gary Player *Grand Slam Golf* 107: . . . under pressure I never hook. I am more prone to cut the ball, if anything.

cut[2] *v. & n.* **1** *v.trans.* To reduce (a field of competitors in a tournament) to a predetermined number by elimination of the high scorers in the first two rounds; to eliminate (a competitor) in this way.

[**1927** Edward B. Tufts *Golf Illustrated* (Jan.) 25: Entries have been so numerous that the Tournament Committee has decided to hold preliminary qualifying rounds of 36 holes two days prior to the tournament. In this manner the field will be cut down to 128 players.]

1975 Mark McCormack *Golf Annual* 195: After a second round of 75 Jacklin was gone, cut from the championship.

1977 *New York Times* (June 11) 14: The starting field of 99 was cut to 65 for the final rounds.

2 n. Elimination of competitors under this system.

1970 Dick Schaap *The Masters* 107: In the Masters, only the leading forty-four golfers, plus ties, survive the halfway cut.

3 n. The score for the first two rounds of a tournament above which competitors are eliminated; the cutoff score.

(a) make the cut To equal or better the cutoff score, thus going on to the last two rounds of a tournament.

1956 Herbert Warren Wind *The Story of American Golf* 514: In 1936 he qualified for the Open at Baltusrol but failed to "make the cut"—that is, he did not finish among the 76 low scorers for the first two rounds and so was not eligible to play the last thirty-six holes.

1977 Al Barkow *Golf Magazine* (June) 49: In 1962 he won his first U.S. Open and the following year in that championship did not make the 36-hole cut.

(b) miss the cut To score above the cut-off score, thus being eliminated from a tournament.

1977 William Wright *Golf Illustrated* (Summer) 8: He completed 41 tournaments without missing a cut.

cutoff n. The score, for the first two rounds of a four-round tournament, which competitors must equal or beat to remain in the tournament for the last two rounds.

1977 Gordon S. White *New York Times* (June 18) S1: Weiskopf just managed to make the two-round cut yesterday, posting 150, the cutoff number that shaved the field from 153 players to 63 for the final two rounds.

D

dead *adj. & adv.* **1** So near the hole that the remaining putt seems unmissable.

1853 *Unidentified newspaper clipping* (in Allan Robertson's album at the R. & A. 49): Hole of Shell was halved, Allan and Tom both bungling putts considered *dead*.
1857 H.B. Farnie *The Golfer's Manual* 62: ... let him putt softly and cautiously, that his ball may lie *dead* for the next stroke.
1899 Willie Tucker *The Outing* (Aug.) 526: Travis, laying his approach putt dead, holed in 4.
1919 Robert K. Risk *Songs of the Links* 25:
   No patent tools had they, but they
      somehow found a way
   To lay their third shots dead.
1927 Robert T. Jones, Jr. & O.B. Keeler *Down the Fairway* 69: But he chipped stone dead and got a half.
1946 Frank Moran *Golfers' Gallery* 122: Mrs. Cheney had to play first and she laid her putt dead.
1974 *The Golfer's Handbook* 432: Willie Park, junior, was perhaps the deadliest putter the game has ever known. He reckoned himself stone dead at two yards.

2 (Falling) to a stop without rolling.

1857 H.B. Farnie *The Golfer's Manual* 79: A ball is said to be dead—1st, when it falls without rolling ...
1895 James P. Lee *Golf in America* 136: ... that the use of this club will give a backward spin and thus cause it to fall dead upon the green.
1902 Horace Hutchinson *Country Life* (Oct. 18) 488: I am not quite sure that on a fairly soft green the Haskell, if it is properly pitched ... will not fall the deader of the two.
1976 J.C. Jessop *Golf* 62: To see the ball pitched high in the air covering the flag and dropping "dead" provides one of the finest thrills in golf.

deep *adj.* (Of a clubface) relatively thick from top to bottom. **—deep-faced** *adj.* (Of a club) having a deep face. **—depth** *n.* The extent to which a club is deep-faced.

1857 H.B. Farnie *The Golfer's Manual* 28: The head of the play club should neither be very deep in the face nor too broad across the back.... In order to strike a ball with a deep-faced play club ...
1907 *Army & Navy Stores Catalogue* 998: Deep-faced mashie.
1913 Horace Hutchinson *Country Life* (Jan. 18) 104: ... although it is rather unusually deep in the face, the impression shows that there was a considerable portion of the ball which did not meet the face at all.
1927 Robert T. Jones, Jr. & O.B. Keeler *Down the Fairway* 204: ... I went in for clubs deeper and deeper in the face.... The face was 1⅝ inches in depth, with a bulge of ⅜ inch, and virtually no loft at all.

1962 Sam Snead *The Education of a Golfer* 72: Now I use a 1½-wood off the tee. This is a regulation deep-faced driver, but with added loft to the face.
1977 Tom Watson *Golf Magazine* (July) 104: This height of tee will, therefore, vary with the depth of driver you use. You should tee the ball lower with a shallow-faced driver than with a deep-faced driver.

deuce *n.* *Chiefly U.S.* A hole in two.

1928 A. Linde Fowler *Golf Illustrated* (Oct.) 40: ... it might be necessary for him to get a 2 to halve and it was in going so firmly for that deuce ... that he missed the putt coming back.
1978 Dennis J. Harrington *Golf Score* (Oct./ Nov.) 55: Here he holed a 60-foot putt for a birdie deuce.

die *v.intrans.* (Of a putt or a putted ball) to cease rolling.

1927 Stewart Maiden (in Jones & Keeler *Down the Fairway* 170): "When the ball dies at the hole, there are four doors; the ball can go in at the front, or the back, or at either side."
1950 Gene Sarazen *28 Holes in 100 Strokes* (in Wind *The Complete Golfer* 1954, 192): My approach putt from eighteen feet died a few inches beyond the hole.
1963 Bob Rosburg *The Putter Book* 111: If I have stroked the ball with the proper momentum, it will be "dying" as it reaches the cup.

dimple *n.* One of the roundish depressions on the surface of a golf ball.

1926 Advertisement *Golf Illustrated* (June) 10: The P.G.A. golf ball ... Dimple or Mesh Marking.
1975 *Bartlett's World Golf Encyclopedia* 366: In 1908 William Taylor ... developed the dimple marking that gave the rubbercore longer and truer flight. ... 370: There are approximately 336 dimples on a golf ball and it has been found that a dimple depth of .012 inches produces the most distance.
1978 A.J. Hagopian *Boston Globe* (Sept. 10)

79: A Uniroyal ball has hexagon shaped dimples while a Wilson has truncated conical dimples.

divot *n.* [*Origin:* Scottish, from Old Scottish *divot, devat,* or *duvate* = "piece of turf," esp. as used for roof insulation or for fuel; ultimate origin unknown.] **1** A piece of turf cut from the ground by the clubhead in the making of a stroke.

1890 Horace Hutchinson *Badminton Golf* 260: No golfer is worthy of the name who does not put back his divot.
1915 A.W. Tillinghast *The Wellington Emerald* (in *Cobble Valley Golf Yarns* 188): ... pointed with his driver at some withered divots lying close behind a wound in the green fairway.
1929 *Golf Illustrated* (May) 24: Time was, when a fellow could amble up to his ball, moisten his hands and carve out a man's size divot.
1962 Richard Armour *Golf Is a Four-letter Word* 89:
The divot is a piece of sod.
That ought to be replaced and trod.
1977 Ben Crenshaw *Golf Magazine* (July) 100: With a good lie, there's no need to take a "soup plate" divot.

2 The cavity left by a divot.

1969 Jack Nicklaus *The Greatest Game of All* 160: ... ended up in a shallow fairway divot.
1978 Tom Watson *Boston Globe* (Aug. 17) 21: "I drove it into a divot."

dogleg or **dog-leg** *n. & v.* **1** *n.* A fairway embodying a sharp turn, or a hole that has such a fairway.

[**1902** *Golf Illustrated* (Aug. 15) 129: This hole has been criticised by some on the ground that the player cannot play straight for the hole, the line for which is rather like a dog's hind leg.]
1908 Horace Hutchinson *Country Life* (Jan. 27) 141: With a "dog-leg" bend to the right it will make this seventeenth a two-shot hole.
1926 A.W. Tillinghast *Golf Illustrated* (Nov.) 18: Probably fifteen years ago I origi-

nated the double dog-leg for a plan of a three-shot hole.

1977 Joanne Carner *New York Times* (June 3): "I have more fun when I can cut the doglegs and hit up and over trouble."

2 *v.intrans.* (Of a hole or fairway) to make a sharp turn.

1962 Sam Snead *The Education of a Golfer* 77: The fourteenth hole doglegs left sharp enough to break your back.

1972 Michael Murphy *Golf in the Kingdom* 28: On the twelfth hole our drive was into the wind, down a narrow fairway that doglegged to the right.

dormie or **dormy** *adj.* [*Origin:* Scottish; further derivation unknown.] In match play, standing as many holes up as there are holes remaining to be played.

1851 *Unidentified newspaper clipping* (in Allan Robertson's album at the R. & A. 40): Tom divided the next three holes, which made Dunnie [i.e., William Dunn] *dormie* at the burn hole, viz., in a position that he could not lose the match, and leaving Tom only the last hole to redeem himself.

1881 Robert Forgan *The Golfer's Handbook* 59: (This word is fancifully derived from *dormio*, to sleep, owing to the security enjoyed by the *dormy* party.)

1936 H.B. Martin *Fifty Years of American Golf* 190: Charles Hitchcock of Yale who was dormie four when the Princetonian pulled out a smashing victory . . .

1969 Jack Nicklaus *The Greatest Game of All* 81: Going to the seventeenth he was dormie: 2 up and 2 holes to play.

1976 *Rules of Golf* Definition 34: A side is "dormie" when it is as many holes up as there are holes remaining to be played.

double-bogey *n. & v.* **1** *n.* A score of two strokes over par for a hole.

1977 *New York Times* (June 13) 43: . . . a shot that went out of bounds and led to a double-bogey 6 on the fourth hole.

2 *v.trans.* To play (a hole) in two strokes over par.

1970 Dick Schaap *The Masters* 113: Then he double-bogeys the fourth to fall back to even-par for the tournament.

double-eagle *n.* A score of three strokes under par for a hole.

1936 H.B. Martin *Fifty Years of American Golf* 386: . . . was apparently breezing along to victory when Sarazen on the par five seventeenth managed to hole out his second shot for a double-eagle.

down *adv.* **1** (In match play) standing a specified number of holes below one's opponent.

1891 *Golf* magazine (Sept. 18) 3: . . . the umpires stood firmly to their guns, and the Kirkaldys were thus two down.

1977 *New York Times* (Aug. 8) 33: Courville missed his second putt at the first hole . . . and was 1 down from the start.

2 Into the hole.

1896 *Golfer's & Angler's Guide* 149: The third, a short approach, and two puts, will put the ball down in five.

1938 E.C. Bentley *The Sweet Shot* (in Wind *The Complete Golfer* 1954, 19): . . . at the last hole sent down a four-foot putt to win the match.

1975 Mark McCormack *Golf Annual* 79: . . . with Irwin safely down in par 4.

downhiller *n.* A downhill shot or putt.

1956 Herbert Warren Wind *The Story of American Golf* 357: . . . it was a better than even bet that Cooper would drop that downhiller for a bird.

downswing *n.* The movement of taking a club from the top of the swing to the point of impact.

1911 James Braid *Advanced Golf* 49: The body seems to want to get in almost as soon as the club begins the down-swing.

1931 Joyce & Roger Wethered *The Game of Golf* 48: The Down-Swing: The next link is from the top of the swing downwards.

1969 Tom Scott & Geoffrey Cousins *The Golf Immortals* 105: . . . hurrying the downswing is a fault of which most golfers are guilty.

draw *v. & n.* **1** *v.trans.* Of a right-handed player, to play (the ball or a shot) so that it curves owing to sidespin from right to left; and the converse for a left-handed player; formerly synonymous with *hook*, now generally used of a controlled and moderate curve.

1842 *Chambers' Edinburgh Journal* (Oct. 8) 18: Then he may stand unfair, or he may *draw* his stroke, and thereby send the ball off the course . . .
1862 Robert Chambers *A Few Rambling Remarks on Golf* 22: . . . when struck with the point or 'toe' of the club, it is said to be 'drawn' or 'hooked,' and flies in to the left.
1881 Robert Forgan *The Golfer's Handbook* 59: DRAW.—To drive widely to the left hand (synonymous with Hook and Screw).
1908 W.W. Tulloch *Life of Tom Morris* 10: With what wile and cunning [Allan Robertson] would, of purpose, heel or draw a ball with the object of getting round a hazard.
1962 Sam Snead *The Education of a Golfer* 77: A ball purposely drawn from right to left will hold its line until late in flight.
1977 Dave Hill & Nick Seitz *Teed Off* 127: At Augusta he draws his drives because it's a right-to-left course.

2 *n.* Controlled and moderate right-to-left curve on a shot by a right-handed player; and the converse by a left-handed player.

1890 H.S.C. Everard *Badminton Golf* 374: . . . he plays sometimes rather for a 'draw,' and gets his back, shoulders, and hips into the stroke.
1912 Harry Vardon *How to Play Golf* 138: . . . the way to impart intentional draw to the ball is to turn the right hand over at the instant of striking—or, at least, turn it half over.
1931 Roger Wethered *The Game of Golf* 68: The touch of "draw" which they put on the ball is caused by swinging the club more from the inside of the line of play and emphasizing the follow through.
1948 Ben Hogan *Power Golf* 24: This

[closed] stance encourages a draw or hook.
1977 Jerry M. Kohlman letter to *Golf Magazine* (June) 115: I. . . usually hit a 5-iron about 155 yards with a slight draw. My problem is that sometimes my draw turns into a hook.

drive *v. & n.* **1** *v.trans. & intrans.* To hit (the ball or a shot) with a full stroke, generally using one's maximum power; especially, to play such a shot from the tee, especially using a driver.

1642 Arthur Johnstone *Epigram on Montrose* (in Alexander Skene *Royall-Burghs of Scotland* 1685, 279):
Some wrestle, some at Pennie-stones do play,
The rolling Balls with Clubs some drive away.
1743 Thomas Mathison *The Goff* 17:
For this the Chiefs exert their skill and might
To drive the balls, and to direct their flight.
1815 *Minutes of the Royal Burgess Golfing Society* (May 13): Mr. Scott betted one guinea with Mr. Dowall that he would drive a ball from the Golf House over Arthur Seat, at 45 strokes. Mr. Scott lost.
1833 George Fullerton Carnegie *The Golfiad* (in *Poems on Golf* 1867, 21):
And good Patullo! He who drove as none,
Since him, have driven—he is also gone!
1888 *Chambers's Journal* (May 26) 322: I would sometimes drive wildly . . .
1911 James Braid *Advanced Golf* 45: They say it is not good to drive a long way if you cannot drive straight. I agree.
1931 Joyce & Roger Wethered *The Game of Golf* 39: To drive long distances is the ambition of every golfer with ordinary human instincts.
1967 Dave Thomas *Modern Golf* 18: Only by consistently driving long and straight can you start to score well.
1975 Mark McCormack *Golf Annual* 47: . . . he missed from four feet after driving into the rough.

2 *v.trans.* To play a tee shot on to (the green).

1910 Walter J. Travis *The American Golfer* (in Wind *The Complete Golfer* 1954, 149): Mr. Blackwell drove the green in both rounds.
1936 H.B. Martin *Fifty Years of American Golf* 108: Gardner drove the green and he was in a position for an easy par three.
1967 Mark McCormack *Arnie* 60: It was possible to drive the green if you caught the ball just right.

3 drive off *phr.v.* To play from the tee, especially at the beginning of a game.

1853 *Unidentified newspaper clipping* (in Allan Robertson's album at the R. & A. 48): . . . spectators congregated to witness the 'driving off' in greater numbers than we have seen on any preceding occasion.
1881 Robert Forgan *The Golfer's Handbook* 19: The match is begun at the teeing-ground in the vicinity of the first hole, by each party driving off his ball in the direction of the second.
1921 Andrew Kirkaldy *Fifty Years of Golf* 93: The amateur boxer was about to drive off . . .
1957 George Houghton *The Truth About Golf Addicts* 56: . . . the first players were due to drive off at half-past twelve.

4 drive (oneself) in. To inaugurate oneself as captain of a golf club by playing a ceremonial tee shot.

1951 S.L. McKinlay *Francis Drives Himself In* (in Wind *The Complete Golfer* 1954, 122): Francis Ouimet, of Boston, Massachusetts, drove himself into the captaincy of the Royal and Ancient Club at eight o'clock yesterday morning. . .
1979 *Golf Illustrated* (Feb. 15) 16: 14-handicap Lawrie Ridley "drove in" as the new captain of Verulam G.C.

5 n. A full shot, especially a tee shot, especially one made with a driver.

1862 Robert Chambers *A Few Rambling Remarks on Golf* 14: The tee . . . on which the ball is to be placed *for the first drive only* . . .
1890 Horace Hutchinson *Badminton Golf* 312: . . . at St. Andrews the majority of the holes are so disposed that they may be reached with two, or maybe three, real good drives.
1922 P.G. Wodehouse *A Woman Is Only a Woman* (in *The Clicking of Cuthbert* repr.

1956, 43): A woman is only a woman, but a hefty drive is a slosh.
1974 *The Golfer's Handbook* 522: The longest recorded drive in America is 426 yards by George Bayer in the 1955 Tucson Open.

drive-and-pitch *attributive.* Designating a hole on which the green can be reached with a drive and a pitch, or a course made up of such holes.

1907 Harold Hilton *My Golfing Reminiscences* 127: . . . the course at Muirfield . . . could not be considered a truly severe test of the game, as . . . there was far too much of the drive and pitch variety of hole in evidence.
1919 Robert K. Risk *Songs of the Links* 55: Golf means the futile drive-pitch course that has "such splendid views" . . .
1956 Herbert Warren Wind *The Story of American Golf* 484: Jones had a violent distaste for drive-and-pitch par fours, gift birdie holes.
1969 Jack Nicklaus *The Greatest Game of All* 245: Arnold was two over par playing the thirteenth, a drive-and-pitch 4.

driver *n.* **1** A player rated as to his or her driving abilities.

1842 *Chambers' Edinburgh Journal* (Oct. 8) 298: Some men are good putters without being good drivers . . .
1927 Robert T. Jones, Jr. & O.B. Keeler *Down the Fairway* 52: Clarence Knowles, who was six feet three and weighed 220 pounds and was the longest driver in the South at that time.

2 Either of the two longest-hitting wooden clubs formerly in use: the play club or the grass-club (or grassed driver).

1857 H.B. Farnie *The Golfer's Manual* 17: There are two members of this class [drivers]; the play club, and the grassed driver.
1881 Robert Forgan *The Golfer's Handbook* 8: Drivers—Play-club, Grassed Driver. . . . 9: Of all the clubs in the "set" the Drivers are the longest, most delicately constructed, and yet most powerful.

driver

(1-2) driver or play club, Willie Dunn,
    c. 1910
(3-4) driver, Ben Hogan, 1979

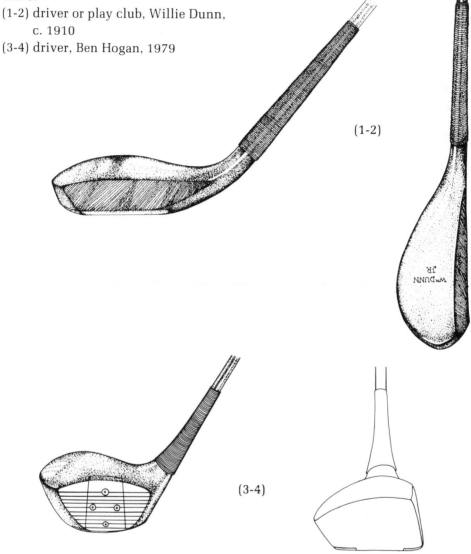

(1-2)

(3-4)

3 The longest-hitting modern wooden club, used primarily from the tee, having loft of 11–12½ degrees, lie of 54–56 degrees, and length of 43 inches, and giving distance of 235–300 yards (men's clubs). Alternate name, number one wood.

1912 Harry Vardon *How to Play Golf* 67:

Once he is master of it, he will find the driver joyous to use.
1931 Henry Cotton *Golf* 95: Therefore I propose to do as I usually do when I have a beginner, and start with a driver.
1979 John Jacobs *Golf World* (Mar.) 24: I would therefore suggest that readers who tend to slice with a driver, should drive with a club with extra loft.

driving cleek. See **cleek.**

driving iron. **1** Any of various iron clubs, no longer in use, that were used for various shots through the green.

1890 Horace Hutchinson *Badminton Golf* 66: . . . driving irons . . . are heavier, shorter, stiffer, with faces more laid back, than the cleek, will drive the ball out of worse places, but will not drive it so far.
1911 James Braid *Advanced Golf* 40: A driving iron is useful for playing up to the hole against a wind, and some players find it the best club for running up . . .
1913 Bernard Darwin *Country Life* (Sept. 20) 401: . . . the Americans are unquestionably very good indeed with their driving irons.
1922 P.G. Wodehouse *Ordeal by Golf* (in *The Clicking of Cuthbert*, repr. 1956, 106): For quite half a minute he stood over his ball, pawing at it with his driving-iron like a cat investigating a tortoise.

2 Alternate name for the number one iron.

1928 A.T. Packard *Golf Illustrated* (Nov.) 51: Hence the exit of the cleek and the entrance of the No. 1 iron with its hitting spot lengthened a half dozen times on the longer face of the club. . . . The driving iron might be classed as a cleek with a hitting spot enlarged.
1948 Ben Hogan *Power Golf* n.p.: The one iron, or driving iron, is the most difficult club in the bag to master.

driving iron
McGregor, 1927

1962 Sam Snead *The Education of a Golfer* 68: In any cuppy position, a driving-iron, 2-iron, or 4-wood was my selection.

driving mashie. An iron club, no longer in use, having somewhat less loft than a mashie-iron, used for driving and for long shots through the green.

1897 *Country Life* (Jan. 23) 83: "There are several kinds of mashies. There is the driving mashie . . ."
1912 Harry Vardon *How to Play Golf* 84: As alternative clubs to the cleek, there are the driving-mashie and the spoon.
1952 Henry Cotton *History of Golf in Great Britain:* By today's standards . . . the driving mashie would be a No. 3 or thereabouts with a medium deep face.

driving putter. A straight-faced wooden club, no longer in use, that was used for driving low shots, especially against the wind.

1833 George Fullerton Carnegie *The First Hole at St. Andrews* (in *Poems on Golf* 1867, 33):
There, to the left, I see Mount Melville
    stand
Erect, his *driving putter* in his hand;
It is a club he cannot leave behind,
It works the ball so well against the
    wind.
1881 Robert Forgan *The Golfer's Handbook* 13: The "Driving-Putter" differs from its companion of the green only in the length of the shaft, which in the one measures 3 ft. 6 in., in the other 3 ft. One function of the Driving-Putter is to "cheat the wind" by sending a low "skimming" ball . . . the Driving-Putter is fast falling into disuse.

driving range. An area or structure provided with equipment for practicing tee-shots and other strokes.

1960 Rex Lardner *Out of the Bunker and Into the Trees* 31: . . . a golf hypochondriac —one of those players who take lessons from club and driving-range pros indiscriminately.
1978 Joe Norwood *Golf Score* (Oct./Nov.)

56: For the past 21 years, I have taught golf at driving ranges, including five which I operated.

drop[1] *v. & n.* **1** *v.trans.* To deposit (a ball) on the course during the play of a hole, as in case of an unplayable lie or when the original ball has been lost.

1744 *Articles & Laws in Playing at Golf* (in Clapcott 1935): 8. If you should lose your ball . . . you are to go back to the spot where you struck last, and drop another ball, and allow your adversary a stroke for the misfortune.
1824 *Rules of the Thistle Golf Club* 49: VII. In all cases where a ball is to be dropt, the party dropping, shall front the hole to which he is playing, and drop the ball behind him, over his head.
1890 Horace Hutchinson *Badminton Golf* 251: You are allowed to take another ball and drop it, with one stroke as penalty, just behind the burn.
1976 *Rules of Golf* 22.2a.: A ball to be dropped . . . shall be dropped by the player himself. He shall face the hole, stand erect, and drop the ball behind him over his shoulder.

2 *n.* An instance of a ball being dropped.

1915 Alexander H. Revell *Pro & Con of Golf* 97: . . . his opponent's ball, which had found an impossible lie off a penalty drop.
1978 Ray Fitzgerald *Boston Globe* (Aug. 14) 24: . . . Morgan had to take a drop.

drop[2] *v.* **1** *v.intrans.* (Of a putt) to hole out.

1948 Ben Hogan *Power Golf* 131: . . . a higher percentage of sinkable putts will start dropping for you.

2 *v.trans.* To hole out (a putt).

1975 Mark McCormack *Golf Annual* 57: . . . he could not drop the putts for birdies.

dub *n. & v.* [Origin: from late 19th-century U.S. slang *dub* = "someone un-skillful or inexperienced at anything"; further origin unknown.] *Chiefly U.S.* **1** *n.* An unskillful player.

1915 A.W. Tillinghast *The Outcasts* (in *Cobble Valley Golf Yarns* 16): "Got around in 75, too. I heard the old dub bragging about it."
1929 Strickland Gillilan *Golf Illustrated* (May) 25: The congenital dub never feels discouragement.
1948 Ben Hogan *Power Golf* xv: Someone once estimated that 90 is the dividing line between a golfer and a dub.
1962 Richard Armour *Golf Is a Four-letter Word* 31: "I've heard," he added, looking at me accusingly, "that some dubs around here are playing winter rules in July."

2 *v.trans. & intrans.* To mishit (the ball or a shot).

1915 Alexander H. Revell *Pro & Con of Golf* 102: The man that seizes your club, after you have dubbed, and says: "Let me show you how that shot should be made, Harry."
1926 James H. Rothschild *Golf Illustrated* (Sept.) 21: And I have learned that when a player most vehemently cries "fore," he will, without exception, dub the ball!
1949 Fred Beck & O.K. Barnes *Seventy-three Years in a Sand Trap* 36: . . . after seeing a friend dub eight or ten shots in succession.

duck *v.intrans.* (Of a ball in flight) to veer suddenly downward.

1848 William Graham *In Praise of Gutta Percha* (in *Badminton Golf* 1890, 28):
They whirred and fuffed, and dooked
    and shied,
    And sklenkit into bunkers.
1916 P.A. Vaile *The New Golf* 250: Sir Ralph says of it: "I tried this smooth ball from the engine and it 'ducked' every time in an extraordinary manner, its length of carry being seldom more than eighty yards."
1968 J.S. Martin *The Curious History of the Golf Ball* 54: . . . it exhibited the same tendency to duck and dart as the earliest smooth gutties had done.

duck-hook *n. & v.* **1** *n.* Tendency of a

shot played by a right-handed player to fly low and to curve sharply to the left and downward; and the converse for a left-handed player.

1962 Sam Snead *The Education of a Golfer* 18: Sometimes I got a duck-hook effect, where the ball shot out low and took a left-hand dip downward into the rough.
1971 Tommy Bolt *The Hole Truth* 31: Arnie would put one of those duck hooks on a shot ...

2. *v.trans. & intrans.* To hit (a ball or shot) with a duck-hook.

1962 Sam Snead *ibid.* 19: After hitting some more drives that skimmed the ground and then duck-hooked at about 150 yards ...
1963 Arnold Palmer *My Game and Yours* 54: Trying to hurry ... I duck-hooked my ball into the woods.
1977 Sue Roberts *Woman Golfer* (Nov.) 11: I hook the ball too, and I know if I swing too fast I'll duck hook.

duff *v.trans. & intrans.* [*Origin:* probably Scottish, and probably related to Scottish schoolboys' slang *dowf* or *duff* = "to bounce a ball up with the fist"; but felt by most golfers as a back-formation from *duffer,* and thus tending to be used in the generalized meaning "to mishit."] To mishit (a shot) by hitting the ground behind the ball and then topping the ball.

1895 W. Dalrymple *Handbook to Golf* 111: ... the innate malignant tendency to duff and muff, and sclaff and miss, and top and heel and toe.
1902 *Golf Illustrated* (Aug. 22) 149: The twelfth is a blind hole, the tee being in a crater. A duffed tee shot gets very badly punished.
1909 E.M. Griffith *With Club and Caddie* 39:
Duffed the approach! O dash it!
What's that? Thirteen; ...
1931 Roger Wethered *The Game of Golf* 75: ... striking the ground behind the ball and completely duffing the shot.
1946 Frank Moran *Golfers' Gallery* 30: Jurado ... duffed his tee stroke at the seventeenth into the burn.
1962 Sam Snead *The Education of a Golfer*

63: Then I duffed the third shot, almost whiffed entirely on the fourth, and took a 6 on the hole. ... *ibid.* 117: Ben had never duffed a putt so many ways since I'd known him.
1970 Tony Jacklin *Jacklin* 24: After a drive into rough I duffed the second into sand.

duffer *n.* [*Origin:* from 19th-century slang *duffer* = "incompetent, unskillful person"; further origin obscure.] An unskillful golfer.

1875 "M.T.S.D." in Clark *Golf: A Royal & Ancient Game* 222:
Why did we e'er buy a set
If we must be duffers yet?
Duffers yet! Duffers yet!
1893 John Thomson *Golfing Poems & Songs* 5:
See yonder lads upon the links,
Go, find a duffer there but thinks,
For a' the jeers and wylie winks,
He'll yet a gowfer be.
1897 Price Collier *The Outing* (June) 296: ... 100 for eighteen holes is the "duffer" mark; anything between 100 and 90 is fair golf.
1908 Arnold Haultain *The Mystery of Golf* (repr. 1965) 3: The old hand is more concerned about how he plays than about why he plays; the duffer is puzzled at the extraordinary fascination which his new-found pastime exercises over him.
1919 Robert Risk *Songs of the Links* 24:
Old Allan and Young Tommy, they were
duffers in their time ...
1948 Ben Hogan *Power Golf* 16: If there is one club in the bag neglected by novices and duffers it is the sand wedge.
1968 Tony Lema *Golfer's Gold* 207: Exactly like 10,000,000 weekend duffers he gets out to the golf course about an hour before his turn to play comes up.
1970 Dick Schaap *The Masters* 205: Littler studies his little chip, steps up to the ball, swings and, inexplicably, like any Sunday duffer, shanks his shot into a bunker.

dunch *v. & n.* [*Origin:* from Scottish *dunch* = "to knock, bump, nudge"; further origin unknown.] **1** *v.trans.* To play (the ball) along the ground with a forceful jabbing or poking motion.

1887 Sir Walter Simpson *The Art of Golf* 132: One of these with a face a yard or two in front of it, is a bad ball, which can only either be dunched along the ground a short distance with a brassy, or popped equally far with an iron.

2 *n.* A dunched shot.

1909 *Golf Illustrated* (May 7) 203: At the short sixth Braid played one of his famous dunches, the result being a win in 3.

1929 C.L. Graves *The Philosophic Foozler* (in *Mr. Punch on the Links* 115): . . . those peculiar vagaries which Mr. Johnny Low, I think it was, described as the 'flub' and the 'dunch.'

1931 Bernard Darwin *The Game of Golf* 141: If, as is highly probable, he cannot play with his iron the formidable "dunch" which gained its onomatopoeic name from Braid's execution of it, he must learn to do the best he can with a longer, quieter swing of his clubs.

E

eagle n. & v. [Origin: by analogy with *birdie*.] **1** n. A score of two under par on a hole.

1926 W. Hastings Webling *Golf Illustrated* (Oct.) 45: Wilbur . . . managed to win the 17th, by running down a long . . . putt, thus earning what he called an "eagle."
1933 A.G. Macdonnell *England, Their England* 136: ". . . half a crown for each birdie, a dollar an eagle, a bob best ball."
1946 Frank Moran *Golfers' Gallery* 106: . . . holing out from eight yards at the third for an "eagle" 2.

2 *v.trans.* To play (a hole) in two under par.

1968 Buddy Hackett *The Truth About Golf* 122: He knew he might get on in two and possibly eagle the hole.

1977 *New York Times* (Aug. 4) D14: Miss Austin . . . eagled the 10th and 16th holes.

eight-iron n. An iron club having loft of 41–44 degrees, lie of 62–63 degrees, and length of 35½ inches, and giving distance of 115–150 yards (men's clubs). Also, a shot made with an eight-iron. Alternate name, pitching niblick.

1954 George Houghton *The Truth About Golf Addicts* 25: An almost impossible lie, but I was undaunted, certain that a stroke with my eight iron would hole out.
1977 Dave Anderson *New York Times* (June 20) 35: He hit an 8-iron and two-putted for par.

eight-iron
Walter Hagen, 1979

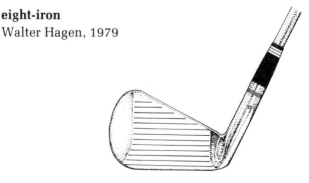

explode *v.trans. & intrans.* To play (the ball) from sand with a steeply lofted club, the clubhead hitting into the sand behind then under the ball and scattering a quantity of sand as the stroke is made.

1890 Horace Hutchinson *Badminton Golf* 146: It is a downward blow, and it is rather the concussion of the sand that explodes the ball up into the air than any actual contact of the club.
1934 Peter Lawless *Little* (in Wind *The Complete Golfer* 1954, 197): He was bunkered . . . Little exploded out.
1948 Ben Hogan *Power Golf* 139: You are now ready to explode the ball out of the bunker.
1977 Sally Little *Golf Magazine* (June) 99: Here I stay more in back of the ball than on the long level shot, so I can explode it upward, taking about two inches of sand.

explosion *n.,* or **explosion shot.** A shot in which the ball is exploded from sand.

1937 Abe Mitchell *Essentials of Golf* 188: It may be advisable at times to play the explosion shot and get the ball up without actually striking it.
1952 Henry Cotton *History of Golf in Britain:* Hagen, while including the explosion shot in his repertoire, had much faith in his ability to flick the ball cleanly off the sand.
1969 Jack Nicklaus *The Greatest Game of All* 139: He played a fairly good explosion and lay four, 12 feet from the flag.

F

face[1] or **clubface** n., or **club face.** The striking surface of a clubhead.

1835 Harry Harewood *Dictionary of Sports* 165: The face of the club is secured by a piece of hard bone . . .
1881 Robert Forgan *The Golfer's Handbook* 9: The head [of the driver] . . . is distinguished from those of the "spoon" family by its "face" being straight and almost perpendicular.
1913 Horace Hutchinson *Country Life* (Jan. 11) 69: For another point of comparison with modern clubs, we may note that these [Hugh Philp woods] are more shallow in the face.
1927 Robert T. Jones, Jr. & O.B. Keeler *Down the Fairway* 204: The face was 1⅝ inches in depth . . .
1976 *Rules of Golf* Appendix II.b: Club faces shall not embody any degree of concavity on the hitting surface.
1977 Raymond Schuessler *Golf Illustrated* (Summer) 23: Open the clubface and choke down on the grip . . .

face[2] n. An exposed bank of sand or steeply sloping side of a bunker.

1743 Thomas Mathison *The Goff* (in Clark *Golf: A Royal & Ancient Game* repr. 1975, 26):
[She] hears the prayers of youths to her address'd,

And from the hollow face relieves the ball distress'd.
1881 Robert Forgan *The Golfer's Handbook* 30: If the ball lies in a thick whin or in a deep sandy face, the Golfer's first and only duty is to get it out. . . . *Ibid.* 59: FACE.— 1st, The sandy slope of a bunker.
1890 Lord Wellwood *Badminton Golf* 41: We all know the tremor with which we confront the face of the bunker which lies between us and the hole.
1912 Harry Vardon *How to Play Golf* 113: When the ball is close to the face of the hazard . . .
1931 T. Simpson *The Game of Golf* 209: The face of a bunker must not be kept too tidy, and it should have a slightly overhanging lip.

fade n. & v. **1** n. Controlled and moderate left-to-right curve on a shot by a right-handed player; and the converse by a left-handed player; also, a shot played with fade.

1933 Alex J. Morrison *A New Way to Better Golf* 127: . . . the "laid back" position of the clubface tends to send the ball away with a slight "fade" to the right.
1948 Ben Hogan *Power Golf* 24: This [open] stance encourages a fade or slice.
1965 Bob Charles *Left-handed Golf* 3: I've retained that fade which I now play for because I like to get just a bit of movement from right to left.

1969 Jack Nicklaus *The Greatest Game of All* 284: He hits wider and wider fades, and ends up by slicing the ball.

1977 John Stobbs *Tackle Golf* 89: . . . that basic fade. . . . The ball sets off low along the left-hand side of the fairway, and then just eases into the middle towards the end of its flight.

2 *v.trans.* To play (the ball or a shot) with fade.

1953 Philip W. Wrenn, Jr. *The New Yorker* (June 20): . . . Hogan faded his drive into that trap.

1975 Henry Cotton *History of Golf* 211: . . . he liked among other things to fade many shots up to the flag.

3 *v.intrans.* (Of the ball or a shot) to curve in a fade.

1977 George Peper *Scrambling Golf* 63: Aim well left of your target, because the ball will fade quite a bit.

fair green. *Obsolete.* The area of a links where the grass is relatively short and free of bushes and hazards; the part corresponding to the modern fairway.

1744 *Articles & Laws in Playing at Golf:* You are not to remove Stones, Bones, or any Break-club for the sake of playing your ball, except upon the fair Green.

1839 *Rules of the Game of Golf* (Hon. Company of Edinburgh Golfers) (in Clapcott 1935, 67): On the fair green, grass or driving course, stones, bones, or any break-club, within a club-length of the Ball may be removed.

1898 *Golf* magazine (Jan.) 51: But the fair green has been entirely neglected and the teeing grounds are going from bad to worse.

1906 Arthur Pottow *Illustrated Outdoor News* (Nov.) 130: . . . another cop bunker stretched across the fair green.

1926 W.S. Stuyvesant, letter to *Golf Illustrated* (Dec.) 35: . . . one player's ball might find a good lie within a foot of the fair green. . . . These are the days of the divot takers and fairgreen butchers.

fairway *n.* [Origin: before its use in golf the word *fairway* was an exclusively nautical term meaning a clear channel between rocks or shallows; it was only at the beginning of this century that the old golfing term *fair green* was generally and rather suddenly abandoned in favor of *fairway*.] The stretch of closely mown ground that is the main avenue from tee to green on a hole.

1907 W. Herbert Fowler (in Leach *Great Golfers in the Making* 161): The most important features of all courses are first, the greens; second, the hazards; and third, the fairway through the green.

1911 James Braid *Advanced Golf* 259: . . . the fairway round such bunkers should be hollowed slightly, so as to draw a ball that comes in that direction towards them.

1915 A.W. Tillinghast *The Home Hole* (in *Cobble Valley Golf Yarns* 50): . . . his hand shook as he built his tee, and the green sweep of the fairway appeared to dance away.

1927 Robert T. Jones, Jr. & O.B. Keeler *Down the Fairway* (title of book).

1931 T. Simpson *The Game of Golf* 207: Most fairways on good courses in the south of England are kept up too well.

1970 Charles Price *Golf* 16: Fairway is turf that has been mowed to a lawn-like consistency.

1978 Hugh Sidey *Time* (Oct. 16) 33: . . . the relaxed mind of Gerald Ford, ensconced last week at the edge of Thunderbird's glorious fairways in Palm Springs.

fairway wood. Any of the wooden clubs that are typically used on the fairway, or a shot played with one of them; any wooden club other than the driver.

1962 Sam Snead *The Education of a Golfer* 67: The fairway wood is one of the toughest of all shots.

1977 Davis Love *Golf Digest* (July) 44: . . . the use of fairway woods is certainly not restricted to the fairway. That might be their primary function but they are equally useful off the tee.

fan *v.trans.* To make a stroke that misses (the ball).

1929 Flos Jewell Williams *Golf Illustrated*

(June) 37: I did not care how far I sent the ball, just as long as I hit it. But if I fanned it! **1949** Fred Beck & O.K. Barnes *Seventy-three Years in a Sand Trap* 88: ... Bartholemew Beekman fanned his tee shot again.

fat[1] *adv & adj.* **1** *adv.* (Hitting the ball) with the clubhead traveling on too low a line, hitting the ground behind the ball and catching the ball below center.

1967 George Plimpton *The Bogey Man* 50: I have often been puzzled by the instructor's phrases. "A bit fat," he'll say. "You hit it just a bit fat." What does that mean?
1969 Jack Nicklaus *The Greatest Game of All* 146: He must have caught the ball a little fat. Halfway in its flight it began to slide off to the right.
1978 Arnold Palmer *Golf Magazine* (May) 50: ... one reason you could be hitting the ball fat in fairway bunkers is you're failing to compensate for the ball being higher than your feet.

2 *adj.* (Of a shot) catching the ball too low.

1967 Dave Thomas *Modern Golf* 103: The fat shot that leaves the ball in the bunker, but shifts a pile of sand on to the green ...
1978 *New York Times* (Aug. 5) 15: ... played a "fat chip" to bogey 16.

fat[2] *adj. & n.* **1** *adj.* Wide and safe; referring to the largest expanse of a putting green, making the easiest target for an approach without striving to get close to the pin.

1977 Lee Trevino in *New York Times* (July 25) 14: "I kept looking at the leader boards, and nobody was doing anything. So I just aimed at the fat part of the greens."

2 *n.* The fat part of a putting green.

1977 Charles Gillespie *Sports Illustrated* (June) 52: Now he attacked the flags instead of the fat and ran off two more birdies.

featherie or **feathery** n. The old feather-stuffed, leather-covered ball, replaced by the gutta percha ball from 1848.

1908 Tom Morris in W.W. Tulloch *Life of Tom Morris* 30: "They werena much like the golf balls we have now, the old 'featheries,' but they could play fine afore the wind."
1968 J.S. Martin *The Curious History of the Golf Ball* 31: ... a 'Gourlay' came to mean the finest featherie money could buy. It was "white as snow, hard as lead, and elastic as whalebone."
1979 *St. Andrews Citizen* (March 10) 1: An old "feathery" golf ball fetched £130 at the sale of antiques held by Macgregor's at St. Andrews ...

fescue n. Any grass of the genus *Festuca*, widely used on golf courses, especially for rough.

1926 "The Professor" *Golf Illustrated* (Sept.) 36: Hard fescue is suitable for the rough, and—like sheep's fescue—should never be used on fairways, greens, tees or approaches.
1967 Mark McCormack *Arnie* 167: Arnold has an ideal game for the British climate and the British courses ... maximum amount of roll on the springy fescue courses.

find v. *trans.* To arrive in (a hazard or some other undesired situation).

1899 Willie Tucker *The Outing* (Aug.) 523: ... playing his second, it also found the bunker.
1915 Alexander H. Revell *Pro & Con of Golf* 97: ... his opponent's ball, which had found an impossible lie off a penalty drop.
1954 Robert Trent Jones (in Wind *The Complete Golfer* 1954, 309): ... they felt they could not afford to play safe, went all out for the pin, and found the water in their bold ventures.
1977 Vinny Giles *Golf Magazine* (Aug.) 12: "What a hole! Too little club finds sand or marsh, too much finds water."

five-iron n. An iron club having loft of 29–32 degrees, lie of 59–61 degrees, and length of 37 inches, and giving distance of 145–180 yards (men's clubs). Also, a shot played with a five-iron. Alternate name, mashie.

1963 Arnold Palmer *My Game and Yours* 81: I used a 5-iron, choking up on it, punched the ball out through the trees . . .
1967 Dave Thomas *Modern Golf* 24: . . . take a five iron on to the practice ground and hit a lot of half shots with it.

five-wood n. A wood club having loft of 21–23 degrees, lie of 55–56 degrees, and length of 41 inches, and giving distance of 190–210 yards (men's clubs). Also, a shot played with a five-wood.

1967 Dave Thomas *Modern Golf* 34: The five wood is particularly useful for the older player, but it is also used most successfully by young men, who are essentially swingers.
1971 Tommy Bolt *The Hole Truth* 77: . . . these days you see a lot of amateur senior golfers using five-woods instead of long irons. It is not a bad idea.

flag n. A marker on a stick or pin, marking the position of a hole.

1854 *Fraser's Magazine* (in Clark *Golf: A Royal & Ancient Game* 1875, 211): . . . a red flag denoting the goal is seen fluttering in the distance.
1908 Arnold Haultain *The Mystery of Golf* (repr. 1965) 1: We played till we could not see the flag.
1977 *New York Times* (Aug. 5) A15: Elder put his approaches within four feet of the flag on the 12th and 14th.

flagstick n. A stick or pin with a marker showing the position of a hole.

1875 *Rules for the Game of Golf* (in Clapcott 1935, 114): XII . . . either party is entitled to have the flag-stick removed when approaching the hole.
1970 Charles Price *Golf* 14: While a flag-stick almost invariably has a flag attached to it, usually with a numeral on it indicating the correct number of a hole, it does not have to. Merion . . . has wicker baskets attached to its flagsticks rather than actual bunting.
1976 *Rules of Golf* 34.4: If the ball rest against the flagstick when it is in the hole, the player shall be entitled to have the flagstick

five-iron
Walter Hagen, 1979

five-wood
Ben Hogan, 1979

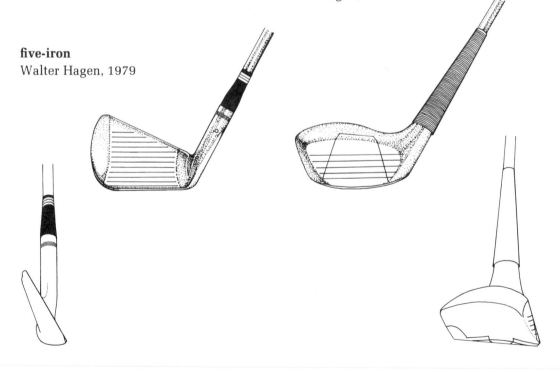

removed, and if the ball falls into the hole the player shall be deemed to have holed out at his last stroke.

flange *n.* A projecting part on the back of an iron clubhead.

1948 Ben Hogan *Power Golf* 138: The sand wedge I mean is a heavy club . . . with . . . a large flange which prevents the club from digging too deeply.
1963 Bob Rosburg *The Putter Book* 19: . . . a Tommy Armour blade putter with the flange on the back.
1977 Arnold Palmer *Golf Magazine* (Aug.) 90: Since the pitching wedge has a thinner flange than the sand wedge, it is better able to cut down and under a buried ball.

flat *adj.* **1** (Of a club) having a relatively wide angle between the head and the shaft; (of the lie of a club) relatively wide-angled.

1857 H.B. Farnie *The Golfer's Manual* 35: The lie of the cleek is decidedly flat.
1887 Sir Walter Simpson *The Art of Golf* 90: In the matter of lie, a tall player's club ought to be upright, a short man's flat.
1977 Dave Hill & Nick Seitz *Teed Off* 180: If the toe is off the ground your lie is too upright. You need a flatter lie so that the club will be squarely on the ground at address.

2 (Of a swing) moving in a relatively horizontal plane.

1890 Sir Walter Simpson *Badminton Golf* 192: . . . trust to a flatter swing to cure rocketing.
1915 Cecil Leitch in Alexander H. Revell *Pro & Con of Golf* 69: I take the club back very slowly and keep it close to the ground farther back than in the case of the ordinary swing. It is altogether a flat swing and shorter than my usual one.
1946 Frank Moran *Golfers' Gallery* n.p.: With her flat swing she lashed the ball with what in a woman golfer seemed a positively terrific power.
1965 *Paul Hahn Shows You How to Play Trouble Shots* 48: There are three regular types of [swing] plane: the flat, the normal, and the upright.

flex *n.* The flexibility or stiffness of the shaft of a club. [*Note:* there is no official scale of flex; different manufacturers use different systems and terms.]

1948 Ben Hogan *Power Golf* 13: The weight of the clubhead should also be in relation to the flex of the shaft.
1977 *Golf Illustrated* (Summer) 36: If a golfer is swinging clubs with the proper flex, the clubhead will move into the ball at the maximum speed that the golfer can control.

flip *n.,* or **flip shot.** A short, delicately hit approach shot of high trajectory played with a highly lofted iron.

1913 Grantland Rice *Golf Instruction* (in H.B. Martin *Golf Yarns* 13):
    The mashie grip, the niblick flip,
    And how H. Vardon plays.
1925 A.W. Tillinghast *Resignation* (in *The Mutt* 70):
    We tried all the grips, the swings, the
        flips
    Of the best men playing the game.
1965 Bob Charles *Left-handed Golf* 60: Who hasn't hit his drive "so far" or missed the green "so close" that he has a little "flip shot" left only to miss this delicate approach because that's precisely what he tried to do: *flip* it? This problem calls for rigid—not floppy—wrists: it cannot be "flipped." Firm up . . .

flip wedge. A flip shot played with a wedge.

1977 George Peper *Scrambling Golf* 113: . . . this mini-cut shot, often called a "flip wedge" . . .
1977 Gordon S. White, Jr. *New York Times* (June 10) A20: . . . flew his ball 180 yards down the fairway so he needed only a flip wedge shot to the green of the par-5 hole.

floater *n.* Any of various balls, no longer in use, that float in water.

1890 H.S.C. Everard *Badminton Golf* 389: . . . Mr. Glennie put the latter into the Swilcan Burn; however, when the party arrived the ball was seen to be a 'floater.'

1913 H.B. Martin *Golf Yarns* 58: The second hole at Great Neck, L.I., course is a mashie pitch over a pond. . . . Even the better players never think of using anything but a floater on this hole.
1929 *Golf Illustrated* (June) 25: The [new standard U.S.] ball, by the way, is not a floater. The floater is larger . . .
1969 J.S. Martin *The Curious History of the Golf Ball* 88: Ladies and light hitters would do better with large floaters, strong men with smaller, denser sinkers.

flub n. & v. [Origin: from U.S. slang *flub* ="to bungle, mismanage"; further origin unknown.] **1** n. A mishit.

1900 Carrie Foote Weeks *The Outing* (July) 387):
C is the Caddie who carries your Clubs;
He calls you a "Corker" in spite of your "flubs."

2 *v.trans.* To mishit (a shot).

1902 *Golf Illustrated* (Aug. 15) 124: Burnett flubbed his drive, getting about 100 yards.
1905 Frederick Upham Adams *John Henry Smith* 26: . . . this is the reason I so often flub my drive on this hole.
1933 Alex J. Morrison *A New Way to Better Golf* 134: Of course any player is likely to flub one now and then.
1949 Fred Beck & O.K. Barnes *Seventy-three Years in a Sand Trap* 23: . . . the man who can, when angry after flubbing a shot, throw a golf club further than anybody else in the world.
1964 Julius Boros *How to Win at Weekend Golf* 17: I knew I couldn't flub any more shots.
1977 *Golf Magazine* (Aug.) 21: On the 13th hole he flubbed a two-foot putt.

fluff v. & n. [Origin: there is only one known earlier occurrence of the verb outside golf, meaning "to bungle one's part in a play" (1888); the word may have been formed independently by golfers; origin obscure.] **1** *v.trans.* To mishit (a shot).

1897 Horace Hutchinson *Country Life* (Feb. 6) 169: . . . uncle squares up to the ball and fluffs it, finally, about half way. . .
1915 Hugh Leslie Dobree in Revell *Pro & Con of Golf* 81: "The odds are a million to one that you fluff your shot . . ."
1931 Roger Wethered *The Game of Golf* 84: After all, to top the ball in a bunker is a less flagrant offence than fluffing it completely.
1946 Frank Moran *Golfers' Gallery* 114: . . . fluffed his second into a bunker.
1969 Jack Nicklaus *The Greatest Game of All* 142: He fluffed his wedge chip, however, advancing the ball only a few yards and leaving it in the rough.
1978 Dave Anderson *New York Times* (June 18) S5: Then he fluffed an 8-iron into the creek.

2 n. A mishit.

1930 Bernard Darwin *Second Shots* 8: He is so prone to the common fluff that among his intimates that particular shot is always named after him.

fluffy *adj.* Sitting up in grass.

1964 Tony Lema *Golfer's Gold* 142: I took the club, put the ball in a nice, fluffy lie, and sent a shot high out over the canal.
1977 Dave Hill & Nick Seitz *Teed Off* 51: A top caddie will . . . remind me that the ball is liable to fly out of a fluffy lie and go farther than usual.

fly[1] *v.trans.* **1** To play clear over (a hazard, green, or other feature)

1890 Horace Hutchinson *Badminton Golf* 323: But if you have boldly and skilfully flown the face . . .
1977 Oscar Fraley *Golf Magazine* (July) 26: Barber feels that most amateurs have that inexplicable fear of flying the green.

2 To hit (the ball or a shot) high.

1962 Sam Snead *The Education of a Golfer* 66: . . . risking trouble on dogleg corners by flying my drives over the trees.
1971 Tommy Bolt *The Hole Truth* 96: Jack just tees his little whitey high and flies it out over those sand traps.

fly[2] *n.* **—on the fly** *phr.* Landing from clear flight without having bounced.

1962 Sam Snead *The Education of a Golfer* 207: Another time, I stymied Runyon, and what did he do but pitch over me with a wedge and into the hole—*on the fly.*
1970 Dick Schaap *The Masters* 87: Chi Chi Rodriguez's approach shot to the first green soars straight at the flag, actually lands in the cup on the fly, then bounces out.

flyer *n.* **1** A shot that flies very high.

1978 John Ahern *Boston Globe* (Sept. 4) 22: . . . lost it all with one bad tee shot, a flyer to the left on the third.

2 flyer lie. A somewhat perched lie from which a player is liable to hit a flyer.

1977 *New York Times* (July 17) S3: When bluegrass envelops a ball it . . . sets up "flyer" lies.

fog *n.* [Origin: Scottish, from Old Scottish *fog* = "moss, second growth of hay"; further origin unknown; not related to *fog* = mist.] *Chiefly Scottish.* A growth of moss or long grass.

1773 *Regulations of the Society of Golfers* (Bruntsfield) (in Clapcott 1935, 24): IX. When a Ball is struck into the Whins or any part where it may be covered, so much of the fogg grass, etc., must be set aside, that the player may have a view of his ball before he playes.
1824 *Rules of the Thistle Golf Club* 48: . . . and where the ball is completely covered with fog or grass.
1890 Horace Hutchinson *Badminton Golf* 60: . . . that accumulation of mossy annoyance which the Scotchman and the golfer can 'fog.'
1899 George S. Sargent *The Outing* (May) 139: . . . essay the task of mowing "fog" and "bent."

follow through *phr.v.* & **follow-through** *n.* **1** *phr.v.* To continue the swing of a club after hitting the ball.

1857 H.B. Farnie *The Golfer's Manual* 48: [On the jerking shot from a buried lie] The player must allow his club to be stopped immediately on hitting the intercepting grass, whin, or whatever obstacle it may be . . . should he attempt to make his club follow through it, as on open ground, the probable consequence would be that the shaft would be shivered.
1899 Findlay S. Douglas *The Outing* (June) 226: Think nothing about following through, but hit hard into the sand.
1915 Alexander H. Revell *Pro & Con of Golf* 25: "Follow through" means to let the club head go out straight to the hole.
1921 Andrew Kirkaldy *Fifty Years of Golf* 156: On his head [statue of Young Tom Morris] is the Balmoral bonnet that so often fell off as he "followed through" with that grand swing of his.
1946 Byron Nelson *Winning Golf* 182: Always follow completely through.
1961 John Stobbs *Tackle Golf* 54: When appropriate, follow through to swing the cutting edge of the club sharply upwards immediately after the ball is hit.

2 *n.* The action of following through; continuation of the swing after hitting the ball.

1912 Harry Vardon *How to Play Golf* 65: If the swing has been properly executed the follow-through will be all right.
1931 Joyce & Roger Wethered *The Game of Golf* 48: The club-head will flow naturally on, and your follow-through will not have been consciously made. It will just happen.
1977 Gene Sarazen *Golf Magazine* (Aug.) 47: Jack has one of the longest follow-throughs you will ever see.

foozle *n.* & *v.* [Origin: the verb occurs independently in U.S. slang (1835) meaning "to mess up (someone's hair)" and (1861) "to fool around with, flirt with (a girl)," but no later U.S. occurrences are known (*Dictionary of American English*). The adjective *foozling* = "messing around, stupid" occurs in *Tom Brown's Schooldays* (1857), presumably representing English public school slang, but this remains an isolated occurrence. The earliest known occurrences in golf (1869 and 1886, see below) are all clearly Scottish; but outside golf there is no trace of any other Scottish usage of the word, nor of any possible Scottish derivation for it. Origin unknown.] **1** *n.* A mishit shot.

1869 *Menu* of the annual dinner of the Cupar Golf Club, Fife (in Forgan *The Golfer's Handbook* 1881, 56): Fowls a la Foozle.
1886 David Jackson *Golf Songs & Recitations* 5:
The *sclaff,* the *foozle,* the *weel sent hame,*
The *ups* and *downs* of this dear game.
1890 Horace Hutchinson *Badminton Golf* 124: . . . on the very rare occasions on which he made a foozle.
1908 Arnold Haultain *The Mystery of Golf* (repr. 1965) 102: They proved to me, the duffer, that to take a foozle philosophically was not to be expected of mortal man.
1912 Harry Vardon *How to Play Golf* 74: . . . the majority of golfers sow the seeds of a foozle in the first movement.
1937 Abe Mitchell *Essentials of Golf* 115: Further, if the ball is lying close, the player fears a foozle with the brassie, with its comparatively flat swing.
1957 George Houghton *The Truth About Golf Addicts* 121: Lost balls, bunker to bunker, fluffs, foozles—all the irritations in the book.

2 *v.trans. & intrans.* To mishit (a shot).

1886 Alexander Lawson *Letters on Golf* 16: . . . many a man who has been missing putts and "foozling" iron shots feels that he has had an enjoyable round because he has been in capital driving form.
1890 Horace Hutchinson *Badminton Golf* 312: . . . the bungler who has foozled one of these drives . . . *Ibid.* 322: . . . if you happen to foozle, woe betide you.
1915 Alexander H. Revell *Pro & Con of Golf* 30: The carefully groomed fellow who draws the club of his choice from a bag bursting with sticks, only to foozle . . .
1922 P.G. Wodehouse *The Rough Stuff* (in *The Clicking of Cuthbert* repr. 1956, 149): Women . . . are apt to giggle when they foozle out of a perfect lie.
1956 Herbert Warren Wind *The Story of American Golf* 509: Snead who had led after the first day with a 71 and then for the nth time had foozled away a splendid chance in the Open with a second round of 78.

1960 Rex Lardner *Out of the Bunker and into the Trees* 39: . . . every time I'd foozle one he'd let me take it over, and every time he foozled, I'd let *him* take it over.
1978 Alex Graham *Fred Basset* (comic strip) in *Boston Globe* (Aug. 14) 20: "Tom had foozled his second, so I had the putt for the match."

3 foozled *adj.* Badly mishit.

1875 "M.T.S.D." *Duffers Yet* (in Clark *Golf: A Royal & Ancient Game* 223):
After grief in sand and whin,
Foozled drives, and "putts" not in . . .
1969 Jack Nicklaus *The Greatest Game of All* 215: I had a 75 which featured a few more hooked tee-shots and a couple of foozled short putts.

fore *interjection* [Origin: Scottish, shortening of *before* = "ahead."] Look out ahead! Used when a player is about to play toward people on the course who might be within range.

1819 *Blackwood's Edinburgh Magazine* (in Clark *Golf: A Royal of Ancient Game* 1875, 126): And clearing, with imperious "fore," the way . . .
1881 Robert Forgan *The Golfer's Handbook* 22: . . . shouts "Fore!" to give the alarm to any one in his way.
1908 Horace Hutchinson *Country Life* (Jan. 18) 105: . . . it is fully understood in Scotland that if you shout "Fore!" at a man and then kill him the Procurator Fiscal's verdict will be "Serve him right."
1929 Richard F. Picard *Golf Illustrated* (May) 24: And instead of screaming "Fore" in their ears and further annoying them, once again show that you belong to a club of gentlemen.
1960 Rex Lardner *Out of the Bunker and into the Trees* 24: A few of the following foursome were waving their clubs and shouting "Fore, Goddamit!"
1975 Dan Jenkins *Dead Solid Perfect* 222: Now one of the U.S.G.A. blue coats strolled to the middle of the tee and held up his arms, motioning politely for quiet among the fans clustered around us behind the ropes. "Fore, please," he said firmly.

forecaddie or **forecaddy** *n. & v.* [Origin: Scottish, shortened from *before-caddie.*]

1 n. A person employed to go ahead of players to mark the lie of balls in play.

1834 *Rules of the Musselburgh Golf Club* (in Clapcott 1935, 66): . . . if stopped by an antagonist or his Cady, the antagonist shall lose the hole. . . . *The fore Cady shall* in regard to this article be held as a third party.

1890 Horace Hutchinson *Badminton Golf* 330: Blackheath, moreover, is the only links on which you habitually play with a fore-caddy, who runs ahead with a red flag, as if you were a traction engine.

1907 Robert Ferguson (in Leach *Great Golfers in the Making* 185): My first job was as a forecaddie, and I daresay it would be a couple of years before I was promoted to a carrying caddie.

1936 H.B. Martin *Fifty Years of American Golf* 264: Secret Service men were often pressed into service [for President Harding] as scorekeepers and sometimes unwittingly as forecaddies.

1970 Dick Schaap *The Masters* 83: . . . the forecaddies for the Masters, the men who, after a player hits a drive, run to where the ball winds up and stand there, holding a flag on the end of a long stick to mark the position.

1976 *Rules of Golf* Definition 7.b.: A "forecaddie" is one employed by the Committee to indicate to players the position of balls on the course, and is an outside agency.

2 v.intrans. To act as forecaddie.

1913 Bernard Darwin *Country Life* (Aug. 16) 241: This office of forecaddying is a most essential one, but it does emphatically demand unselfishness, because the forecaddie combines the maximum of exertion with the minimum of interest.

1971 *Bartlett's World Golf Encyclopedia* 419: Know distances, hazard, where to "fore-caddie" . . .

form n. [*Origin:* doubtless borrowed from horse-racing.] A golfer's general standard of play, assessed on past performance and to some (varying) extent on style.

1890 Lord Wellwood *Badminton Golf* 50: A man's form is so quickly known that he is soon correctly handicapped.

1915 Alexander H. Revell *Pro & Con of Golf* 22: What is meant by "good form" is an approved stance, and a use of the clubs with a style approaching, if not strictly following, the best standards.

1922 P.G. Wodehouse *A Woman Is Only a Woman* (in *The Clicking of Cuthbert* repr. 1956, 27): . . . to develop such equal form at the game that the most expert critics are still baffled in their efforts to decide which is the worse player.

1936 H.B. Martin *Fifty Years of American Golf* 154: Willie Park, Jr., the former British Open Champion, who was regarded as an authority on form, picked out the best [U.S. Amateur] prospects according to his own idea of style.

1948 Horton Smith *Golfing* (May) n.p.: I think that O.B. Keeler made an accurate observation that main attention is now paid to "form" instead of to "style."

1962 Sam Snead *The Education of a Golfer* 179: Cy'd shot a 35-37-72, good enough to win all the bets he'd purposely lost the previous week. He'd done as good a job of disguising his real form as you'll ever see.

1975 Henry Cotton *History of Golf* 53: He also had the enviable ability to win when he was playing below form.

four-ball n. A match between the better balls of two sides, each consisting of two players.

1899 *Country Life* (Aug. 26) 251: The match was a four-ball one, for £20 a side.

1921 Andrew Kirkaldy *Fifty Years of Golf* 99: I had always plenty of faith in Ben when we were partnered in two-ball foursomes, before that monstrosity the four-ball foursome had been thought of.

1968 Stephen Potter *Golfmanship* 92: In a 4-ball at Beaconsdale, Virginia, we were four down against Dowell and Cussman, two Southerners.

1976 *Rules of Golf* Definition 28: Four-ball: A match in which two play their better ball against the better ball of two other players.

four-iron n. An iron club having loft of 27–28 degrees, lie of 58–60 degrees, and length of 37½ inches, and giving distance of 155–190 yards (men's clubs). Also, a shot played with a four-iron. Alternate name, mashie-iron.

1937 Abe Mitchell *Essentials of Golf* 116: The No. 4 should have a medium deep face and should be as deep at the heel as at the toe.
1972 Dutch Harrison *Golf Digest* (June): He pulled out a 4-iron and knocked that thing six inches from the flag.

four-iron
Walter Hagen, 1979

four-putt *v.trans. & intrans.* To take four putts on (a green or hole).

1962 Sam Snead *The Education of a Golfer* 209: I'd 3-putted only four greens out of 108 and 4-putted only one.
1967 George Plimpton *The Bogey Man* 193: Gene Sarazen . . . recalls Vardon as the most atrocious putter he had ever seen. "He didn't 3-putt, he 4-putted."
1979 Tom Place *Golf International* (March 8) 12: . . . lo and behold, he proceeded to FOUR PUTT the 15th green.

fours n. A score averaging four strokes for each hole.

1899 *Golf Illustrated* (June 16) 6: . . . everybody reckons the score now by "fours," and not, as used to be done, by "fives." Players prefer to say that they are two over "fours" for nine holes, to the old-fashioned "seven under," and this has only happened because the four standard is much more commonly reached or approached than formerly.
1907 Harold Hilton *My Golfing Reminiscences* 97: . . . going to that hole he had to do an average of fours to tie.
1928 George W. Greenwood *Golf Illustrated* (July) 27: For the 106 holes . . . Perkins's score was an average of two over 4's.
1946 Frank Moran *Golfers' Gallery* 19: Seventy-two holes of the Old Course in three under 4's was rather a staggerer for many of the old-timers.
1969 Tom Scott & Geoffrey Cousins *The Golf Immortals* 63: . . . at 56 he was able to average fours for four rounds of the Open Championship.

foursome n. A match between two sides, each consisting of two players playing one ball by alternate strokes.

1857 H.B. Farnie *The Golfer's Manual* 65: Sometimes four engage—two against two—and this combination is called a foursome.
1891 *Golf* magazine (Sept. 18) 3: Of all forms of Golf matches perhaps a first-class foursome affords the greatest interest to the critical spectator.
1936 H.B. Martin *Fifty Years of American Golf* 263: It was during the midst of an enjoyable foursome at Chevy Chase that [President Wilson] was informed by messenger of the sinking of the *Lusitania*.
1977 Charles Price *Golf Magazine* (July) 65: One of her favorite tournaments was the Worplesdon Foursome, an event in which a man and a woman played alternate shots with the same ball in matches against another pair.

four-wood n. A wood club having loft of 18–20 degrees, lie of 55–57 degrees, and length of 41½ inches, and giving distance of 200–230 yards (men's clubs). Also, a shot played with a four-wood. Alternate name, spoon.

1948 Ben Hogan *Power Golf* 140: In using

four-wood
Ben Hogan, 1979

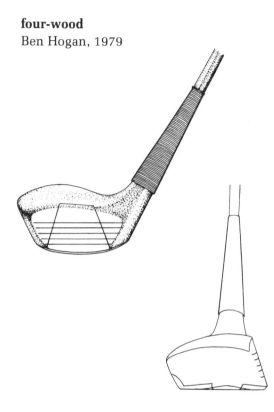

the four-wood . . . out of a bunker make sure that you hit the ball, not the sand behind it.
1979 Liz Kahn *Par Golf* (March) 23: . . . he placed a four wood firmly behind the ball . . .

freak *adj.* Contrary to the traditions or the rules of golf, or both.

1915 Alexander H. Revell *Pro & Con of Golf* 22: 'A freak player is a blot on the landscape.'
1919 Robert K. Risk *Songs of the Links* 59:
There arrived weird permutations, twin
    and triple combinations—
The driving-iron, driving-mashie-cleek;
There followed very soon, that
    "albumeenious spoon,"
And every other day some putting freak.
1922 P.G. Wodehouse *The Long Hole* (in *The Clicking of Cuthbert* repr. 1956, 114): I was revolted. About that time a perfect epidemic of freak matches had broken out in the club. . . . Playing freak golf-matches is to my mind like ragging a great classical melody.

1927 Robert T. Jones, Jr. & O.B. Keeler *Down the Fairway* 205: . . . it was, in plain language, a stupid attempt to correct a faulty position with a freak club.
1946 Frank Moran *Golfers' Gallery* 67: Those freak tees . . . to see a golf ball pegged up a foot high and hit with an abnormally deep-faced club was strange indeed.
1976 J.C. Jessop *Golf* 90: Freak putters have been invented, and there are many freak styles of putting.

fried-egg *adj.* Half-buried in sand.

1960 Rex Lardner *Out of the Bunker and into the Trees* 146: The ball was half-buried in the sand. . . . "What we call a fried-egg lie," I told her cheerily.
1977 Gordon S. White *New York Times* (Aug. 28) S4: McEvoy then blasted away at a fried-egg lie and put the American ball even farther away.

frog hair. *Slang, chiefly U.S.* The short grass of the apron of a green.

1962 Sam Snead *The Education of a Golfer* 7: So I put the shot . . . into the frog hair around the green.
1977 Gordon S. White *New York Times* (Aug. 8) 33: . . . he pushed a tee shot 330 yards, so far that it landed on the frog hair of the 11th green.

front *adj.* Designating the first nine holes of an eighteen-hole course.

1977 Betsy Rawls *Golf Magazine* (June) 101: The hardest par on the front nine . . .

full *adj.* (Of a stroke or swing) using the farthest extent of backswing and follow-through; (of a shot) played with a full swing and generally full application of power.

1793 *Addendum* to Thomas Mathison *The Goff* (3rd edition): . . . he could play off from the tee, at a full stroke, twelve successive balls, and lay every one of them within the space of two or three club-lengths from one another.

1857 H.B. Farnie *The Golfer's Manual* 50: . . . such Golfers have invariably a bad style of using this tool [driving iron], the general mistake being a *full swing.*

1896 *Baily's Magazine* (Sept.) 243: . . . if you get on the upward slope, you may take a driver or brassie and have a full shot, while if, on the other hand, the ball chances to lie on the further side of the mound, you have to content yourself with a comparatively short stroke with cleek or iron.

1912 Harry Vardon *How to Play Golf* 33: A distance of 330 yards is often described as bad, because, under normal circumstances, it requires more than one full shot and less than two less strenuous strokes.

1916 P.A. Vaile *The New Golf* 83: A half or three-quarter shot with the cleek is frequently much better than a full shot with the iron.

1950 Sam Snead *How to Hit a Golf Ball* 52: The chief difference between a full-iron shot and a half-iron shot is in the length and amount of power in the swing.

1977 Sandra Palmer *Golf Digest* (July) 34: Since the men are stronger to begin with, they don't have to practice their full shots as much, so they have more time for putting.

G

gallery *n. & v.*   **1** *n.* The body of spectators at a match or tournament.

1890   Lord Wellwood *Badminton Golf* 43: This being the home hole, a large gallery is looking on . . .
1908   Arnold Haultain *The Mystery of Golf* repr. 1965, 116:   How many golfers, too, either resent or welcome the existence of a "gallery."
1927   Robert T. Jones, Jr. & O.B. Keeler *Down the Fairway* n.p.:   . . . word had got about that the new kid from Dixie was breaking up the tournament, and almost the entire gallery assembled to follow me.
1977   Dan Jenkins *Sports Illustrated* (June) 43:   By now Palmer had collected a gallery of perhaps 100, most of them walking side by side with him down the fairways.

2 *v.trans. & intrans.*   To be a spectator (at a match or tournament).

1962   Sam Snead *The Education of a Golfer* 91:   . . . a long-distance glimpse of King George VI when he'd galleried the 1937 British Open.
1970   Dick Schaap *The Masters* 64:   . . . qualified to play in the 1970 Masters. "It sure beats gallerying," says Rosburg.

galleryite *n.*   A spectator at a match or tournament.

1928   A.T. Packard *Golf Illustrated* (June) 76:   Hundreds of galleryites noted the shots and broke for commanding positions at the first hole.
1969   Paul D. Peery *Billy Casper, Winner* 170:   A galleryite was heard to remark, "This can't be the same man. Casper never smiles."

game *n.*   **1** Golf itself, or any contest at golf, either by match play or by stroke play.

1793   *Preface* to Thomas Mathison *The Goff* (3rd edition):   The game of goff has been known and practiced in Scotland for upwards of four hundred years.
1872   John Henry Walsh *British Rural Sports* 635:   A game may be said to terminate at a fixed number of these holes . . .
1976   *Rules of Golf* 1:   The Game of Golf consists in playing a ball from the teeing ground into the hole by successive strokes in accordance with the Rules.

2 A player's standard of performance.

1907   J.H. Taylor in Leach *Great Golfers in the Making* 73:   The match with Mr. Hutchinson, perhaps, made it dawn on me that I might be the fortunate possessor of a game that was rather better than that of my contemporaries.
1922   P.G. Wodehouse *A Woman Is Only a Woman* (in *The Clicking of Cuthbert* repr. 1956, 26):   I have known cases where marriage improved a man's game, and others where it seemed to put him right off his stroke.

1946 Percy Boomer *On Learning Golf* 20: Her own game is the essence of perfect mental and physical balance.
1977 John S. Radosta *New York Times* (July 25) 14: Trevino also has added a disciplined regimen of work on rebuilding his game.

3 (a) long game. Performance of drives and other long shots; play through the green.

1881 Robert Forgan *The Golfer's Handbook* 28: We have dwelt thus at length on the *long* game because . . . "far and sure" driving is most difficult of attainment.
1913 Bernard Darwin *Country Life* (Jan. 11) 69: He is a very sound and steady player in the long game.
1926 Lucille MacAllister *Golf Illustrated* (Sept.) 29: On the whole Miss Collett played the prettier and more efficient long game.
1977 Sandra Palmer *Golf Digest* (July) 33: "We have to practice our long games more than the men to keep up our strength."

(b) short game. Performance of approaches and putts.

1890 Lord Wellwood *Badminton Golf* 35: . . . his short game was deadly, especially his putting.
1915 Christy Mathewson in Revell *Pro & Con of Golf* 27: . . . I would recommend to the beginner that he practice the short game as much as possible, the approach and putting.
1936 H.B. Martin *Fifty Years of American Golf* 271: Commodore Heard worked on the theory that it was the short game that counted most and perfection in the pitch and putt saved many strokes.
1977 George Peper *Golf Magazine* (June) 68: The short Challenger course, at 2,200 yards, is a good place to give your driver and 2-iron a rest and tune up your short game.

gateway *n.* The part of a fairway that leads to the green, especially if flanked by hills or hazards.

1912 Harry Vardon *How to Play Golf* 34: But he would have to keep straight, and the open gateway to the green would not be expansive.
1973 Arnold Palmer *Go for Broke* 11: . . . a treacherous bunker guarding the gateway to the green.

gimme *n.* *Slang, chiefly U.S.* A short putt, that is often conceded without holing out.

1929 W.H. Faust *Golf Illustrated* (April) 25: Bill carelessly tapped his ball toward the hole, following the usual custom of considering a putt of that short distance a "gimme."
1964 Tony Lema *Golfer's Gold* 16: There are no "gimmes" on the pro tour.
1973 *Bartlett's World Golf Encyclopedia* 411: The "gimme putt' is the most frequent violation of this rule [Rule 1], which is the very definition of golf.
1978 Jack Craig *Boston Globe* (Aug. 14) 23: Mahaffey's decisive four-birdie string included two gimme putts.

globe *n.* **—miss the globe** *phr.* *Slang, probably obsolete.* To make a stroke that fails to hit the ball.

1862 Robert Chambers *A Few Rambling Remarks on Golf* 23: Now, as nearly every beginner, from over-anxiety, 'misses the globe' the first shot . . .
1895 James P. Lee *Golf in America* 179: Miss the globe.—To fail to strike the ball either by swinging right over the top of it or by hitting the ground behind.
1920 Robert Marshall *The Enchanted Golfer* 38: "Ye've missed the globe," was his comment. "An' it's a black disgrace to a gowfer."

gobble *n.* *Slang, obsolete.* A hard-hit putt that holes out.

1857 H.B. Farnie *The Golfer's Manual* 62: On the other hand, when the golfer is a couple of strokes or more behind, his only chance lies in a bold put—a rapid gobble over level ground.
1893 J. Stuart Balfour *Golf, Spalding's Athletic Library* (May) 13: Gobble.—A rapid straight "putt" into the hole, such that, had the ball not gone in, it would have gone some distance beyond.

glove *n.,* or **golf glove.** A glove generally worn by a right-handed golfer on the left hand, and by a left-handed golfer on the right hand, to enhance the grip.

1899 Advertisement *Golf Illustrated* (June 23) 58: Wear the New Simplex Golf Glove. For Left Hand, the most Perfect Glove made. . . . Right Hand Glove also supplied if required.
1979 Alex Hay *Golf Illustrated* (U.K.) (Feb. 15) 10: Recently I have been involved in the production of a new golf glove which has a snakeskin palm.

golf *n. & v.* [Origin: Scottish, from Old Scottish *golf, golve, gowf, gouf* (and other spellings); probably borrowed from medieval Dutch *colf*="club," and *spel metten colven*="game (played) with club," name of a Dutch game resembling golf.] **1** *n.* A game, probably evolved from Dutch antecedents, first recorded in Scotland in the 15th century, and played under codified rules since the middle of the 18th century; now consisting of hitting a golf ball, using an array of golf clubs, by successive strokes into each of nine or eighteen holes on a golf course. [See *Rules of Golf* (1976), published by the Royal and Ancient Golf Club of St. Andrews, Scotland, and the United States Golf Association, Far Hills, New Jersey.]

1457 *Acts of the Parliaments of Scotland* II.48: At the fut bal ande the golf be vtterly criyt done and nocht vsyt.
1504 *Accounts of the Lords High Treasurers of Scotland*: To the King to play at the golf with the Erle of Bothuile, iii French crounis.
1575 *Diurnall of Remarkable Occurrents* 285: Certane horsmen of Edinburgh . . . past to the links of Leith, and thar tuik nyne burgessis of Edinburgh playand at the golf.
1596 *Records of Elgin*: Walter Hay . . . accusit for playing at the boulis and golff upoun Sondaye in the tym of the sermon.
1642 *Muniments of the University of Glasgow* II. 466: That the Schollers be exercised in lawful games, such as gouffe, archarie, and the lyk.
1658 Thomas Harbottle (of Tuttle Fields, London) *Petition* (Feb. 9) (in *The Golfer's Handbook* 1974, 78): . . . to the Defaceing of the sd ffeilds, the hindrance of the meeting of the Gentry for their recreation at Bowles, Goffe, and Stowball.

1687 Thomas Kincaid *Diary* (Jan. 21) (in *Book of the Old Edinburgh Club* XXVII (1949) 133): I found that the first point to be studied in playeing at the golve is to hitt the ball exactly.
1690 *Seafield Correspondence* 64: Ife . . . you have a mind for a touch at long gauff tomorrow, lett me know.
1743 Thomas Mathison *The Goff* 1:
   GOFF, and the Man, I sing, who em'lous plies
   The jointed club; whose balls invade the skies.
1744 *Articles & Laws in Playing at Golf* (title of the rules of the Gentlemen Golfers of Leith).
1771 Tobias Smollett *Humphrey Clinker* (repr. 1902) 236: Hard by, in the fields called the Links, the citizens of Edinburgh divert themselves at a game called Golf, in which they use a curious kind of bats tipped with horn, and small elastic balls of leather, stuffed with feathers.
1779 *Rivington's Royal Gazette* (April 21) (in H.B. Martin *The Story of American Golf* 1936, 45): To the GOLF PLAYERS. The season for this pleasant and healthy Exercise now advancing, Gentlemen may be furnished with excellent CLUBS and the veritable Caledonian BALLS.
1819 Peter Morris *Peter's Letters to His Kinsfolk* 203: . . . we saw several elderly citizens playing at the old Scots game of golf, which is a kind of gigantic variety of billiards.
1890 Andrew Lang *Badminton Golf* 13: Golf has thus historical records far more ancient than cricket can display.
1898 Charles B. Macdonald *Golf* magazine (Jan.) 23: In the old university town of St. Andrews the word golf is pronounced "Goff" . . . such is the pronunciation today.
1919 Robert K. Risk *Songs of the Links* 20:
   And Betty has written a letter, to say
      that our match is off,
   Unless I can give her wholly the love
      that belongs to golf.
1928 Will Rogers *Autobiography* 181: Rail splitting produced an immortal President in Abraham Lincoln: but Golf, with 29 thousand courses, hasent produced even a good A Number-1 Congressman.
1968 Stephen Potter *Golfmanship* 6: This analysis of a few of the pronunciations of the word 'golf' may be useful: . . . gŏff: English 'upper-class' or O.K. pronunciation, 1890–

1950 . . . gouf: Lowland Scots who wish to preserve accent . . . garlf: Northern Idaho.

1976 *Rules of Golf* 1: The Game of Golf consists in playing a ball from the teeing ground into the hole by successive strokes in accordance with the Rules.

2 *v.intrans.* To play golf.

1769 *Minutes of the Town Council of St. Andrews* (Nov. 29) (in H.S.C. Everard *History of the R. & A.* 1907, 39): It is also agreed that the part of the Links as presently golfed upon shall be kept entire, and not ploughed up nor enclosed by the Town of St. Andrews or their tenants.

1881 Robert Forgan *The Golfer's Handbook* 55: [Ninety] is understood to have been the age of a general officer who golfed at St. Andrews as long as he could walk.

1912 Harry Vardon *How to Play Golf* n.p.: Sometimes one sees ladies golfing in large straw hats.

1968 Buddy Hackett *The Truth About Golf* 42: Once I was golfing with a shifty-looking stranger . . .

golf ball. See **ball.**

golf car. See **car.**

golf cart. See **cart.**

golf club. See **club.**

golf course. See **course.**

golfdom n. The world of golf.

1853 *Fifeshire Journal* (June 30): We don't imagine that Allan's right to the sceptre of golfdom was ever doubted by the many who know he has discomfited all who have challenged him.

1898 W.G. Van T. Sutphen *The Hong-Kong Medal* (in *The Golficide* 75): . . . all golfdom had assembled to see the battle.

1907 Arthur Pottow *Recreation* (May) 549: So that, after the game had been domiciled here but a few years an American player had won the Blue Ribband of Golfdom.

1926 James H. Rothschild *Golf Illustrated* (Sept.) 21: But my advent into Golfdom has been nothing if not educating.

1927 *Golfdom, the Golf Business Magazine* (title of magazine).

1977 *New York Times* (Sept. 30) 55: [headline] Adoption of Sudden-Death Play-offs Drives A Wedge In Golfdom's Ranks.

golfer n. [With Scottish variant spellings.] A player of golf.

1744 *Scots Magazine* (April) 197: The act appoints . . . that [the Captain of the Goff] . . . have . . . the determination of disputes among goffers.

1771 Tobias Smollett *Humphrey Clinker* (repr. 1902) 236: Among others, I was shown one particular set of golfers, the youngest of whom was turned of fourscore.

1810 *Minutes of the Musselburgh Golf Club* (Dec. 14) (in Clark *Golf: A Royal & Ancient Game* repr. 1975, 91): The Club resolve to present by subscription a new Creel and Shawl to the best female golfer who plays on the annual occasion on 1st Jan. next.

1833 George Fullerton Carnegie *Golfiana* (in Clark op. cit. 157):

Let none judge us rashly, or blame us as scoffers,
When we say that, instead, there are
Links full of golfers.

1890 Tom Morris *Badminton Golf* 431: "Aye! as ye say, sir, born and bred in St. Andrews, an' a gowffer a' ma days."

1915 "A Wandering Briton" in Revell *Pro & Con of Golf* 54: It is asserted that the best American golfers are not so keen as the British, but that they are coming on fast, and that with their thoroughness, keenness, and determination there is no telling what they may do.

1926 Roger Wethered *Golf Illustrated* (Sept.) 20: I am afraid that the truth of the matter is that we are less efficient golfers than the Americans.

1968 Buddy Hackett *The Truth About Golf* 12: Golfers like to bug each other and frequently they say things which in any other circumstances would destroy friendships.

1971 Henry Longhurst *My Life and Soft Times* 43: ... my father, a keenly indifferent 16-handicap performer and precisely the average golfer for whom all golf writers should to my way of thinking deem themselves to be writing.

golfiana *plural n.* Matters, literature, or artifacts belonging to golf.

1833 George Fullerton Carnegie *Golfiana* (title of collection of poetry).
1881 Robert Forgan *The Golfer's Handbook* 50: *Golfiana* (chapter heading).
1912 "Bibliophile" *Golf* magazine (Nov.) 1: GOLFIANA—The collection of books, prints, and all manner of things having an antiquarian interest to golf is not a hobby much pursued in this country.
1973 *Bartlett's World Golf Encyclopedia* 436: Finally, for the collector of golfiana, we list a major reference resource ...

golfic *adj. Rare, probably obsolete.* Relating to golf.

1892 *Golf* magazine (Feb. 5) 330: But to return to matters golfic ...

golfing *n. & adj.* **1** *n.* The playing of golf.

1793 Anon. *Song in Praise of Golf* (in Thomas Mathison *The Goff*, 3rd edition, 24):
But truth bids the muse from
    henceforward proclaim
That golfing of field sports stands
    foremost in fame.
1881 Robert Forgan *The Golfer's Handbook* 22: Golfing, he will find, is a mysterious art.
1907 Robert Ferguson in Leach *Great Golfers in the Making* 193: I believe that golfing—that is, good golfing—is a gift.
1921 Andrew Kirkaldy *Fifty Years of Golf* 25: I may now tell a story of Mr. Asquith, who was very fond at one time of golfing ...

2 *adj.* Of or relating to golf.

1888 *Chambers's Journal* (May 26) 322: The regular golfing jokes that have served successive generations ...
1913 Henry Leach *The American Golfer*

(Oct.) n.p.: America has indeed graduated now as a first-class golfing power.
1925 Logan Pearsall Smith *Words and Idioms* 149: ... from Scotland has come that wealth of golfing terms which have recently been added to the language.
1946 Frank Moran *Golfers' Gallery* 165: Jones had somehow got the secret of golfing greatness.
1975 Barry Goldwater *Reader's Digest* (Dec.) 186: ... to stop weakening the cause of justice by putting men on the bench who may happen to be golfing partners of Congressmen.

golf lawyer. A golfer who makes pettifogging use of the rules.

1899 *Country Life* (Oct. 7) 418: The golfing lawyer will not even yet be defrauded of the exercise of his natural, if perverted, intelligence.
1922 P.G. Wodehouse *The Long Hole* (in *The Clicking of Cuthbert* repr. 1956, 110): "If there's one thing that gives me a pain squarely in the centre of the gizzard," he burst out ... "it's a golf-lawyer ..."
1949 Fred Beck & O.K. Barnes *Seventy-three Years in a Sand Trap* 73: One of the familiar types is the Golf Lawyer, or Rulebook Demon.

golf widow. A woman whose husband neglects her for golf.

1890 *Badminton Golf* 45: A golf widow [caption to drawing].
1919 Robert K. Risk *Songs of the Links* 30:
But the young golf widows, O my
    brothers,
  They are weeping bitterly,
They are weeping in the playtime of the
    others,
  While you're swiping from the tee.
1936 H.B. Martin *Fifty Years of American Golf* 194: After a few years of patient suffering the women folk of Yonkers arose *en masse* to remonstrate in earnest, as they were no longer reconciled to being known as "golf widows" ... So there was nothing left to do but to start a golf course of their own.
1969 Paul D. Peery *Billy Casper: Winner* 38: And Liz Chase says that she and Shirley

[Casper] have been golf widows since fourteen.

1974 Advertisement *The Golfer's Handbook* ix: Whitsand Bay Hotel and Golf Club.... Owned and run by golfers, but not forgetting golf widows and widowers and their families, for whom other facilities include games rooms.

---

goose-neck or **goose-necked** *adj.* (Of an iron club) having the neck curved so that the heel is slightly offset from the line of the shaft.

1899 Price Collier *The Outing* (Jan.) 423: ... and hears with delight again the familiar *patois* about Silvertowns, remade balls, goose-neck putters, one-piece drivers, et *hoc genus omne.*

1907 *Army & Navy Stores Catalogue* 999: Goose-necked putters.

1941 Patty Berg *Golf* 71: I prefer a "goose-neck" putter (one whose putting blade is behind the point at which the head joins the shaft).

1956 Herbert Warren Wind *The Story of American Golf* 254: [Dorothy Hurd] chipped with "Thomas," a goose-necked mashie with a small face.

1977 Joe Martin letter to *Golf Magazine* (June) 7: ... a goose-neck niblick I have owned since 1918.

---

gorse *n.* *Chiefly British.* A spiny evergreen shrub, *Ulex europaeus*, having bright yellow flowers, found on many golf courses, especially those of the linksland type. [Note: the same plant is also called *whin* in Scotland and usually *furze* in the United States.]

1972 Michael Murphy *Golf in the Kingdom* 21: Gorse, a low brambly shrub of the genus *Ulex*, is common to Scottish wastelands and golfing links. It is said by some to grow as well in the fields of hell.

---

grain *n.* The direction in which the blades of grass on a putting green predominantly point or lie.

1948 Ben Hogan *Power Golf* 134: When you putt against the grain it stands to reason you have to hit the ball a little harder to reach the hole.

1963 Bob Rosburg *The Putter Book* 51: Grain is the term given to grass that lies flat on greens, instead of growing upright as is desirable.

---

grainy *adj.* Having strong grain.

1969 Jack Nicklaus *The Greatest Game of All* 214: I found I could read the grainy greens all right and I putted them reasonably well.

---

grass *n.* *Obsolete.* The loft of a wooden clubface.

1895 W. Dalrymple *Handbook to Golf* 52: ... the lofting is given by what is technically known as the "grass" of the face.

---

grass-club *n.*, or **grassed club** or **grassed driver.** *Obsolete.* A driver with slightly more loft than the straight-faced driver or play club.

1837 *Encyclopaedia Edinensis* (in Donald Walker *Sports & Games* 179): The most common kind is the grass club, which consists of a long tapering shank...to the smaller extremity of which is fixed a broad head.

1867 "R.C. Jr." *The Short Hole* in *Poems on Golf* 54:
> Yours, by no blunder this time
> counteracted,
> Is with the grass-club lofted over all.

1881 Robert Forgan *The Golfer's Handbook* 10: The "grassed driver" is likewise used to effect distance.... It differs from the play-club in having a slightly stiffer handle and heavier head, and in its face being sloped back a little from the perpendicular.

1895 James P. Lee *Golf in America* 117: WOODEN CLUBS. The driver or play club. Grassed driver ...

1913 Horace Hutchinson *Country Life* (Jan. 11) 69: Now the clubs that our forefathers generally recognized as necessary to golfing salvation were ... (2) the grassed club (that is to say, a club with the face very slightly laid back, or "grassed," and in other respects identical with the driver.)

grassed *adj. Obsolete.* (Of a wooden clubface) lofted.

1857 H.B. Farnie *The Golfer's Manual* 31: Their driving clubs may be also grassed more than is customary, to ensure elevation to a stroke.
1881 Robert Forgan *The Golfer's Handbook* 60: GRASSED—said of a club whose face is "spooned" or sloped backward.
1891 *Golf* magazine (Feb. 20) 356: . . . as all golfers know, the ordinary cleek has a good deal of loft on it, or, in other words, the face is sloped back, or grassed.

green *n.* **1** *Chiefly Scottish.* A golf course.

1743 Thomas Mathison *The Goff* 14:
Thrice round the green they urge the
  whizzing ball . . .
1833 George Fullerton Carnegie *Golfiana* (in Clark *Golf: A Royal & Ancient Game* 1875, 141):
The green has its bunkers, its hazards,
  and rubs . . .
1868 *Minutes of the Edinburgh Burgess Golfing Society* (in Clark op. cit. 111): The Committee appointed to report on the Braid Hills as a Golfing Green, played there today, and enjoyed the game amazingly.
1890 Tom Morris *Badminton Golf* 431: Three years efter Allan deed I cam to keep the Green here . . .
1915 "A Wandering Player" in Revell *Pro & Con of Golf* 117: . . . three hours and ten minutes were taken over a match that had a clear green in front of it all the way.
1931 T. Simpson *The Game of Golf* 175: From the point of view of all-round excellence the course at Pullborough should rank as at least the equal of any inland green in this or any other country.
1946 Frank Moran *Golfers' Gallery* 54: What about Robert Maxwell, the giant of Muirfield who had been well-nigh invincible on his own green?

1974 *The Golfer's Handbook* 436: [Braid and Herd] lost to Vardon and Taylor in a match for £400 over four greens.

2 green *or (officially)* **putting green.** The clear area of short grass on which a hole is situated; now generally mown and rolled to the smoothest possible texture.

1815 *Regulations* (Aberdeen) (in Clapcott 1935, 51): . . . all loose impediments may be removed on the putting green, which is declared to be 15 yards from the hole all round.
1833 George Fullerton Carnegie *The Golfiad* (in Clark loc. cit.):
We reach the green at last, in even
  strokes . . .
1857 H.B. Farnie *The Golfer's Manual* 14: These holes are placed on especially smooth tables of turf called putting greens.
1887 "Rockwood" (in Charles Chambers *Golfing* 48): I thought of hazards surmounted and battles snatched literally from the fire on the putting-greens of my youthful days.
1901 Horace Hutchinson *Country Life* (July 13) 39: . . . had not Taylor been unfortunate in his ball striking the rail guarding the green at the last hole.
1926 William D. Richardson *Golf Illustrated* (Oct.) 39: Jones had 29 two-putt greens and five one-putt greens.
1963 Bob Rosburg *The Putter Book* 50: The average green on a full-size, modern course is bigger—5,000 square feet and up—and usually elevated, sloped and contoured.
1976 *Rules of Golf* Definition 25: The "putting green" is all ground of the hole being played which is specially prepared for putting or otherwise defined as such by the Committee.

green committee. A committee of members of a golf club responsible for the maintenance and management of the course. [*Note:* the term "greens committee" is erroneous. The reference here is to green=the course, not to the putting greens. See def. 1 of green.]

1864 *Minutes of the Royal & Ancient Golf Club of St. Andrews* (May 4) (in Clark *Golf: A Royal & Ancient Game* repr. 1975, 80):

Major Boothby moved, That Tom Morris of Prestwick, formerly of St. Andrews, be brought here as a professional golfer . . . on the understanding that he shall have the entire charge of the Golf Course under the Green Committee.
1901 Horace Hutchinson *Country Life* (July 20) 93: All the green committees in the kingdom ought to go to Mitcham for an object-lesson.
1929 Richard A. Picard *Golf Illustrated* (May) 24: . . . I peep cautiously around to see if a member of the Green Committee is watching me.

green fee. A fee charged to a player for use of a golf course. [*Note*: the term "greens fee," although now widespread, is erroneous. The fee is charged, not merely for the putting greens, but for the use of the whole course. See def. 1 of green.]

1913 Bernard Darwin *Country Life* (May 10) 685: . . . clubs deriving the larger part of their income from visitors' green fees.
1962 Sam Snead *The Education of a Golfer* 227: . . . the Revenuer insisted on paying his own greens fee.
1974 Advertisement *The Golfer's Handbook* ix: Gleneagles Hotel, Perthshire . . . Reduced green fees for hotel guests.
1977 *Golf Magazine* (July) 21: . . . they had purchased green fees and electric cars for 18 holes.

greenkeeper *or* **green-keeper** *n.* An employee of a club or course who is responsible for the maintenance and management of the course. [*Note*: the term "greenskeeper" is erroneous. The official is in charge of the whole course, not merely of the putting greens. See def. 1 of green.]

[**1875** Robert Clark *Golf: A Royal & Ancient Game* 71: . . . a proposal was made to invite Tom Morris, then at Prestwick, to become Keeper of the St. Andrews green.]
1890 Horace Hutchinson *Badminton Golf* 283: The green-keeper, engaged by the club

at a certain annual salary to look after the ground, manage the tees . . .
1903 Arthur Ruhl *The Outing* (June) 292: Each one must get his little ticket from the greens keeper.
1926 Personal advertisement *Golf Illustrated* (Sept.) 52: Professional & Greenskeeper—Wishes change, ten years experience . . . capable of producing superior fairways and putting greens.
1946 Bernard Darwin *British Golf* 12: There were few courses that needed [the professional's] services as a green-keeper.
1967 Mark McCormack *Arnie* 29: Arnold's father, who had been greenskeeper, was soon to be made head professional.
1975 Herb Graffis *The P.G.A.* 106: The National Association of Greenkeepers (later to be called golf course superintendents) was formed in 1927.

greenkeeping *or* **green-keeping** *n.* The science and profession of maintaining and managing a golf course. [*Note*: on the erroneous term "greenskeeping," see *Note* at greenkeeper.]

1907 W. Herbert Fowler in Leach *Great Golfers in the Making* 162: I have for some time taken a keen interest in green-keeping, and found it a most fascinating subject.
1936 H.B. Martin *Fifty Years of American Golf* 139: . . . the extensive research work done each year, which has removed greenkeeping from the realm of mysticism, quackery and humbug and placed it on a scientific basis.
1969 Tom Scott & Geoffrey Cousins *The Golf Immortals* 47: Modern greenkeeping has made it easier for a man who studies the art to be a good putter.

greenside *adj.* Situated beside a putting green.

1977 Arnold Palmer *Golf Magazine* (Aug.) 90: . . . where you have a good lie in a greenside trap and no lip to worry about.

greensome *n.* See quotation below.

1974 *The Golfer's Handbook* 113: The greensome is a species of four-ball competition. Both players in a combination play tee shots, and afterwards continue with one of the balls which is nominated . . . (This type of competition is "unofficial" and not covered by the Rules.)

grip n.   **1** The part of the shaft of a club by which the player holds it, including the leather, rubber, or synthetic material encasing it to form a handle.

1881 Robert Forgan *The Golfer's Handbook* 60: GRIP.—1st, The part of the handle covered with leather by which the club is grasped; 2nd, the grasp itself.
1908 Horace Hutchinson *Country Life* (Jan. 11) 69: . . . the cork grips which I find many people using now. There are many other grips, rubber is the material principally in use.
1926 Advertisement *Golf Illustrated* (June) 70: HEWIT'S IDEAL GRIPS, of solid pigskin . . .
1973 *Bartlett's World Golf Encyclopedia* 363: Most grips today are of rubber or leather. . . . The weight of the grip is one of the three major factors in overall swing-weight.
1976 *Rules of Golf* Appendix II.d: The grip consists of that part of the shaft designed to be held by the player and any material added to it for the purpose of obtaining a firm hold.

2 The way in which a player's hands are positioned in holding the club.

1888 *Chambers's Journal* (May 26) 322: His counsel, I hope, has been worked long since into flesh and blood movement—grip, swing, loft, and putt.
1890 Horace Hutchinson *Badminton Golf* 81: Certain points may be noted about the grip . . .
1916 P.A. Vaile *The New Golf* 8: It is however impossible to dogmatize about the matter of grip.
1921 Andrew Kirkaldy *Fifty Years of Golf* 153: You will have noticed, if you have ever seen Herd play, that his grip is according to the old-fashioned St. Andrews style—no overlapping, no interlocking, or other contraption.
1931 Robert & Joyce Wethered *The Game of Golf* 51: The importance of grip and stance is that they shall aid and abet the swing.

1977 *Golf Illustrated* (Summer) 37: Generally speaking, there are three types of grip, the overlapping, interlocking and palm (or baseball). . . . the majority of golfers prefer the overlapping method.

groove[1] n. & v.   [*Origin:* U.S., borrowed from baseball; see quotation 1929 under *grooved adj.*]   **1** n. The consistent path or sequence of movements followed by the swing of a consistently accurate player.

1928 Robert T. Jones, Jr. *Golf Illustrated* (June) 21: The swing never has a chance to get started in the proper groove . . .
1931 Joyce & Roger Wethered *The Game of Golf* 43: The idea of the swing should be so clearly mapped out in the brain that the arms and body know their lesson and slip of their own accord into their fixed groove.
1933 Alex J. Morrison *A New Way to Better Golf* 29: . . . to produce a successful shot the head of the club must move in an accurate and consistent "groove."
1946 Percy Boomer *On Learning Golf* 24: . . . whether it is muscular memory, or the wearing of certain grooves or channels in the mind . . . it is obvious that the more often the same succession of movements can be repeated the clearer the memory will be.
1970 Dick Schaap *The Masters* 126: Jack Nicklaus is on the practice tee, firing ball after ball down the range, searching for his groove.

2 v.trans.   To habituate (the swing or a stroke) into a consistent and accurate pattern by practice.

1941 Patty Berg *Golf* 49: Be sure to "anchor" feet and the head as an aid to "grooving" your swing.
1948 Ben Hogan *Power Golf* 55: Once you've grooved your swing you shouldn't be conscious of making any fundamental changes, no matter what club you are using.
1967 Johnny Pott in Plimpton *The Bogey Man* 194: "You're down there trying to groove the shot, to tone up the muscle memory."
1977 Dave Hill & Nick Seitz *Teed Off* 153: I've seen him stand on a putting green for an hour in 100-degree heat sinking one-foot putts. I asked him what he was doing and he said he was grooving a stroke.

groove² n.   A linear scoring on a club-face.

1976 *Rules of Golf* Appendix III.1.b: *Iron Clubs* 1. A series of straight grooves in the form of V's may be put in the face of the club.
1977 Gordon S. White, Jr. *New York Times* (Aug. 12) A17:   . . . Burns's irons were found to have grooves that were too wide.

grooved adj.   Habituated by practice into a consistent and accurate pattern.

1929 Archie Compston *Golf Illustrated* (May) 37:   . . . Macdonald Smith, whom I look on as the outstanding example of what the Americans call the "grooved swing"—an idea they have borrowed from the baseball swing of Babe Ruth, who swings his bat in exactly the same groove every time, waiting to pick the ball that comes within the arc of its sweep.
1971 Tommy Bolt *The Hole Truth* 122:   Even as grooved as my left wrist is during a golf swing . . .
1977 Dave Hill & Nick Seitz *Teed Off* 125:   He has his swing so well grooved that he gives the appearance of being almost mechanical. His movements appear to be programmed.

gross adj. & n.   (A score) actually made, before deduction or addition of handicap strokes.

1890 Horace Hutchinson *Badminton Golf* 278:   Each club should have a book, indexed and ruled in columns for names, dates, gross scores, handicap allowances, and nett scores, respectively
1977 George Peper *Golf Magazine* (Aug.) 42:   Although his gross score is lower than yours, you win, because 88 minus your handicap of 17 is a net 71.
1978 *Daily Hampshire Gazette* (June 3) 20:   Low gross was 48 for Martha Hayes and Millie Wolf.

ground v.trans.   To touch the head of (a club) to the ground behind the ball at address.

1890 Horace Hutchinson *Badminton Golf* 140:   . . . in a bunker, where you are not allowed to 'ground' the club at all.
1922 P.G. Wodehouse *A Woman Is Only a Woman* (in *The Clicking of Cuthbert* repr. 1956, 33):   "I mean to say—no offence, old man—but no grounding niblicks in bunkers."
1950 Gene Sarazen & Walter Hagen (in Wind *The Complete Golfer* 1954, 168):   "You can't do that, kid—remove leaves from a hazard and ground your club," he barked at me.
1976 *Rules of Golf* Definition 1:   A player has "addressed the ball" when he has taken his stance and has also grounded his club, except that in a hazard a player has addressed the ball when he has taken his stance.

ground under repair.   An area on the course undergoing work for maintenance or alteration; for a lie in which, relief is permitted under the rules.

1976 *Rules of Golf* Definition 13:   "Ground under repair" is any portion of the course so marked by the committee concerned. . . . It includes material piled for removal and a hole made by a greenkeeper, even if not so marked.

gutta n.   Gutta percha, or a gutta percha ball.

1856 *Unidentified newspaper clipping* (in Allan Robertson's album in the R. & A. 71):   The guttas having been teed by them, both of the competitors struck off in gallant style.
1867 "R.C. Jr." *The Short Hole* in *Poems on Golf* 54:
> One bunker wide and bushy yawns
> between,
> Where Tyro's gutta is too often found.

1897 Horace Hutchinson *Country Life* (Jan. 16) 49:   "Gutta's made the game cheap, and that's only another way of saying popular."
1932 Francis Ouimet *A Game of Golf* (in Wind *The Complete Golfer* 1956, 93):   I learned then and there . . . why it was that the rubber-cored ball was vastly superior to the solid gutta.

gutta percha *n. & adj., pron.* /per-cha/ *often also* /per-ka/ [*Origin:* from Malay *getah-percha:* *getah* = "sap" + *percha* = name of the tree that yields gutta percha.] —*n.* A hard, resilient, easily molded substance derived from the sap of several Malaysian trees of the family Sapotaceae, of which golf balls were made from 1848 until the beginning of the 20th century. —*adj.* Made of gutta percha.

1848 William Graham *In Praise of Gutta Percha* (in Clark *Golf: A Royal & Ancient Game* repr. 1975, 216):
Hail, GUTTA PERCHA! precious gum!
O'er Scotland's links lang may ye bum;
1849 Charles Roger *History of St. Andrews* 79: [*Footnote:*] For about a year, golf balls, and also heads of clubs, have been constituted of gutta percha, but whether this material may be ultimately preferred, time alone can determine.
1852 *Minutes of the Bruntsfield Links Golf Club* (July 24) (in Clark op. cit. 104): . . . it was agreed that there should be second, third, and fourth prizes, to consist of six, four, and two Gutta Percha balls respectively.
1890 Lord Wellwood *Badminton Golf* 32: Now, wherein consists the difficulty of hitting that unresisting little piece of gutta-percha?
1912 Harry Vardon *How to Play Golf* 13:

. . . us who started to play in the days of the gutta-percha ball.

gutty *or* **guttie** *n.* A gutta percha ball.

1886 Alexander Lawson *Letters on Golf* 8: . . . sends the ball out of sight by cutting deep into the turf and covering the "guttie," which remained unmoved.
1890 Andrew Lang *Badminton Golf* 28: The earlier 'gutties' took on paint badly . . .
1908 Arnold Haultain *The Mystery of Golf* repr. 1965, 104: But man, the master-mechanic of this terrestrial globe, versed in all the laws of parabola and ellipse, can no more govern the flight of his pigmy gutty than he can govern the flight of the summer swallow.
1912 Harry Vardon *How to Play Golf* 17: No, deeply as I grieve at the passing of the gutty, I do not see how it is to be reinstated.
1975 Herb Graffis *The P.G.A.* 14: Occasionally an old gutta-percha ball, or "gutty," is played [by the Hickory Hackers].

gutty-perky *n. & adj.* *Scottish.* Variant of gutta percha.

1899 *Golf Illustrated* (June 23) 45: No wonder James Braid, who saw the shot, protested against a "sinfu' waste of gutty-perky."
1933 John Ressich *Thir Braw Days* 98: The gentleman that brocht thae gutty-perky ba's till St. Andrews wis a Mr. Petrie . . .

H

hack *v.trans. & intrans.*   To hit (the ball) violently and crudely, especially in rough or in a bad lie; make generally incompetent shots; play poor golf.

1907   Willie Park in Leach *Great Golfers in the Making* 107:   . . . he hacked away at his ball until he took 9 to the hole.
1915   Hugh Leslie Dobree in Revell *Pro & Con of Golf* 80:   "You depart toward the whins and hack the ball back on to the fairway again."
1919   Robert K. Risk *Songs of the Links* 27:
The circumjacent caddies grin
To see me hack my way through whin.
1949   Fred Beck & O.K. Barnes *Seventy-three Years in a Sand Trap* 100:   It is midday, and but a handful of listless players may be spied in the distance, hacking their way along.
1975   Mark McCormack *Golf Annual* 60:   . . . at the 6th he took a horrid 8, his second shot burying itself in a steep bank. He hacked and hacked until he reached the green in five . . .
1977   John S. Radosta *New York Times* (June 17) A18:   After hacking out to the fairway, he reached the green in three.

hacker *n.*   An unskillful player.

1954   Geoffrey Houghton *The Truth About Golf Addicts* 46:   When you have conditioned yourself at Ferndown (even hackers feel like tigers after a couple of rounds) . . .

1977   Dave Hill & Nick Seitz *Teed Off* 171:   I don't mind playing with hackers at all.

half *n.*   **1** In match play, a tied score on a hole, each side being credited with a half.

1896   *Baily's Magazine* (Aug.) 169:   In this state of affairs Park, being dormy one, played for a half.
1931   Henry Cotton *Golf* 106:   . . . you have your opponent struggling for a half.

2 The first or last nine holes of a round of eighteen.

1899   *Golf Illustrated* (June 16) 15:   The outward half he covered in grand form, the total for this half being 36.
1974   *The Golfer's Handbook* 507:   Tony Jacklin who had a first-round outward half of 29 at St. Andrews in 1970 . . . Other halves in 30 in the Open Championship have been recorded.

half shot.   A shot made with a reduced swing, somewhat less full than a three-quarter shot.

[**1857**   H.B. Farnie *The Golfer's Manual* 18:   The short spoon . . . is used for those short and difficult half strokes on to the putting green over a hazard.]

1890 Horace Hutchinson *Badminton Golf* 115: . . . a half-shot of medium distance and of medium loft—that is to say, a stroke which will loft the ball a certain distance and will then allow it to run; it is the position for the typical half shot.
1931 Joyce & Roger Wethered *The Game of Golf* 69: Half shots with all the iron clubs, whatever their loft, are played exactly on the same lines as the fuller shots. To reduce the power the back swing must be shortened.
1976 J.C. Jessop *Golf* 55: The term "half-shot" is really a misnomer. It implies a half-swing, and that the ball travels half the distance of a full shot. It is neither: the swing is more than half, and the ball travels, consequently, much more than half the distance of a full shot.

halve *v.* **1** *v.trans. & intrans.* In match play, to play (a hole) in a tied score.

1823 James Grierson *Delineations of St. Andrews* 220: If the ball be struck into the hole at the *like*, or an equal number of strokes on both sides, the hole is said to be *halved*, and goes for nothing.
1862 Robert Chambers *A Few Rambling Remarks on Golf* 7: If . . . they both arrive at the hole and put their balls in in an equal number of strokes, in which case the hole is said to be *halved*, and scores to neither.
1928 A. Linde Fowler *Golf Illustrated* (Oct.) 41: He felt that at the short 12th hole it might be necessary for him to get a 2 to halve.
1962 Sam Snead *The Education of a Golfer* 46: We halved No. 36 to complete one of the worst flops of my life.

2 *v.trans. & intrans.* To tie (a match).

1851 *Unidentified newspaper clipping* (in Allan Robertson's album at the R. & A. 40): Seeing that he could not halve the match, Tom [Morris] gave his ball a kick in disgust.
1897 Horace Hutchinson *Country Life* (June 12) 636: "I was at the championship at Muirfield," said the Colonel, "where Taylor and Vardon halved—tied for first place."
1911 James Braid *Advanced Golf* 292: The match was halved.
1967 Mark McCormack *Arnie* 175: . . . Palmer was a winner in three matches and halved his fourth.

handicap *n. & v.* [Origin: doubtless borrowed from horse-racing.] **1** *n.* A compensation in strokes assigned to players on the basis of their past and current performance, designed to enable players of different abilities to compete together on approximately equal terms.

1842 *Minutes of the Bruntsfield Links Golf Club* (Dec. 17) (in Clark *Golf: A Royal & Ancient Game* 1875, 100): Matches were then arranged (handicap) to compete for the Prize Clubs presented by Mr. Stewart.
1890 Horace Hutchinson *Badminton Golf* 276: There is coming into general prevalence a stupid mechanical system of never cutting off men's handicaps except after a win.
1915 Alexander H. Revell *Pro & Con of Golf* 2: Until a man brings his handicap down to sixteen, there should be no addition to the number [of clubs] used . . .
1933 A.G. Macdonell *England, Their England* 126: . . . a handicap of plus one when he was sixteen had marked him out as a coming man.
1977 *Golf Digest* (Aug.) 31: A survey by the Metropolitan [New York] Golf Association of its members shows an average handicap of 19.3 for men and 32.9 for women.

2 *v.trans. & intrans.* To assign a handicap or handicaps to (a player or players).

1890 Lord Wellwood *Badminton Golf* 50: A man's form is so quickly known that he is soon correctly handicapped.
1907 Harold Hilton *My Golfing Reminiscences* 28: In this year (1889) I came on a great deal in my game, and when I finished up the year I was handicapped within two strokes of Johnnie Ball.
1921 Andrew Kirkaldy *Fifty Years of Golf* 172: Two golfers were starting out on a game, and were considering how to arrange the handicapping so as to make a good match . . .

handicapper *n.* **1** One who assigns handicaps, as a member of a handicapping committee.

1890 Horace Hutchinson *Badminton Golf* 276: One of the besetting nuisances of the handicapper's life is the improving player.

2 A player who has a stated handicap.

1977 *Golf Digest* (Aug.) 20: Miss Novinger is a 3-handicapper at the Kirksville Country Club.

hanging *adj.* [Origin: from an old use of the word in descriptions of landscape: *a hanging meadow, hanging woods,* etc.="situated on a steep slope."] (Of a ball or lie) situated on ground that slopes down in the direction of the line of play.

1857 H.B. Farnie *The Golfer's Manual* 79: HANGING—When the ground rises in any way behind the ball.
1890 Lord Wellwood *Badminton Golf* 37: . . . let him try to . . . loft a hanging ball.
1911 James Braid *Advanced Golf* 111: But when the lie is very hanging, when, in fact, the ball is at rest on a quite steep hill, it is time to go in for a very unusual type of shot.
1931 Bernard Darwin *The Game of Golf* 37: It is a very different matter when the ball lies close or hanging or cupped.
1970 Tony Jacklin *Jacklin* 45: Nicklaus pitched to eleven feet from a hanging lie.

hazard *n.* **1** *Obsolete.* Any obstructive or difficult feature of a golf course, considered part of the inherent challenge of the course; for which no relief was generally allowed under the rules; and including (with specified exceptions on each course) both natural features such as bunkers, permanent water, gorse, and molehills, and incidental features such as paths and fences.

1744 *Articles & Laws in Playing at Golf* 13: Neither Trench, Ditch or Dyke, made for the preservation of the Links, nor the Scholar's Holes or the Soldier's Lines, Shall be accounted a Hazard, But the Ball is to be taken out Teed and play'd with any Iron Club.
1862 Robert Chambers *A Few Rambling Remarks on Golf* 6: . . . on each the ground is diversified by knolls, sand-pits, or other apparent impediments (termed in golfing phraseology *hazards*) the avoiding of which is one of the most important objects of the game.
1893 *Rules for the Game of Golf* (R. & A.)

15: A "hazard" shall be any bunker of whatever nature:—water, sand, loose earth, mole hills, paths, roads or railways, whins, bushes, rushes, rabbit scrapes, fences, ditches, or anything which is not the ordinary green of the course, except sand blown on to the grass by wind, or sprinkled on grass for the preservation of the Links, or snow or ice, or bare patches on the course.

2 Either of two features of a golf course now designated as specific difficulties for the player—a sand trap (or bunker), or a body or channel of water—play from which is governed, under penalties, by Rule 33.

1976 *Rules of Golf* Definition 14: A "hazard" is any bunker or water hazard. Bare patches, scrapes, roads, tracks and paths are not hazards. Rule 33: When a ball lies in or touches a hazard or water hazard, nothing shall be done which may in any way improve its lie. Before making a stroke, the player shall not touch the ground in the hazard or water in the water hazard with a club or otherwise [etc.].

head or **clubhead** or **club-head** *n.* The part of a club with which the ball is struck, made of wood or some substitute or of iron.

1687 Thomas Kincaid *Diary* (Jan. 20) (in *Book of the Old Edinburgh Club* XXVII, 1949, 133): Your club most be almost streight, that is, the head most make a verie obtuse angle with the shaft. (Jan. 25, 135): I glewed the club head . . .
1835 Harry Harewood *Dictionary of Sports* 166: These are called *putters*—being short and heavy, of the same form, but larger in the head. . . .
1858 *Unidentified newspaper clipping* (in Allan Robertson's album at the R. & A. 87): . . . those with iron heads are the cleek, sand-iron, and track-iron.
1890 Horace Hutchinson *Badminton Golf* 78: The club-head wants to be travelling, when it meets the ball, in the direction in which it is intended the ball should go.
1913 Bernard Darwin *Country Life* (Oct. 11) 504: . . . the length of a ball's flight is determined by the velocity at which the club-head is travelling at the moment of impact.

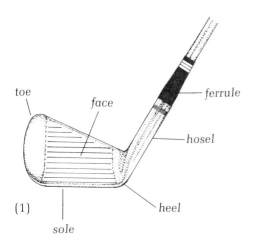

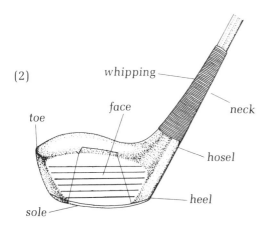

head

(1) four-iron, Walter Hagen, 1979
(2) three-wood, Ben Hogan, 1979.

1931 Joyce & Roger Wethered *The Game of Golf* 46: You are moving the club head. Therefore try to have the sense of the club head, if you can, rather than of your hands and the shaft of the club.
1976 *Rules of Golf* 2.2.a. The golf club shall be composed of a shaft and a head . . . Appendix II.a. The length of a clubhead shall be greater than the breadth.

heel *n. & v.* **1** *n.* The near end of a club-head at address, immediately below the neck.

1857 H.B. Farnie *The Golfer's Manual* 34: The head [of an iron] should be deep in the face, more so at the point than the heel, as the former is the more powerful hitting part.
1890 Horace Hutchinson *Badminton Golf* 75: When the club is laid with its *heel*—not the centre of its face—to the ball . . .
1911 James Braid *Advanced Golf* 149: . . . if another part, either nearer the toe or the heel, comes back to the ball, there has been an unintended deviation in the backward swing.
1953 Bobby Locke (in Wind *The Complete Golfer* 1954, 269): Never hit a putt with the heel of the club.
1967 George Plimpton *The Bogey Man* 174: I hit my drive off the heel of the club.

2 *v.trans.* To hit (the ball or a shot) off the heel.

1862 Robert Chambers *A Few Rambling Remarks on Golf* 22: . . . he is apt . . . when standing too near the ball, to 'heel' or strike it with that part of the clubhead nearest the shaft.
1893 John Thomson *Golfing Poems & Songs* 2:

The man in a hurry can never dae weel,
He'll heel her, or tap her, then a's to the deil.

1908 Arnold Haultain *The Mystery of Golf* 114: . . . during the contest he heeled ball after ball.

hickory *n. & adj.* —*n.* The wood of a North American tree of the genus *Carya*, used from the early 19th century to the 1920s for making the shafts of golf clubs; also, a club with a hickory shaft. —*adj.* Made of hickory.

1835 Harry Harewood *Dictionary of Sports* 165: The upper part is generally of some very pliant tough wood, as hickory.
1869 Anon. *Golfiana; or A Day at Gullane* 7:

My "hickory" I've wielded high,
On Prestwick's wilds so benty . . .

1890 Horace Hutchinson *Badminton Golf* 65: on the whole, however, no improvement can be made upon split hickory for shafts.

1912 Harry Vardon *How to Play Golf* 45: So long as we can obtain good hickory for our shafts, we ought to be glad.
1915 *New York Sun* in Revell *Pro & Con of Golf* 35: Good hickory is becoming scarcer every year.
1937 Henry Longhurst *Golf* 4: A perfect piece of straight-grained hickory was a joy to behold and a joy to feel in the hands. . . . Faced with the choice between steel and an increasingly indifferent hickory, the beginner can come to only one decision. He must choose steel.

high. See **hole-high** *and* **pin-high.**

hit *v.trans.* **1** To play (a stroke or shot).

1946 Frank Moran *Golfers' Gallery* 6: I saw him hit stroke after stroke.
1970 Dick Schaap *The Masters* 189: Gene Littler and Bert Yancey both hit perfect drives.

2 To play (a club).

1961 Eric Brown *Knave of Clubs* 18: I realized that if he hit his brassie properly he would make the green.
1975 Dan Jenkins *Dead Solid Perfect* 29: "Let me see you hit that driver . . ."
1977 Robert Kotz in *New York Times* (June 22): "I was going to hit my 6-iron and my caddie said, 'Hit the 4.' So I hit the 5 right to the green."

hitter *n.* A player who uses maximum power in driving. *Compare* **swinger.**

1903 Harold Hilton *The Outing* (Apr.) 124: To do full justice to the old club it was almost necessary to trust to the swing of the club. The *hitter* was all over the place.
1964 Julius Boros *How to Win at Weekend Golf* 35: But many of today's better players —Arnold Palmer, Jack Nicklaus, Gary Player, for example—happen to use a power swing to various degrees. These are "hitters." They take the club back quite fast and return it to the ball even faster, using every iota of their god-given power.
1969 Tom Scott & Geoffrey Cousins *The Golf Immortals* 225: [Gary Player] suggests that every golfer, even a beginner, should try to hit the ball as hard as he can . . . he maintains that if one becomes a swinger from the word go it is difficult, if not impossible, to become a hitter when this becomes necessary.

hog's back (*Brit.*) or **hogback** (*U.S.*) n. A ridge of ground, or a hole having a ridge on the fairway.

1901 *Country Life* (Jan. 19) 93: The old sixth hole had a hog's-backed bank before it, and not a straight hog's back, but one that slanted perilously to a bunker on the right.
1931 Bernard Darwin *The Game of Golf* 157: Ask for any type of hole you like--a plateau, a valley, a hog's back, a punchbowl . . .
1969 Jack Nicklaus *The Greatest Game of All* 25: My approach shot, a 4-iron that finished 40 feet from the hole, left me with a difficult putt over a hogback.
1977 Johnny Miller *Golf Magazine* (July) 43: The hogback fairway tosses tee shots to the right and left.

hold *v.trans. & intrans.* **1** (Of ground) to absorb the impact of (a shot) with little bounce or roll.

1962 Sam Snead *The Education of a Golfer* 202: . . . the hard, fast greens wouldn't hold normal pitches.
1969 Jack Nicklaus *The Greatest Game of All* 156: . . . the greens had been watered to make them hold better.

2 (Of a shot) to impact on (ground) with little bounce or roll.

1970 Dick Schaap *The Masters* 186: Littler feels the proper shot for him is a two-iron, but he wants loft to try to hold the green.

holding *adj.* Tending to hold a ball on impact with little bounce or roll.

1973 Pat Ward-Thomas *Bartlett's World Golf Encyclopedia* 254: The grass was richer, the fairways heavier, and the greens more holding.

hole n. & v.   **1** n. The small excavation into which the ball is played; formerly of irregular size and shape, now defined as a cylinder 4¼ inches in diameter and at least 4 inches deep.

1744 *Articles & Laws in Playing at Golf* 7: . . . you are to play your Ball honestly for the Hole, and not to play upon your Adversary's Ball, not lying in your way to the Hole.
1858 *Unidentified newspaper clipping* (in Allan Robertson's album at the R. & A. 90): Your object is to drive your tiny gutta percha ball . . . till you reach within a short distance of the six-inch hole.
1893 *Rules for the Game of Golf* (in Clark *Golf: A Royal & Ancient Game* repr. 1975, 294):   3. . . . The hole shall be 4¼ inches in diameter, and at least 4 inches deep.
1977 Larry Dennis *Golf Digest* (July) 52: . . . telling us to roll our putts at a speed which allows the ball to die into the hole.

2 n.   In match play, the score obtained by the side that plays a hole in fewer strokes than the other or others.

1743 Thomas Mathison *The Goff* 14:   And thrice three holes to great *Castalio* fall; The other six *Pygmalion* bore away . . .
1851 *Unidentified newspaper clipping* (in Allan Robertson's album at the R. & A. 40): Dunne . . . smiled satisfactorily, having the credit of taking the match by two holes.
1961 John Stobbs *Tackle Golf* (repr. 1977) 122:   Expect him to play some admirable shots and get a hole or two back.

3 n.   One of the nine or eighteen segments of a course, from each teeing ground to each putting green.

1863 "J.S." *The Links of St. Rule* (in Clark *Golf: A Royal & Ancient Game* 1875, 136): . . . the shortest "hole" being about one hundred, and the longest about four hundred yards.
1891 *Golf* magazine (March 20) 13:   One of the longest holes in the Carnoustie course— the fifth, or Bowling-green hole—was recently taken by Mr. Dewars . . . at the phenomenally low figure of three strokes.
1926 *Golf Illustrated* (Sept.) 11:   Beautiful holes are already being discussed as works of art.
1954 Robert Trent Jones (in Wind *The Complete Golfer* 1954, 301):   It is my feeling that

to copy holes in detail, moving mountains of earth in trying to parallel the original, is a waste of time and effort.
1970 Charles Price *Golf* 14:   Speaking *generally*, a hole is also the entire area from the teeing ground . . . through the green to the putting surface.

4 n.   The play of a hole.

1911 James Braid *Advanced Golf* 219:   . . . it is . . . good to try to forget one's bad holes as quickly as possible.
1921 Andrew Kirkaldy *Fifty Years of Golf* 163:   . . . stepping out in their meal hours to have a few holes.
1967 George Plimpton *The Bogey Man* 244: They began talking about golf holes with a kind of quiet intensity that made me think of retired colonels recalling old campaigns on distant battlefields.
1977 Gordon S. White *New York Times* (June 22):   King's most spectacular hole was the 17th, a lengthy par 3 of 200 yards over water from tee to green. His 2-iron tee shot went over the green into a bunker. He blasted out and over the green to the front fringe. Then he chipped into the cup to save par.

5 v.trans. & intrans.   To play (the ball or a shot) into the hole.

1687 Thomas Kincaid *Diary* (Jan. 21) (in *Book of the Old Edinburgh Club* XXVII, 1949, 134):   . . . they will serve . . . for holling the ball.
1744 *Articles & Laws in Playing at Golf*:   7. At Holling, you are to play your ball honestly for the Hole.
1842 *Chambers' Edinburgh Journal* (Oct. 8) 297:   . . . he and his opponent contending which shall get it *holed* by the smallest number of strokes.
1890 Lord Wellwood *Badminton Golf* 35: . . . holeing putts of six or eight feet.
1911 James Braid *Advanced Golf* 218:   You cannot afford to lose the chance of holing with your approach.
1946 Frank Moran *Golfers' Gallery* 10: Hagen meant to try hard at holing the recovery from the sand.
1966 Gary Player *Grand Slam Golf* 40:   . . . chipped back and had to hole from about 12 feet for the par.
1969 Jack Nicklaus *The Greatest Game of All* 249:   If I missed and Arnold holed, I was thinking, we'd be all even.

6 *v.trans.* To play (a round or course) in a specified number of strokes.

1767 Minutes of the R. &. A. (Sept. 3) (in Clark *Golf: A Royal & Ancient Game* 1875, 74): This day the Silver Club was played for, and gained by James Durham of Largo, Esq., by holing the Links at 94 strokes.
1807 *Regulations . . . of the Edinburgh Burgess Golfing Society* (in Clapcott 1935, 39): 2. . . . the player holing two rounds at the fewest number of strokes is to be the winner.
1849 Charles Roger *History of St. Andrews* 78: The gentlemen who have holed the links at the fewest number of strokes, are declared the winners.
1957 Henry Longhurst *The Best of Henry Longhurst* 118: . . . that Hogan had not only played a round of golf, but had holed the Colonial Club's course at his home town of Fort Worth, Tex., in 71.

holeable *adj.* (Of a putt) within reasonable distance for holing out.

1891 *Golf* magazine (Sept. 18) 13: . . . had not Hugh missed quite a holeable putt.
1912 Harry Vardon *How to Play Golf* 105: But only the player who has missed hundreds of holeable putts in a season is in a position to appreciate it.
1927 Robert T. Jones, Jr. & O.B. Keeler *Down the Fairway* 50: And I could tell you right now of missed putts—I mean holeable putts —which would have given me a 60 at the worst.
1975 Mark McCormack *Golf Annual* 178: . . . a voice in the crowd calling out "Rubbish" when he missed a holeable putt.

holed *adj.* Having been legitimately played into the hole.

1976 *Rules of Golf* Definition 4: A ball is "holed" when it lies within the circumference of the hole and all of it is below the level of the lip of the hole.

hole-high *adj. & adv.* Level with the hole.

1895 "Calamo Currente" *Half Hours With an Old Golfer* 88: . . . his ball had such spin when it fell, That it . . . was nearly hole high in the dell. [*Footnote:*] up to the hole.
1919 Robert K. Risk *Songs of the Links* 19:
  When drives are all hole-high and
    straight . . .
1926 Lucille MacAllister *Golf Illustrated* (Sept.) 29: Miss Collett with her spoon was hole high.
1962 Sam Snead *The Education of a Golfer* 63: On No. 2, a 512-yarder, two big wallops put me hole high, just off the green.
1974 *The Golfer's Handbook* 545: This particular shot finished hole-high.

hole in one. A hole played in one stroke.

1893 John Thomson *Golfing Poems & Songs* 21:
  Holes in one were quite common, the
    longest in two . . .
1921 Andrew Kirkaldy *Fifty Years of Golf* 132: But would I wager to do a hole in one to order?
1975 Herb Graffis *The P.G.A.* 240: [In 1944] Only 835 holes-in-one were recorded for the P.G.A. prize.

hole in one *phr. v.* To play a hole in one stroke.

1974 Peter Dobereiner *The Golfer's Handbook* xli: Gene Sarazen . . . holed in one at the Postage Stamp in full view of the TV cameras.

hole out *phr.v.* To play (a shot) into the hole.

1844 *Rules for the Game of Golf* (Blackheath) (in Clapcott 1935, 85): IX.—In holing out, no mark of any kind shall be made to direct the player to the hole.
1890 Horace Hutchinson *Badminton Golf* 252: You have a perfect right to ask a golfer to hole out every single putt.
1907 Harold Hilton *My Golfing Reminiscences* 25: I chased my ball up and down that drain for some minutes, and finally holed out in thirteen.
1936 H.B. Martin *Fifty Years of American Golf* 387: One of the greatest thrills in golf is holing out the tee shot.

1976 *Rules of Golf* 6.2: A hole is halved if each side holes out in the same number of strokes.

holer *n.* A successful putter.

1977 Dave Hill & Nick Seitz *Teed Off* 158: He was a born holer.

home *adv. & adj.* **1** *adv.* Into the hole.

1833 George Fullerton Carnegie *The Golfiad* (in *Poems on Golf* 1867, 25):
'Tis bad, but still we may get home at
    four.
1919 Robert K. Risk *Songs of the Links* 16:
Where the longest putts get home, dear
    lass . . .
1970 Dick Schaap *The Masters* 189: With body English and a smooth stroke, Billy Casper sends home his four-footer.

2 *adv.* On or onto the green.

1890 H.S.C. Everard *Badminton Golf* 335: . . . long drivers now frequently carry the whole lot of bunkers which can catch a tee shot, and get easily home in two.
1915 A.W. Tillinghast *A Woman's Way* (in *Cobble Valley Golf Yarns* 75): The drive that he hit there is still pointed out to incredulous visitors, and he was home with his iron.
1977 John S. Radosta *New York Times* (July 8) A13: . . . Hayes got home with a 3-iron 15 feet from the cup.

3 *adv.* Incoming; on or through the last nine holes.

1893 *Baily's Magazine* (July) 65: Mr. Hilton accomplished the first round in 82, being 38 "out" and 44 "home."
1927 Robert T. Jones, Jr. & O.B. Keeler *Down the Fairway* 56: He came home in 33.

4 *adj.* Referring to the last nine holes.

1975 Mark McCormack *Golf Annual* 50: Nor was Irwin devastating on the home nine.

5 *adj.* Referring to the eighteenth hole.

1890 Lord Wellwood *Badminton Golf* 43: This being the home hole, a large gallery is looking on.
1977 Joseph C. Dey *Golf Digest* (Aug.) 18: The 1969 Ryder Cup at Birkdale was all square as the last singles came to the home green.

home-and-home *adj. & adv.* (Of a match) made up of rounds played on the home courses of both sides.

1870 *St. Andrews Gazette* (Apr. 30): A match is on the *tapis* between Willie Park, of Musselburgh, and Bob Kirk, of Blackheath, London, for £100 a side, to be played "home and home" in Blackheath and Musselburgh.
1895 *Baily's Magazine* (Jan.) 77: A very interesting "home-and-home" match was recently played between J. Cuthbert, the Stanmore professional, and John Milne, of Neasden.
1907 Harold Hilton *My Golfing Reminiscences* 140: . . . Willie Park . . . recently had beaten Willie Fernie in a home-and-home match.
1921 Andrew Kirkaldy *Fifty Years of Golf* 123: There I met and played Taylor, whose green was close at hand. We played home and home matches.

honor (*U.S.*) or **honour** (*Brit.*) *n.* The privilege of driving off first from the tee, usually assigned at the first hole by lot, and thereafter belonging to the winner of each previous hole.

1862 Robert Chambers *A Few Rambling Remarks on Golf* 8: . . . he gains that hole, and so takes precedence (the *honour*) in striking off towards the next.
1881 Robert Forgan *The Golfer's Handbook* 60: HONOUR.—The right to play off first from the tee, which belongs to the winner of the last hole.
1899 Willie Tucker *The Outing* (Aug.) 524: Douglas, having the honor, drove a fine ball.
1922 P.G. Wodehouse *A Woman Is Only a Woman* (in *The Clicking of Cuthbert* repr. 1956, 35): James, who had the honour, shook visibly as he addressed his ball.
1962 Sam Snead *The Education of a Golfer* 10: Little and Burke, two of the biggest hitters in the business, had the honor at the first tee.
1975 Dan Jenkins *Dead Solid Perfect* 222: The blue coat looked toward Donny and said, "Mr. Smithern, it's your honor, I believe."

hood *v.trans.* To tilt (a club or clubface) forward, reducing its effective loft.

1969 Tom Scott & Geoffrey Cousins *The Golf Immortals* 63: The technique of using the wedge is now familiar to all . . . the hooded clubface at the address, ball played off the right heel, and a low trajectory shot designed to stop on the second bounce.
1977 George Peper *Scrambling Golf* 71: Hood the club. Don't close the face, hood it, by tilting it down toward the ball a bit. The hooding will delay slightly the "take" of the backspin and thus delay the rise of the ball.

hook *v. & n.* **1** *v.trans. & intrans.* Of a right-handed player, to play (the ball or a shot) so that it curves owing to sidespin strongly from right to left, often having started in a path to the right of the target line; and the converse for a left-handed player.

1863 *The Links of St. Rule* (in Clark *Golf: A Royal & Ancient Game* 1875, 138): . . . the Captain hookit his ba' into the "Principal's Nose."
1890 Sir Walter Simpson *Badminton Golf* 194: There are many golfers who have no need to guard against hooking.
1911 James Braid *Advanced Golf* 77: There are many golfers of the first rank who hook regularly as part of their fixed golfing system.
1946 Frank Moran *Golfers' Gallery* 17: He hooked his drive into a sandy waste.
1977 Dave Hill & Nick Seitz *Teed Off* 134: Beard's game is simple. He aims fifteen yards right of his target and hooks the ball back in where he wants it.

2 *v.intrans.* (Of a ball or shot) to be hooked.

1961 *R. & A. Decisions* (in *The Golfer's Handbook* 1974, 933): In a stroke competition A and B drove from the 15th tee and both balls hooked.
1977 Gordon S. White *New York Times* (June 10) A20: . . . his tee shot had hooked a bit too much around the slight dogleg and landed in soaked, four-inch grass.

3 *n.* A shot that hooks, or a tendency to hook one's shots.

1900 *The Outing* (July) 445: . . . that so long as he played for a "hook" on his ball, as he does, he never would be first-class.
1912 Harry Vardon *How to Play Golf* 150: . . . the ugly hook which sends the ball off the course to the left is perhaps the most frequent of faults.
1946 Byron Nelson *Winning Golf* 182: To play the desired hook (curve to the left) I must first assume a *closed* stance, as shown.
1967 Arnold Palmer in McCormack *Arnie* 64: I tried to go back to a shot I have played a thousand times before, a hard, controlled hook.
1971 Tommy Bolt *The Hole Truth* 170: That hook might beat some folks some days, but before it is over, it will take you right down with it.

hooker *n.* A player who habitually hooks.

1913 Bernard Darwin *Country Life* (May 31) 792: . . . but the hooker must now restrain himself even as the slicer did on the way out.
1946 Frank Moran *Golfers' Gallery* 5: . . . proved again how much the classic links can be a hooker's course.
1977 Dave Hill & Nick Seitz *Teed Off* 134: Beard's grip is bad. It's a hooker's grip, a strong left-hand grip (turned to the right on the club).

hose *n.* [*Origin:* the word *hose* = "tube," was from the 18th century used of the sockets of shafted iron tools such as spades or rakes (O.E.D.). See also *hosel.*] The socket of an iron clubhead.

1890 *Badminton Golf* 447: Hose.—The socket, in iron-headed clubs, into which the shaft fits.
1895 James P. Lee *Golf in America* 178: (Same def. as 1890 above).
1915 A.W. Tillinghast *The Spur* (in *Cobble Valley Golf Yarns* 163): . . . patented monstrosities that were designed to prevent hitting in the hose, or socketing them, as most know the disease.
1979 Ian T. Henderson & David I. Stirk *Golf in The Making* 179: In consequence, some of the later cleeks are smaller in the hose.

hosel *n. & v.* [*Origin:* Scottish *hosel,
hoozle, houzle*="socket of a shafted iron
tool." Sc.N.D. derives it from the verb
house="to fix in a socket or *housing.*" If
this is correct, *hosel* is not related to the
synonymous *hose* (see preceding entry),
and their resemblance is a coincidence.]
1 *n.* The socket or neck of an iron clubhead.

1929 *Spalding's Athletic Library* 122:
Hosel—The socket in iron-headed clubs into
which the wood or steel shaft fits.
1973 *Bartlett's World Golf Encyclopedia*
363:   Then the hosel (that part of the forging
which receives the shaft) is ground to size
and drilled to receive the shaft.
1977 Ralph Maltby *Golf Magazine* (June)
78:   Hosel length also increases from the 2-
iron (shortest) to the pitching wedge (longest).
1979 George Gibson in Henderson & Stirk
Golf in the Making 173:   Two big hammer
men were in the centre of the smithy at the
call of the forgers when beating out the
heated bar in readiness for making the hosel.

2 *v.trans.*   To hit (the ball) off the hosel;
shank.

1977 George Peper *Scrambling Golf* 119:
This will help prevent you from leaning or
tipping forward and "hoseling" the ball.

I

impediment. *See* **loose impediments.**

inland *adj.*   (Of a course) not situated by the sea; not being a seaside linksland course of the traditionally classic Scottish kind.

1892 *Baily's Magazine* (Feb.) 91:   No one who knows anything about the game would for a moment contend that inland links are as good as those on the seashore.
1900 Willie Tucker *The Outing* (June) 286: But all cannot be next the sea, and for inland courses select a line of old pasture fields . . .
1930 Advertisement *Golfer's Year Book* 4: When the heat and monotony of inland courses sap your golf game of some of its zip, come to cool, beautiful Montauk Beach. . . . Two magnificent 18-hole links with soil, turf, topography and setting identical with Britain's famous championship seaside courses.
1969 Jack Nicklaus *The Greatest Game of All* 220:   Muirfield with its splendid turf, its moderate undulations, its honest "inland" character—that was my kind of course.
1971 Henry Longhurst *My Life and Soft Times* 86:   Our second port of call was the great Pine Valley, perhaps the greatest inland course in the world.

inside *prep.*   Nearer the hole than (one's opponent or one's opponent's ball).

1890 Horace Hutchinson *Badminton Golf* 223:   Caddies and professional advisers generally are very fond of advising their masters to 'get inside' the opponent—that is, to play to get their ball nearer to the hole than their opponent's.
1908 Pentland Peile *Clanbrae* 36:   . . . making a grand approach well inside the Minister's ball.
1926 William D. Richardson *Golf Illustrated* (Oct.) 39:   Von Ems was inside Bobby on eleven greens in the morning.
1956 Herbert Warren Wind *The Story of American Golf* 264:   He was nicely inside Brownlow on the green, eighteen feet away to his opponent's thirty-five.
1962 Sam Snead *The Education of a Golfer* 130:   In some of the eighteen-hole matches my ball would be inside his from tee to green on fifteen holes—and Locke would win, 1 up.

interlocking *adj.*   Of a grip for a right-handed player, having the little finger of the right hand interlocked with the forefinger of the left hand; and the converse for a left-handed player.

1916 P.A. Vaile *The New Golf* 6:   I do not believe in any of the interlocking grips.
1969 Jack Nicklaus *The Greatest Game of All* 292:   I honestly believe that the interlocking grip is a better grip than the Vardon.

iron *adj. & n.* **1** *adj.* (Of a club) having the head made of iron, or in modern times of steel.

1744 *Articles & Laws in Playing at Golf* 13: Neither Trench, Ditch or Dyke . . . Shall be accounted a Hazard, but the Ball is to be taken out Teed and play'd with any Iron Club.
1790 *Hoyle's Games* 288: . . . there are six Sorts used by good Players; namely . . . the *Heavy Iron Club,* when [the ball] lies deep amongst Stones or Mud; and the *Light Iron ditto,* when on the surface of chingle or sandy Ground.
1858 *Unidentified newspaper clipping* (in Allan Robertson's album at the R. & A. 87): . . . those with iron heads are the cleek, sand-iron, and track-iron.
1895 James P. Lee *Golf in America* 117: IRON CLUBS. Iron-putter . . . Cleek . . . Driving iron . . . Medium or ordinary Iron . . . Lofting Iron . . . Niblick . . . President . . . Mashie.
1931 Horace Hutchinson *The Game of Golf* 27: When I commenced golfing, about 1870, three iron clubs only were considered generally necessary to golfing salvation—cleek, iron, and niblick.
1950 Dai Rees *Golf My Way* 50: Consider first the wooden club shot through the green, where the ball, instead of being teed up, is lying on the turf, but too far for the green to be reached by a shot with an iron club.
1976 *Rules of Golf* Definition 36: An "iron" club is one with a head which usually is relatively narrow from face to back, and usually is made of steel.

2 *n.* Any of the numerous clubs, in past and present use, having iron or steel heads.
(a) *Before 1850* Any iron-headed club, typically having a rather massive lofted head, used primarily for playing out of difficulties; two types being the *heavy iron* and the *light iron.*

[**1790** *Hoyle's Games* see under def. 1 above.]
1793 *Records of the Honourable Company of Golfers* (May 4) (in Clark *Golf: A Royal & Ancient Game* 1875, 57): It is the unanimous opinion of this Company that no Member shall play on the Links with Irons all . . .
1824 *Rules of the Thistle Golf Club* 48: . . . the player is entitled to drop it behind the hole, and play with an iron, without losing a stroke.
1833 George Fullerton Carnegie *The Golfiad* (in *Poems On Golf* 1867, 24):
"Give me the iron!" either party cries,
As in the quarry, track, or sand he lies.
1837 *Encyclopaedia Edinensis* (in Donald Walker *Sports & Games* 180): There are also two kinds of irons, a light and a heavy, for extricating the ball from a stony situation or from among bushes.
1842 *Chambers' Edinburgh Journal* (Oct. 8) 298: The ball being found deep in the loose earth of the cart-track, he calls for the *iron;* that is, a club with a comparatively short handle and a heavy spoon-like termination of iron, designed for exercising great force on a ball lying in a difficult situation.

(b) *1850–1890* Any of the iron-headed clubs, proliferating into increasingly specialized varieties: the *heavy iron, bunker iron,* or *sand iron,* used primarily for playing from bad lies and bunkers; the *rut iron, track iron,* or *iron niblick,* gradually becoming an independent type; and the *light iron, driving iron,* and *lofting iron,* used for various shots through the green and for pitching and approach shots.

Note: In this period the cleeks, iron niblicks, and iron putters were introduced, and all collectively could be referred to as *irons;* but "the irons" were those given above (i.e., not including cleeks, niblicks, and putters). See also separate entries at **cleek, niblick, putter, sand iron, driving iron, lofter.**

1857 H.B. Farnie *The Golfer's Manual* 18: Irons . . . are three in number; the bunker iron; the driving iron; and the cleek or click. The first of these is especially at home in a bunker—in a thicket whin—amongst the stones of a road—or, in fact, in any scrape where a wooden-headed tool would be useless. . . . The driving-iron nearly resembles him of the bunker, in everything but weight; it is used among difficulties also, but only when the ball is intended to be . . . sent some distance. . . . Ibid. 50: In these two predicaments [bad whins or bunker] the heavy iron must be used unavoidably in the manner of a pickaxe. . . . Ibid. 59: [quarter stroke] The baffing-spoon is . . . the club especially fitted

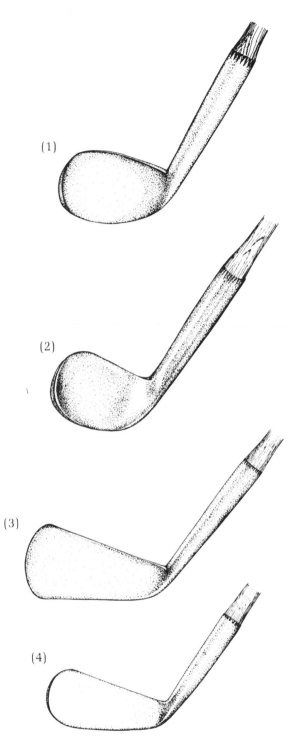

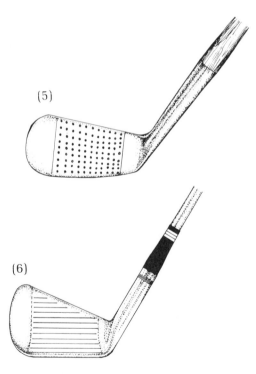

iron
(1) heavy iron, c. 1840
(2) track iron or iron niblick, c. 1860
(3) bunker iron or sand iron, c. 1860
(4) lofter or lofting iron, R. Forgan, c. 1895
(5) mid-iron ("the iron"), J.M. Inglis, Montgomery, Ala., c. 1920
(6) a representative modern iron, four-iron, Walter Hagen, 1979

for this stroke; another, however, is used. . . . This club is the light iron.

1858 *Unidentified newspaper clipping* (in Allan Robertson's album at the R. & A. 85): He laid his ball 'dead' with his iron. . . . Ibid. 88: Brown jerks his ball out of the whins with his iron.

1881 Robert Forgan *The Golfer's Handbook* 15: To inexperienced eyes, a cleek and an iron seem very much alike; but careful inspection will show that, while the handles are the same, the head on an Iron is both broader at the point and more sloped back in the face than that of a Cleek. . . . The "Sand Iron" . . . is mainly employed to extricate a ball from sandy ruts and bunkers. . . . The "Driving Iron" is lighter and less sloped in the face than the "Sand Iron." . . . The "Lofting Iron" is a light weapon, well sloped in the face, and intended almost solely for playing quarter-strokes (and "stimies").

1890 H.S.C. Everard *Badminton Golf* 335: To Allan [Robertson] was due in a great measure the introduction of irons and cleeks for the approach to the hole, these shots previously having been played with baffy spoons. Horace Hutchinson Ibid. 64: . . . there are heavy irons and light irons, driving irons, lofting irons, and sand irons.

(c) *1890–1930* Any iron-headed club, including cleeks, mashies, niblicks, and putters. But "the iron" in this period was specifically used of the moderately lofted club called also the "ordinary iron" or the "mid-iron," the ancestor of the modern two-iron. See separate entry at **mid-iron.**

1893 John Thomson "The Caddie" in *Golfing Poems & Songs* 3:
That drive went awa just a beautiful ba',
And the iron stroke up was as bonnie.

1898 Willie Tucker *The Outing* (Aug.) 441: The Ordinary Iron, or Mid-iron, as it is termed, is, in the majority of cases, the most difficult club to manipulate with accuracy.

1899 Findlay S. Douglas *The Outing* (June) 221: To-day the average golfer carries six irons in his bag, viz., driving cleek, driving iron, mid-iron, mashie, putting cleek and niblick.

1911 James Braid *Advanced Golf* 139: Generally one will play this shot [pitch-and-run] with an iron or mashie.

1912 Harry Vardon *How to Play Golf* 79: . . . that the easiest shots in golf were those made from the tee with a brassie and from the fairway with an ordinary iron. The latter club is a general favourite.

1916 P.A. Vaile *The New Golf* 83: The iron is used when the shot is beyond the range of the mashie.

1921 Andrew Kirkaldy *Fifty Years of Golf* 34: I remember he put the ball in the hole with his iron about eighty yards away.

(d) *1930–present* Any iron- or steel-headed club, now making up a numbered set of nine, having graduated lofts, lies, and lengths of shaft; the number one iron through the number nine iron (each having a vestigial name inherited from earlier times); the wedges and sometimes the putter being also counted as irons. See also separate entries at **one-iron, two-iron,** etc.

1961 John Stobbs *Tackle Golf* (repr. 1977) 36: Still practising with your irons and pushing out the range longer and longer as you get control of them . . .

1967 Dave Thomas *Modern Golf* 33: Nine people out of ten with exceptionally strong arms and wrists are not able to hit a golf ball anything like as well with wooden clubs as they are with irons.

J

jerk *v. & n.* **1** *v.trans* To play (the ball) from rough, sand, or a bad lie, with a downward cut, the clubhead digging into the ground beneath the ball.

1857 H.B. Farnie *The Golfer's Manual* 32: A jerking stroke is managed by hitting the *obstacle* as *close behind* the ball as possible, and well below its centre, with a quick half swing. . . . The player must allow his club to be stopped immediately on hitting the intercepting grass, whin, or whatever obstacle it may be.

1889 Alexander Lawson *Letters on Golf* 23: It is better to jerk the ball out with your niblick than to attack it with your cleek.

1895 James P. Lee *Golf in America* 131: This is best accomplished by what is known as a "jerking" stroke, wherein the club strikes with a quick cut immediately behind the ball and comes to a dead stop on reaching the ground.

2 *n.* A jerked shot.

1887 Sir Walter Simpson *The Art of Golf* 139: Most bunkered balls, then, are best dislodged by a good hard jerk.

jigger *n.* **1** A moderately lofted, shallow-faced, short-shafted iron club no longer in use, that was used especially for approaching.

1905 Frederick Upham Adams *John Henry Smith* 18: . . . dainty maidens who do not know the difference between a follow-through and a jigger.

1907 *Army & Navy Stores Catalogue* 997: Special Approaching Cleek or "Jigger."

1926 "A Former Golf Moron" *Golf Illustrated* (Sept.) 26: I began studying the mashie, the jigger, and the niblick.

1937 Abe Mitchell *Essentials of Golf* 117: The jigger resembles a cleek in appearance, but is shorter in the shaft and has the weight of a No. 4.

2 A club used for chip shots.

jigger
face and back of "Braid" jigger, J. Carstairs, Leven, c. 1920

K

kick v. & n. [*Origin:* probably borrowed from cricket, in which *kick*="to bounce erratically on the pitch."] **1** *v.intrans.* To bounce unpredictably or undesirably.

1901 R.H. Lyttelton *Cricket & Golf* 137: . . . if he lofts so that the ball pitches short of the green it may kick to the right or left.
1912 Harry Vardon *How to Play Golf* 32: . . . it is bitterly disappointing to see a good stroke kick into a bunker.
1922 P.G. Wodehouse *Sundered Hearts* (in *The Clicking of Cuthbert* repr. 1956, 62): . . . the sort of feeling you get when your drive collides with a rock in the middle of a tangle of rough and kicks back into the middle of the fairway.
1967 Mark McCormack *Arnie* 57: The ball hung in the air and looked good, but it landed just short of the apron and kicked back into the creek.

2 *n.* An unpredictable or undesirable bounce.

1899 Willie Tucker *The Outing* (Aug.) 526: Travis played a perfect shot, but got a bad kick on the grade of the green, and stopped dead.
1913 Bernard Darwin *Country Life* (May 31) 792: . . . to avoid the kicks and stops and darts from the banks and braes on the left-hand side.
1928 *Golf Illustrated* (May) 53: By pitching the ball wherever possible one eliminates all chances of a bad kick off any uneven ground.

L

lag *v.trans & intrans.* To play (a putt) so as to get close to but short of the hole.

1962 Sam Snead *The Education of a Golfer* 126: All I wanted was to . . . lag for the safest possible position on my second putt.
1969 Jack Nicklaus *The Greatest Game of All* 95: . . . lagging a longish putt if the situation demanded it or charging it when the percentages were favorable.
1977 George Peper *Scrambling Golf* 141: So gear yourself to making every putt you ever address. Never, never lag the ball. Lagging is associated with a fear of three-putting.

lag putt. A putt played so as to get close to but short of the hole.

1975 Mark McCormack *Golf Annual* 134: Trevino . . . hit the green, 30 feet behind the pin. His lag putt was 40 inches short.

lag putting. The making of lag putts.

1963 Bob Rosburg *The Putter Book* 136: And in only 10 per cent of the cases did the first putt stop more than two feet from the hole. This is "lag" putting at its best, and it goes on every day in professional golf.

laid back. (Of a clubface) lofted, or tilted back by the player to increase the effective loft.

1898 Willie Tucker *The Outing* (Aug.) 440: . . . the face of the mashie is laid back, and the club gripped tightly in both hands.
1913 Horace Hutchinson *Country Life* (Jan.) 104: . . . to vary the experiment by going from a nearly vertical-faced club, like a driver, to a club with a very much laid-back face, like a broad-faced niblick.
1934 *From a Hundred and Two to Eighty-two* . . . 44: Face of club head laid back to cut readily thru sand to lift ball.
1946 Byron Nelson *Winning Golf* 160: Note that the clubface is open (laid back).

lay *v.trans.* To deposit (a ball or shot) in a stated place by playing a stroke.

1779 Hugo Arnot *History of Edinburgh* 361: . . . measuring the strength of the stroke, and applying it in such direction as to lay the ball in smooth ground.
1890 Lord Wellwood *Badminton Golf* 43: . . . one of your opponents . . . has laid his ball about a foot from the hole on the far side.
1912 Harry Vardon *How to Play Golf* 165: I kept laying my approaches within holing distance.
1931 Roger Wethered *The Game of Golf* 73: . . . redeeming his ill fortune time and again by laying his shorter pitches close enough to the hole to obtain par figures.
1956 Herbert Warren Wind *The Story of American Golf* 545: . . . he laid his seven-iron second hole-high, eleven feet to the right of the cup.

For **lay dead** *phr., see* **dead** (def. 1).

lay back *phr.v.* To tilt (a clubface or clubhead) back so as to increase its effective loft.

1857 H.B. Farnie *The Golfer's Manual* 59: The stroke is done by taking a short grasp of the iron, laying the head well back, and hitting the ball clean.
1907 John L. Low (in Leach *Great Golfers in the Making* 2): I used to lay the face of the club back and let fly.
1950 Dai Rees *Golf My Way* 59: The clubface, too, is laid back just a trifle for all shots with 5, 6, 7 and 8 irons.

layout *n.* A golf course, especially when considered in terms of architecture.

1926 Ramsey Herberhart *Golf Illustrated* (June) 40: Salzbrunn has one of the longest of the German courses . . . that fine layout . . .
1954 Robert Trent Jones (in Wind *The Complete Golfer* 1954, 307): . . . the greens are extremely small, perhaps the smallest of any of our championship layouts.
1970 Tony Jacklin *Jacklin* 173: Gary went to the course ten days before the championship and made extensive notes on the lay-out.

lay up *phr. v.* To play a shorter shot than might be attempted; typically, to play for a good lie short of a hazard or other difficulty rather than striving to make the green in one shot.

1897 Price Collier *The Outing* (Aug.) 424: There is a running stream between you and the green. . . . If you were playing a medal round you would lay up in 2, be safely on the green in 3 . . .
1970 Dick Schaap *The Masters* 42: In 1969, he made a conscious decision not to attack the par-fives, to lay his second shots up short of the hazards, then wedge up and try to get his third shots close enough for putts at birdies.
1977 Dave Hill & Nick Seitz *Teed Off* 119: A good par-5 should give a man a challenge and also a choice. I'm speaking now of the second shot. You should have the option . . . to go for the green or lay up.

layup *n.* A shot that is laid up, or a hole on which such a shot may often be chosen.

1966 Gary Player *Grand Slam Golf* 101: I shall never go back to using a 3-wood off the tee unless the hole is a lay-up.
1977 John S. Radosta *New York Times* (July 18) 19: . . . that was exactly how Floyd played the hole—drive, layup with a No. 6-iron, pitching wedge to 20 feet and two putts.

length *n.* Long hitting.

1902 Horace Hutchinson *Country Life* (Sept. 13) 351: . . . has become a steadier player than he was, though without losing any of his length and brilliancy.
1912 Harry Vardon *How to Play Golf* 139: Good golfers and excellent fellows are becoming intoxicated with the passion for length.
1969 Jack Nicklaus *The Greatest Game of All* 56: Length has certainly helped me immensely in tournament golf.

lie[1] *v. & n.* **1** *v.intrans.* (Of a ball in play) to be at rest in some stated position or situation on the course; (also of a player).

1743 Thomas Mathison *The Goff* 21:
Full fifteen clubs' length from the hole
he lay.
1744 *Articles & Laws in Playing at the Golf:* 10. If a Ball be stopp'd by any person, Horse, Dog or any thing else, the Ball so stopp'd must be played where it lyes.
1887 Sir Walter Simpson *The Art of Golf* 132: But alas! The ball does not always lie well.
1976 *Rules of Golf* 16: The ball shall be played as it lies except as otherwise provided for in the Rules or Local Rules.

2 *v.intrans.* (Of a player during the play of a hole) to have played a specified number of strokes on the hole.

1891 *Golf* magazine (Mar. 20) 13: . . . both players . . . lay at two each on the edge of the green.
1963 Arnold Palmer *My Game and Yours* 78: If he lifted the ball he would lie 3.
1970 Dick Schaap *The Masters* 114: He is

lying four, and he still hasn't reached the green.

3 *n.* The stationary position of a ball in play on the course, described in terms of the nature of the ground, slope, vegetation, etc., and the ease or difficulty of playing it.

1828 *Laws of Golf* (Blackheath) (in Clapcott 1935, 54): IX.—In playing, no mark shall be used to beat down or make any mark in the sand or soil, whereby to improve the lie of the Ball.
1857 H.B. Farnie *The Golfer's Manual* 18: . . . the thousand and one bad *lies* which the best directed stroke will get into.
1890 Horace Hutchinson *Badminton Golf* 54: . . . the ball has to be driven from every variety of lie, sandy, grassy, rushy, or stony.
1911 James Braid *Advanced Golf* 104: . . . lies which call for abnormal stances occasionally result from good shots down the course.
1976 J.C. Jessop *Golf* 99: Lies in the semi-rough or rough vary, but you must consider yourself lucky if the lie is at all favourable.

lie² *n.* The angle at which a clubhead is set on the shaft; measured precisely as the angle between the shaft and the horizontal, when the club is correctly soled for address.

1857 H.B. Farnie *The Golfer's Manual* 29: Regarding the lie of a club intended for effecting distance, whether it should be flat or upright, little can be said . . . the rule being, the longer the club, the flatter the lie.
1890 Horace Hutchinson *Badminton Golf* 58: The 'lie' is the result of the angle formed by the head with the shaft. When head and shaft are at an obtuse angle the club is termed a 'flat-lying' club, when they more nearly form a right angle the club is said to be 'upright,' or to have an 'upright lie.'
1912 Harry Vardon *How to Play Golf* 41: The frequency with which one sees a golfer using wooden instruments of different degrees of 'lie' is extraordinary.
1929 *Spalding's Athletic Library* n.p.: The clubs in each group are perfectly related in weight, pitch, lie, balance and feel.
1963 Bob Rosburg *The Putter Book* 24:

lie²

two-iron, lie 58 degrees

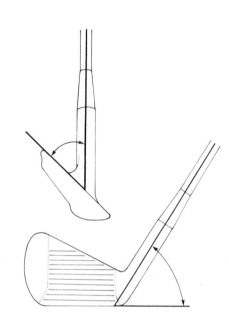

Shafts may be attached to the putter head at various angles (lies).
1977 Dave Hill & Nick Seitz *Teed Off* 180: If the toe is off the ground your lie is too upright. You need a flatter lie so that the club will be squarely on the ground at address.

lift *v. & n.* **1** *v.trans. & intrans.* To pick up (a ball in play), as when accepting a penalty for an unplayable lie, or when improving a lie under "winter rules."

1744 *Articles & Laws in Playing at Golf* 6: If your Balls be found anywhere touching one another you are to lift the first Ball, till you play the last.
1824 *Rules of the Thistle Golf Club* 48: V. The player, in every case, shall be entitled to lift his ball, drop it at such distance as he thinks proper behind the hazard, and lose one stroke.
1874 *The Times* (Oct. 5) (in Clark *Golf: A Royal & Ancient Game* 1875, 258): You may as well lift it at once and submit to the penalty.

1891 *Golf* magazine (July 10) 295: . . . at the next hole Reid bunkered his ball and lifted.
1911 James Braid *Advanced Golf* 305: I think that perhaps I was injudicious not to have lifted from the place, and lost two strokes.
1974 *The Golfer's Handbook* 469: . . . put their respective approach shots into the Swilcan Burn and each had to lift out and count a penalty stroke.
1977 Dwayne Netland *Golf Digest* (Aug.) 27: Because the course had been afflicted by a severe winter, players were allowed to lift and clean on the fairway.

2 *n.* An act or instance of lifting a ball.

1977 Gordon S. White *New York Times* (June 5): She was permitted a lift and then made her third shot.

like *n.* *Obsolete.* The same number of strokes for a hole (as an opponent). —
to play the like *phr.* To play a stroke that brings one's score for a hole level with that of one's opponent.

1790 *Hoyle's Games* 290: [A and B are partners in a foursome against C and D.] A strikes off first—C next; but perhaps does not drive his Ball above half the distance A did, on which account D, his partner, next strikes it, which is called *one more*, to get it as forward as that of their Antagonists, or as much beyond it as possible; if this is done then B strikes A's ball, which is called playing the *like*, or equal, of their Opponents.
1823 James Grierson *Delineations of St. Andrews* 220: If the ball be struck into the hole at the *like*, or an equal number of strokes on both sides, the hole is said to be halved.
1899 Willie Tucker *The Outing* (Aug.) 523: Holabird, playing the odd . . . laid within 8 feet of the hole. Macdonald, playing the like, was short.
1912 Harry Vardon *How to Play Golf* 159: . . . the man who now has to supply the "like."
1926 William D. Richardson *Golf Illustrated* (Oct.) 39: . . . [von Elms] was inside on seven of the nine greens and on six of the seven holes Bobby had the advantage of playing the like.

like as we (or **they**) **lie.** *Obsolete.* Having played an equal number of strokes for a hole.

1858 *Unidentified newspaper clipping* (in Allan Robertson's album at the R. & A. 88): They arrive within a few yards of the last hole 'the like as they lie.'
1881 Robert Forgan *The Golfer's Handbook* 60: LIKE-AS-WE-LIE—When both parties have played the same number of strokes.
1891 *Golf* magazine (Sept. 18) 13: Both sides were like as they lay in three.
1929 *Spalding's Athletic Library* 122: Like-as-we-lie—When both sides have played the same number of strokes.

line *n.* **1** (On the putting green) the correct path of a putt to the hole.

1881 Robert Forgan *The Golfer's Handbook* 31: The first thing the Golfer has to attend to on the Putting-Green is to study the "line" or direction which, in his judgment, allowing for curves or inequalities in the ground, will most probably land his ball safely at the bottom of the hole.
1907 Jack White in Leach *Great Golfers in the Making* 152: The great thing is to find the line, and my own success with the putter is, as I have already indicated, almost entirely due to my gift for finding the line, and being very sure about it almost at once.
1969 Jack Nicklaus *The Greatest Game of All* 200: I hit my putt well, the ball had the line and struck the back of the cup and dropped.

2 (Through the green) the correct direction of a shot toward the putting green; the correct, or most desirable, route along which the ball should be played on a particular hole.

1893 John Thomson *The Caddie* in *Golfing Poems & Songs* 3:
I can hand the richt club, and gie the
richt line . . .
1916 P.A. Vaile *The New Golf* 148: Coming to one of the greens Taylor got off the line a bit and for his approach found his way to the green blocked by a great tree.
1921 Andrew Kirkaldy *Fifty Years of Golf* 65: I was afraid of Mr. Travis all the way

because of his deadly accuracy. He hardly ever left the line.

1933 John Ressich *Thir Braw Days* 84: Noo, there was a north-east wind that we're verra apt for tae get yonder i' the winter, an' this cairried Davie's ba' off the line.

1969 Tom Scott & Geoffrey Cousins *The Golf Immortals* 144: Every tee-shot was an adventure, for she [Didrickson] hit with all the power she could muster, confident that if . . . she got off the line, she had the power and the courage to get out of trouble.

1976 Hamish Dunn in *Golf Collectors' Society Bulletin No. 31* (July) 4: 'Sorr, yer laine is just overr yon tree on the left.'

line up *phr.v.* To study the line of (a putt).

1971 Henry Longhurst *My Life and Soft Times* 31: . . . the man lining up a putt to tie for the Open . . .

links n. [Origin: Scottish, from Old Scottish *links, lynkis* = "ridges, hummocks," also "rough open ground," from Old English *hlincas*, plural of *hlinc* = "ridge, bank, hummocky ground." (The word exists also in some dialects and place names in England. It is not related to *link* = "bond, piece of chain.")]

1 *Usually plural, Scottish.* Rough open ground; especially, a tract of low-lying seaside land on the east coast of the Lowlands held by a town as a common and used from the Middle Ages onward for sports, including archery, bowls, and golf. Such land is characteristically sandy, treeless, undulating or hummocky, often with dunes, and the typical ground cover is bent grass, with gorse bushes.

1651 Sir R. Gordon *Genealogical History of the Earldom of Sutherland*: About this toun [Dornoch] along the sea coast ther ar the fairest and largest linkes (or green feilds) of any pairt of Scotland, fitt for archery, goffing, ryding and all other exercise.

1771 Tobias Smollett *Humphrey Clinker* (repr. 1902) 236: Hard by, in the field called

the Links, the citizens of Edinburgh divert themselves at a game called Golf.

1823 James Grierson *Delineations of St. Andrews* 217: The ground over which golf is played, is in Scotland called links, and is usually a particular sort of sandy soil in the neighbourhood of the seashore, its surface mostly covered with short coarse grass, here and there interrupted by breaks, pits, and inequalities. These interruptions are necessary to impart interest to the game.

1952 Sir Guy Campbell *The Birth of the Linksland Courses* (in Wind *The Complete Golfer* 1954, 81): . . . the area known as St. Andrews links. . . . As the sea retreated from it the process of natural reclamation progressed until today the links area is bounded by a long belt of fertile farmland, an expanse of saltings, the Eden estuary and St. Andrews Bay.

2 *Usually singular.* A golf course laid out on Scottish links (def. 1), or on similar seaside terrain elsewhere.

1744 *Scots Magazine* (Apr.) 197: That he have the sole disposal of the booking-money, the determination of disputes among goffers, . . . and the superintendency of the links.

1767 *Minutes of the Royal & Ancient Golf Club of St. Andrews* (Sept. 3): This day the Silver Club was played for, and gained by James Durham of Largo, Esq., by holing the Links at 94 strokes.

1861 H.B. Farnie *Fife Coast* 115: The links lying at the house door, is a very famous one in the annals of golf.

1893 John Thomson *Golfing Poems & Songs* 11:

The fair links of Dornoch is dearer to me
Than the best of the greens in the south
    countrie.

1898 Charles B. Macdonald *Golf* magazine (Jan.) 23: Links was originally plural, but now to golfers it signifies the ground the game is played over, and is, therefore, also used in the singular.

1931 Bernard Darwin *The Game of Golf* 148: Nearly every self-respecting Scottish links possesses a burn.

1970 Charles Price *Golf* 23: A links is a golf course built on linksland, the sandy deposits by the sea left by centuries of receding oceanic tides. . . . Genuine links are rare in the United States.

1970 Tony Jacklin *Jacklin* 58: Basically he

does not like links courses and is not a good wind player.

3 *Usually singular.* A golf course of any kind.

1890 Horace Hutchinson *Badminton Golf* 330: At neither Wimbledon nor Blackheath is there any sand ... therefore there are no bunkers, properly so called. This may indeed be said of all inland links.
1895 *The Outing* (July) 89: Golf in America has entered upon a new phase. . . . On the one hand a commencement has been made in laying out private links, and on the other hand, the first municipal links are in progress.
1936 H.B. Martin *Fifty Years of American Golf* 133: There were always a few [clubs] who insisted that it was a great sacrifice to give up their links to the U.S.G.A. for a week.
1952 Christopher· Rand *The Hong Kong Golf Club* (in Wind *The Complete Golfer* 1954, 124): The main links of the Royal Hong Kong Golf Club are at Fanling in the New Territories.

linksland n.   The seaside terrain typical of Scottish links (def. 1).

1969 Jack Nicklaus *The Greatest Game of All* 219: I don't much care for courses that represent the extreme in British linksland conditions.
1977 Robert Sommers *Golf Magazine* (Aug.) 51: The Eastern end of Long Island is quite possibly the closest approximation of real British linksland that exists in North America.

linksman n.   A golfer.

1915 Alexander H. Revell *Pro & Con of Golf* 53: To learn what we are as linksmen, compared with older foreign golf brothers, it is sometimes necessary to "see oursel's as ithers see us."
1978 *Reader's Digest* (Jan.) 146: Perhaps the most inspired golf dreamer of them all is Loyal "Bud" Chapman, a 54-year-old amateur linksman from Minneapolis.

lip n. & v.   **1** n. The edge of the hole.

1895 "Calamo Currente" *Half Hours With an Old Golfer* 106:
> He does his best, but oh! that horrid lip!
> The curling ball disdains the trifling dip.

1908 W.W. Tullock *Life of Tom Morris* 111: The sixth was halved also, Tom's ball lying on the lip of the hole with the like.
1927 John C. Koefoed *Golf Illustrated* (Feb.) 11: ... why Macdonald Smith lost his North-South title in 1926 through missing a putt on the very lip of the cup?
1962 Sam Snead *The Education of a Golfer* 118: I didn't even have to try for the putt— just nudged it up to the lip and tapped it in.

2 v.trans., or **lip out** phr.v.   (Of a putt) to run round part of the lip of (the hole) and fail to drop; (of a player) to play such a putt.

1891 *Golf* magazine (Oct. 9) 51: ...two unlucky shortish putts lipping the hole without going in.
1916 P.A. Vaile *The New Golf* 42: ...the topped put, which often "rims" or "lips" the hole and runs out again.
1977 Larry Dennis *Golf Digest* (July) 54: ... you eventually will get the ball rolling faster than the ideal speed and, even though you may be hitting the hole, the putts will start lipping out.
1978 Neil Amdur *New York Times* (July 15) 11: Owen lipped the 18th hole with a birdie putt.

loft v. & n.   **1** v.trans. & intrans. To play (a ball or shot) with a lofted club so that it flies in a steep trajectory.

1857 H.B. Farnie *The Golfer's Manual* 18: The long and middle spoons are often pressed into doing duty for a grassed driver, from their ability to "loft" the ball.
1898 Willie Tucker *The Outing* (Aug.) 440: The mashie is ... used to loft a ball over stone walls, fences, or to play a stymie.
1908 Arnold Haultain *The Mystery of Golf* (repr. 1965) 56: And as to that mashie shot, where you loft high over an abominable bunker ...
1946 Frank Moran *Golfers' Gallery* 184: ... at the previous hole, where she was stymied ... she lofted successfully.
1960 Rex Lardner *Out Of the Bunker and Into the Trees* 147: Marge now ... lofted an

loft²

(1) driver, loft 12 degrees

(2) nine-iron, loft 47 degrees

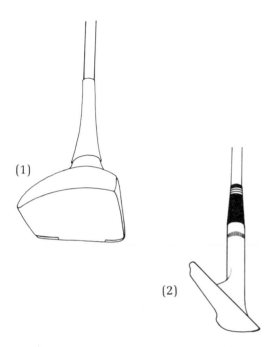

(1)

(2)

iron that stopped dead four feet from the pin.
1977 Gordon S. White *New York Times*
(July 10) S41: Dalrymple selected his 9-iron
for the second shot and lofted it easily to the
green.

2 *n.* The degree to which a clubface is
laid back from the vertical; measured
precisely as the angle between the face
and a line parallel to the shaft.

1907 John L. Low in Leach *Great Golfers in
the Making* 3: . . . a beginner who learns to
play every sort of approach with a club of
medium loft will gain a great deal more experience that the golfer who starts with the
assistance of variously lofted clubs.
1913 Bernard Darwin *Country Life* (Jan. 18)
105: I am now disposed to think that it is
greater shallowness rather than greater loft
that we want through the green.
1927 Robert T. Jones, Jr. & O.B. Keeler *Down
the Fairway* 182: He employs a club with
notably less loft than the conventional type of
mashie-niblick, and his shot is notably less
steep.

1965 Bob Charles *Left-handed Golf* 52:
. . . the long irons . . . Their lofts are, respectively, 17, 20, 23, and 27 degrees.

lofted *adj.* (Of a club) having relatively
steep loft on the face.

1911 James Braid *Advanced Golf* 44: . . .
some men, when they fail with the mashie,
are put on to a lofted jigger, and do excellently with it.

lofter *n.* or **lofting iron.** A lofted iron club,
no longer in use, that was used chiefly
for approaching.

1889 Alexander Lawson *Letters on Golf* 29:
Quite lately it was announced that young
Willie Park had at length succeeded in fash-
ioning a lofter that will do all that is desired.
1890 Horace Hutchinson *Badminton Golf*
59: The 'baffy,' with which the golfer of old
used to approach the hole, is now replaced by
the lofting-iron.
1903 Harold Hilton *The Outing* (Apr.) 124:
. . . the lofting iron, with its broad, homely
face, had to give way to the pitching mashie.
1933 John Ressich *Thir Braw Days* 90:
Noo, he had a great muckle loftin' iron wi' a
face like a fryin'-pan an' about as wechty as
ain o' auld Balsillie's sermons.

long *adj. & adv.* **1** *adj.* (Of a shot or ball)
traveling a long distance.

1779 Hugo Arnot *History of Edinburgh*
361: But the game does not depend solely
upon the striking of the longest ball.

lofter

R. Forgan, St. Andrews, c. 1895

1867 *The First Hole at St. Andrews* in *Poems on Golf* 32:
> And swears by Ammon, he'll engage to drive
> As long a ball as any man alive!

1915 A.W. Tillinghast *The Wellington Emerald* (in *Cobble Valley Golf Yarns* 196): "...I got away some longer and straighter balls than ever before in my life."

1927 Robert T. Jones, Jr. & O.B. Keeler *Down the Fairway* 206: I think that is the longest ball I ever hit, for carry.

2 *adv.* A long way; far.

1839 Song in *Minutes of the Bruntsfield Links Golf Club* (Sept. 28) in Clark *Golf: A Royal & Ancient Game* 1875, 100:
> Come all you Golfers stout and strong
> Who putt so sure and drive so long ...

1969 Jack Nicklaus *The Greatest Game of All* 267: Compared to most golfers, I hit the ball quite long.

1977 Gordon S. White *New York Times* (Aug. 7) 4: Jerry was hitting the ball somewhat longer than he does these days.

3 *adj.* (Of a player) far-hitting.

1867 "H.J.M." *The Golfer at Home* in Clark op. cit. 169: There is the "long driver," who hits as far in two strokes as the "short driver" does in three.

1913 Bernard Darwin *Country Life* (Sept. 20) 401: Mr. Anderson, a fine, straight wooden-club player, but not very long with his irons ...

1931 Joyce Wethered *The Game of Golf* 135: Only the longest ladies can come within striking distance of these greens off the tee shot.

1975 Dan Jenkins *Dead Solid Perfect* 29: "Let me see you hit that driver. Looks like you might be pretty long."

4 *adj.* (Of a club) relatively straight-faced and far-hitting.

1897 Price Collier *The Outing* (Oct.) 88: ... by making the length of the hole such that a poor shot off the tee ... cannot be retrieved merely by taking a longer club for the second shot.

1948 Ben Hogan *Power Golf* 58: Fundamentally, the brassie is the longest club off the fairway.

5 *adv.* (Of a course) as if it were longer, owing to weather conditions.

1914 Bernard Darwin *Country Life* (Jan. 3) 31: ... the course is particularly long just now, there being very little run in the ground.

1975 Mark McCormack *Golf Annual* 80: Both had gone out in 37, two over par but no disgrace in the teeming rain and on a course playing as long as it ever can.

long driving. The making of long drives.

1857 H.B. Farnie *The Golfer's Manual* 41: Long driving, if it be not the most deadly, is certainly the most dashing and fascinating part of the game.

1908 Arnold Haultain *The Mystery of Golf* (repr. 1965) 38: ... developing his muscles for his summer's golf—his ambition was long driving.

1962 Sam Snead *The Education of a Golfer* 17: The big feature was a long-driving contest, including the strongest swingers from west-central Virginia.

1977 *Golf Digest* (July) 37: Evan (Big Cat) Williams, winner of last year's National Long Driving Contest ...

long-driving *adj.* Capable of long drives.

1890 Horace Hutchinson *Badminton Golf* 220: ... a staunch old golfer about to be partnered with a slashing long-driving young opponent.

1929 *Golf Illustrated* (Apr.) 44: The long-driving young player is the professional ...

long irons. The relatively straight-faced and long-hitting irons (see quots.)

1941 Patty Berg *Golf* 9: I prefer this stance for playing long irons (nos. 1, 2, 3, 4) ...

1946 Byron Nelson *Winning Golf* 30: ... long irons (numbers 1, 2, 3).

1965 Bob Charles *Left-handed Golf* 52: Gaining in popularity because they combine distance with accuracy are the long irons, numbers one through four.

1977 Davis Love *Golf Digest* (July) 44: There is less tendency to overwork your hands with fairway woods than with long irons.

loop n. A round of golf.

1968 Buddy Hackett *The Truth About Golf* 60: And the caddy says, "I've already had a couple of loops today and I don't want to go any more."
1973 *Bartlett's World Golf Encyclopedia* xix: . . . the caddie ranks swell with schoolboys who hope to get two loops a day if the caddiemaster nods their way.

loose impediments. Unattached natural objects which might obstruct a stroke, and which may generally, under the rules, be removed, except in hazards.

1809 *Rules of the Honourable Company of Edinburgh Golfers* (in Clapcott 1935, 42): 50. . . . all loose impediments may be removed in putting.
1976 *Rules of Golf* Definition 17: The term "loose impediments" denotes natural objects not fixed or growing and not adhering to the ball, and includes stones not solidly embedded, leaves, twigs, branches and the like, dung, worms and insects and casts or heaps made by them.

M

makable *adj.* (Of a putt) reasonably possible to hole.

1977 Dave Stockton *Golf Digest* (Aug.) **40:** The range for a makable putt—one you're trying to sink as opposed to just getting it close—varies with an individual's skill and the putting surface.

make *v.trans.* **1** *Obsolete.* To play (a round or course) in a stated number of strokes.

1824 *Rules of the Thistle Golf Club* 45: On comparing these cards, he who shall be found to have made the ten holes in fewest strokes, to be declared the gainer of the Medal.
1905 Frederick Upham Adams *John Henry Smith* 54: Carter is a rattling good fellow and a fine golfer—he has made Woodvale in seventy-seven.

2 To score (a stated score).

1962 Richard Armour *Golf Is a Four-letter Word* 27: . . . and one day [I] broke a hundred—made a 99, to be exact.
1966 Gary Player *Grand Slam Golf* 32: Straightforward four. I made six, and my entire world seemed to disintegrate.
1977 *New York Times* (Aug. 5) A15: . . . made birdie 4 on the second.
1977 Tom Watson *Golf Magazine* (Aug.) 73: . . . got two bad breaks and made bogey.

mallet putter
(1) Braid-Mills aluminum, 1915
(2) Auchterlonie Special (modern, reproducing wooden putter of c. 1880)

(1)

(2)

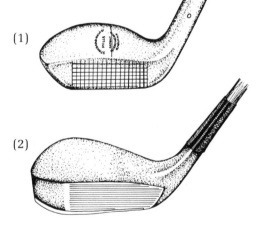

mallet *n., often attributive,* or **mallet-head.** A putter having a head that is considerably wider and heavier than that of a blade putter.

1963 Bob Rosburg *The Putter Book* 21: Manufacturing imagination has turned out a great many kinds of mallets.

1970 Tony Jacklin *Jacklin* 161: In the Open he used a new mallet putter.
1970 Dick Schaap *The Masters* 204: . . . using a mallet-head putter.

marker *n.* **1** A person who acts as scorer in a stroke competition.

1807 *Regulations of the Edinburgh Burgess Golfing Society* [medal rules] (in Clapcott 1935, 39): That the competitors play in single parties and each party to have a marker.
1976 *Rules of Golf* Definition 18: A "marker" is a scorer in stroke play who is appointed by the Committee to record a competitor's score. He may be a fellow-competitor. He is not a referee.

2 One of a pair of objects placed at a teeing ground, between which players should tee their balls.

1929 W.H. Faust *Golf Illustrated* 25: "Take it over," said the referee, pointing to the tee which was still stuck in the ground. "You teed your ball three inches ahead of the markers."
1976 *Rules of Golf* Definition 33: The "teeing ground" . . . is a rectangular area . . . the front and sides of which are defined by the outside limits of two tee-markers.

3 A small object such as a coin used to mark the position of a ball that has been lifted from the putting green.

marshal *n.* An official appointed to control a gallery.

1950 Gene Sarazen (in Wind *The Complete Golfer* 1954, 193): I waited until the marshals had herded the swarming gallery away from the right-hand side.
1977 Max Conrad *Golf Digest* (July) 12: A marshal asked the gallery to move back.

mashie *n.* [*Origin:* Scottish, diminutive of *mash*="sledgehammer"; perhaps originally suggested by the contemporary billiards term *massé*="downward jabbing stroke played with the cue held nearly vertical to impart maximum back-

mashie

(1) ordinary mashie, c. 1890
(2) George Sinclair Special, 1910

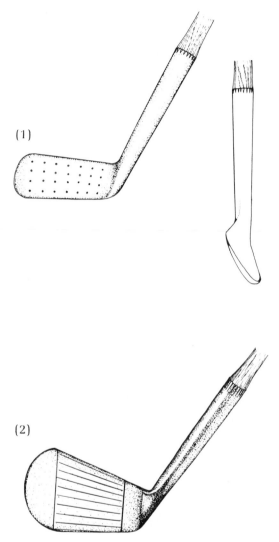

(1)

(2)

spin."] **1** A lofted iron club, no longer in use, introduced about 1880 and used for pitching with backspin.

1881 Robert Forgan *The Golfer's Handbook* 17: The "Mashy" is used for the same purposes as the Niblick proper, and only differs from it in its sole and face being straight instead of rounded. . . . The Mashy, however, is one of those fanciful clubs that have been invented in recent years, and is entirely unnecessary in the golfer's set.

1890 Horace Hutchinson *Badminton Golf* 67: The mashie may be said to be a hybrid growth. But a few years back it was almost unknown. Now its use is universal.

1903 Walter Camp *The Book of Sports & Games* 248: Your mashie, for approaching purposes, should be essentially a weapon of balance, while your niblick, for digging purposes, should be essentially a weapon of weight.

1915 Alexander H. Revell *Pro & Con of Golf* 11: The writer believes the mashie is the most important club in the bag.

1937 Abe Mitchell *Essentials of Golf* 146: In playing the pitch-and-run the club to use is the mashie.

1975 Henry Cotton *History of Golf* 22: J.H. Taylor . . . perfected play with the mashie . . . which he used with a short swing and a firm punching stroke, quite unlike the accepted long sweeping swing of the day.

2 Alternate name for the number five iron.

1926 Advertisement *Golf Illustrated* (June) 11: No. 5, Mashie.

1961 John Stobbs *Tackle Golf* (repr. 1977) 31: Take a mashie, that is (in vulgar modern terminology) a 5-iron.

mashie-iron n.   **1** An iron club, no longer in use, somewhat less lofted than a mashie, that was used for driving and for full shots through the green.

1899 Walter Camp & Lilian Brooks *Drive & Puts* 84: "If you must get distance, take your mashie-iron . . ."

1911 James Braid *Advanced Golf* 44: There is a good deal more to be said for the mashie iron. . . . It is really a deep-faced mashie with less loft than an ordinary mashie —about the same as a mid-iron.

1926 Lucille McAllister *Golf Illustrated* (Oct.) 23: . . . she often used a wood for distances that appeared no more than a mashie-iron in length.

2 Alternate name for the number four iron.

1926 Advertisement *Golf Illustrated* (June) 11: No. 4 (Mashie Iron).

1972 *Encyclopaedia Britannica* 10:557: Irons . . . Number Four (Mashie Iron).

mashie-niblick n.   **1** An iron club, no longer in use, having a loft between those of a mashie and a niblick, used for pitching.

1907 *Army & Navy Stores Catalogue* 999: Heavy soled Mashie Niblick. . . . If your ball is lying in an almost unplayable position, try one of these mashie niblicks.

1927 Robert T. Jones, Jr. & O.B. Keeler *Down the Fairway*: For years I have been wishing I could play a mashie-niblick shot the same as a mashie shot.

1937 Henry Longhurst *Golf* 123: Compston considers the straightforward mashie-niblick pitch to represent the easiest movement in the game.

2 Alternate name for the number six iron or the number seven iron.

1926 Advertisement *Golf Illustrated* (June) 11: No. 6, Mashie Niblic.

1972 *Encyclopaedia Britannica* 10:557: Irons . . . Number Seven (Mashie Niblick).

mashie-niblick
"Wilson Cup Defender," c. 1925

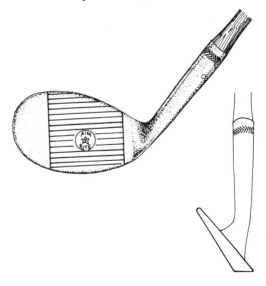

match n.   **1** A contest between two sides composed of one, two, or occasionally more players, in which the score is by holes, and now usually played over a stipulated round.

1786 *Regulations of the Crail Golfing Society* (in Clapcott 1935, 36):   That three rounds of the Links shall decide all Matches . . .
1823 James Grierson *Delineations of St. Andrews* 219:   A match may consist of two or more players, but no proficient at golf ever plays in one exceeding four, that number being allowed to be the most elegant and convenient.
1872 John Henry Walsh *British Rural Sports* 636:   . . . many important matches for high stakes are played there [St. Andrews], throughout the year, by the best players in the kingdom.
1911 James Braid *Advanced Golf* 214:   . . . after all, it is at the end of the round that matches are won, and not at the beginning.
1976 *Rules of Golf* 6.3:   A match (which consists of a stipulated round, unless otherwise decreed by the Committee) is won by the side which is leading by a number of holes greater than the number of holes remaining to be played.

2 The golfers playing a match.

1976 *Rules of Golf* Section I Etiquette: Any match playing a whole round is entitled to pass a match playing a shorter round.

matched adj.   (Of clubs) designed and made in a graded, numbered series with consistent specifications and swing-weights.

1929 Advertisement *Golf Illustrated* 63:   . . . a set of Matched Clubs will help you . . .
1946 Byron Nelson *Winning Golf* 18:   It is wise to buy "matched" irons and "matched" woods.
1952 Henry Cotton *History of Golf in Britain*:   The matched set, numbered 1–9, first blew in from America and so did the ballyhoo with it.

match play.   The original form of competition in golf, in which the contest is between two sides and the score is by holes.

1890 Horace Hutchinson *Badminton Golf* 213:   The primary difference between match play and medal play is that, whereas under the former conditions the score is counted by the result of the holes, under the latter the result is estimated by the sum total of the strokes played.
1931 T. Simpson *The Game of Golf* 191:   . . . in these islands where, at all events until quite recently, the sporting spirit of match play has always held the first place. The card and pencil has tended to supersede the spirit of match play and may for that reason be looked on as a regrettable evil to which a measure of tolerance must be shown.
1975 Henry Cotton *History of Golf* 145:   By 1973 the U.S.G.A. had reverted to match play, considering this form of golf to be more in keeping with the traditions of the game.
1977 Dave Hill & Nick Seitz *Teed Off* 97:   I'd like to see match play stay alive in golf, but not in a major championship.
1979 *Golf Illustrated* (Feb.) 15:   "I quite like matchplay," says [Mark] James, who numbered among his many amateur victories . . . the Lincolnshire matchplay title in 1972.

match player.   A golfer considered in terms of ability at match play rather than stroke play.

1956 Herbert Warren Wind *The Story of American Golf* 177:   Hagen's reputation as a match-player reached such proportions that each error he made was interpreted as a deliberate move to set up some stratagem.
1975 Mark McCormack *Golf Annual* 81:   Player finally closed out his man, 4 and 3. Crenshaw's generous comment: "He is the greatest match player I have ever seen."

meadowland n., attributive.   (Of a golf course) consisting of rich grassland.

1954 Robert Trent Jones (in Wind *The Complete Golfer* 308):   The Augusta National is the epitome of the type of course which appeals most keenly to the American taste, the meadowland course.
1973 Pat Ward-Thomas *Bartlett's World Golf Encyclopedia* 256:   Muirfield is not an-

cient, neither is it a links in the strict sense of the word. There are sandhills, and the sea is nearby, but the rich turf is more meadowland than seaside in character.

medal *n.* An honorary prize competed for by stroke play by members of a club or by entrants in a tournament.

1771 *Minutes of the Royal & Ancient Golf Club of St. Andrews* (Oct. 2): This day a Gold Medal, value Seven Guineas, given by the Society of Golfers, was played for and gained by Mr. Beveridge holing the Links at 101 strokes.
1897 Horace Hutchinson *Country Life* (Jan. 16) 50: At Rye the monthly medal was taken by Mr. H. Waldron, with 16 allowed, and nett 82.
1967 Mark McCormack *Arnie* 37: ... all major championships present the winner[s] with medals.

medal play. Golf competition in which the contest is among many competitors simultaneously and the score is by the total of strokes for the round or rounds.

1816 (in Clapcott 1935, 52): SPECIAL RULES FOR MEDAL PLAY MADE 4th MAY, 1816, Aberdeen Golf Club.
1853 *Unidentified newspaper clipping* (in Allan Robertson's album at the R. & A. 45): The medal play was above the common run in excellence.
1896 Price Collier *The Outing* (Dec.) 277: Medal play is an innovation. Many a crusty old golfer in Scotland pretends even now that he does not know what you mean by medal play.
1921 Andrew Kirkaldy *Fifty Years of Golf* 58: It was a two-round competition under medal play.
1962 Sam Snead *The Education of a Golfer* 169: When it's medal play, such as the Masters, where total strokes decide the winner, only a sucker takes a chance of multiplying one sorry shot with another.
1974 *The Golfer's Handbook* 87: "MEDAL PLAY" has crept into golf language as a synonym for "STROKE PLAY." "Stroke play" is the correct term, according to the Rules and tradition.

middle *adj.* (Of clubs) having medium range and loft.

1965 Bob Charles *Left-handed Golf* 54: The middle irons are the five, six and seven.
1969 Tom Weiskopf *Go For the Flag* 58: When we talk of the middle irons, we mean the four, five, and six.

middle spoon or **mid-spoon** *n.* A wooden club, no longer in use, having a loft between those of the long spoon and the short spoon.

1881 Robert Forgan *The Golfer's Handbook* 11: The "Middle Spoon" is a very strong club, and is especially useful in "forcing" a ball out of a grassy rut, and in playing a three-quarters stroke.
1890 Horace Hutchinson *Badminton Golf* 59: There was the 'long spoon,' the 'mid spoon,' and the 'short spoon.'

mid-iron *n.* **1** An iron club, no longer in use, somewhat more lofted than a driving iron.

1899 Findlay S. Douglas *The Outing* (June) 221: To-day, the average golfer carries six irons in his bag, viz., ... mid-iron ...
1912 Harry Vardon *How to Play Golf* 168: After the driver, ... the most valuable implement during the winter is a fairly powerful mid-iron.

mid-iron
J. M. Inglis, Montgomery, Ala., c. 1925

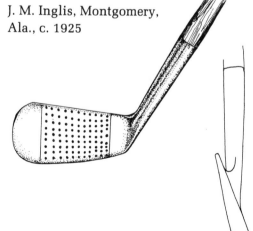

2 Alternate name for the number two iron.

1927 Robert T. Jones, Jr. & O.B. Keeler *Down the Fairway* 196: The No. 2 is what used to be called a midiron.
1972 *Encyclopaedia Britannica* 10:557: Irons . . . Number Two (Midiron).

3 Middle iron.

1962 Sam Snead *The Education of a Golfer* 47: . . . midirons, short irons and the putter are your scoring weapons nearly 60 per cent of the time.

mid-mashie n. Alternate name for the number three iron.

1926 Advertisement *Golf Illustrated* (June) 11: No. 3, Mid-mashie.
1972 *Encyclopaedia Britannica* 10:557: Irons . . . Number Three (Mid Mashie).

misclub v.intrans. To play a wrong club.

1977 Gene Littler *New York Times* (Aug. 15) 38: ". . . I misclubbed at least half a dozen times."
1979 Florida *Times-Union* (Apr. 13) E1: He misclubbed on his second shot at 15, using a 6-iron instead of a 5-iron.

misread v.trans. To read (a green or putt) wrongly.

1969 Jack Nicklaus *The Greatest Game of All* 153: Either we had misread the line or I had misgauged the speed of the green.

missable adj. (Of a putt) sufficiently long to be somewhat challenging.

1907 Harold Hilton *My Golfing Reminiscences* 41: Again, against Leslie Balfour and Horace Hutchinson, Johnnie only just got home by holing very missable putts on the last green.
1946 Frank Moran *Golfers' Gallery* 139: . . . he confidently put down a missable putt to take the title.
1966 Gary Player *Grand Slam Golf* 111: I pitched my ball inside his, about eight feet from the hole, a good missable distance.
1975 Mark McCormack *Golf Annual* 219: . . . he conceded DeWitt Weaver a missable 2-foot putt.

muff v.trans. To mishit (a shot).

1913 R.E. Howard *Country Life* (Sept. 13) 369: After a round in which he has muffed nearly all his tee shots.
1949 Fred Beck & O.K. Barnes *Seventy-three Years in a Sand Trap* 24: . . . he muffed his shot, ground his teeth, and let fling.
1962 Sam Snead *The Education of a Golfer* 35: Even after muffing 2 or 3 wood shots . . .

Mulligan n. [Origin obscure.] Permission by a player (forbidden under the rules) to an opponent to replay a misplayed shot, especially a tee-shot.

1960 Rex Lardner *Out of the Bunker and Into the Trees* 39: I don't even know if there *was* a Mulligan. But he gave his name to a wonderful gesture—letting you play a bad first drive over, and no penalty.
1977 *Golf Digest* (Aug.) 70: "For a comedian, Hope moans a lot about the way the fates treat him in golf," Fugazy says with a grin. "He will take six mulligans if you let him."

N

Nassau *n.* [Origin obscure.] A three-part bet on a round of golf, in which an equal stake is wagered on the first nine holes, on the last nine, and on the whole round.

1915 A.W. Tillinghast *The Outcasts* (in *Cobble Valley Golf Yarns* 16): "Stung Blodgett all three ways for a ball, Nassau."
1926 W. Hastings Webling *Golf Illustrated* (Oct.) 16: I understood after a little explanation from Wilbur what "five dollars, Nassau" meant.
1975 Dan Jenkins *Dead Solid Perfect* 29: Then he said we'd play Zark and Ruffin a $50 Nassau.

neck *n.* The tapered projecting part of a wooden clubhead into which the shaft is fitted.

1881 Robert Forgan *The Golfer's Handbook* 61: NECK.—The crook of the head where it joins the shaft.
1965 Bob Charles *Left-handed Golf* 112: Then comes the critical operation of drilling the hole in the neck of the head to accept the shaft.

net (*U.S.*) or **nett** (*Brit.*) *adj. & n.* (A score) resulting from deduction or addition of handicap strokes.

1890 Horace Hutchinson *Badminton Golf* 278: Each club should have a book, indexed and rules in columns for names, dates, gross scores, handicap allowances, and nett scores, respectively.
1962 Richard Armour *Golf Is a Four-letter Word* 44: It was a medal play, eighteen-hole tournament, with a cup for low gross and twenty-five dollars for low net.
1970 Tony Jacklin *Jacklin* 86: I did the last nine holes in par figures for a nett sixty-three.
1977 *Golf Magazine* (June) 30: ... middle-handicapper Greenday managed an 84 for net 67.

niblick *n.* [*Origin:* Scottish, probably a diminutive of *nib* = "nose," the literal meaning being "short-nose," since the original (wooden) niblick was much shorter in the nose than any other wooden club.] **1 (a)** A short-headed, steeply lofted wooden club, no longer in use, used for playing out of ruts and tight lies. **(b)** A round-faced, steeply lofted and concave-faced iron club, no longer in use, used like the wooden club; also called track-iron.

1857 H.B. Farnie *The Golfer's Manual* 19: Before quitting the subject of spoons, we shall notice an antiquated connection of the family, now seldom to be met with, unless as a

niblick
(1) wooden niblick, c. 1860
(2) iron niblick or track-
   iron, c. 1860
(3) T. Stewart, 1890
(4) Berwick, c. 1925

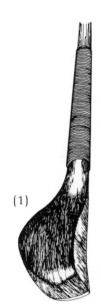

(1)

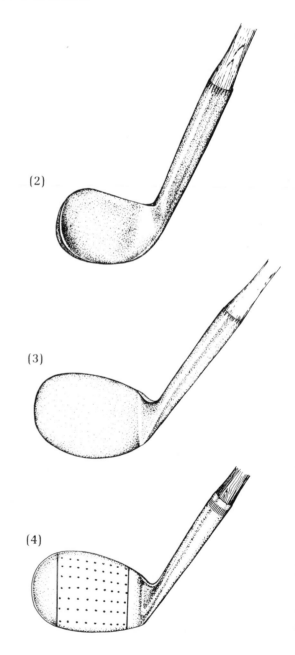

(2)

(3)

(4)

supernumerary in the pack of an oldster. It is called a NIBLICK; has a tough yet effective driving shaft; and an exceedingly small head well-spooned back. Its use is or rather *was,* to drive a ball out of a rut or cap large enough to admit the "diminished head."

1858 *Unidentified newspaper clipping* (in Allan Robertson's album at the R. & A. 90): The niblick is of very important service when the ball lies in a cart-rut, horseshoe print in sand, or any round deep hollow not altogether beyond the player's reach. [*Footnote:*] The niblick of St. Andrews is a short, spooned, *wooden* club; that of Musselburgh, a short, stout, *iron*-headed club, used for driving balls out of cart-ruts, etc. At St. Andrews, this little iron-headed club is termed a *track-iron.* We, however, prefer the Musselburgh terminology.

1881 Robert Forgan *The Golfer's Handbook* 8: *Wooden clubs:* Drivers, Spoons, Niblicks, Putters. —*Niblicks:* Wooden Niblick, Brassy Niblick. *Irons:* Cleeks, Irons, Niblicks. — *Niblicks:* Iron Niblick, [Mashy].

1895 James P. Lee *Golf in America* 117: WOODEN CLUBS . . . Baffing Spoon, Niblick, Brassy . . . IRON CLUBS . . . Lofting Iron, Niblick, President.

2 A deep-bladed iron club, no longer in use, developed from the earlier iron niblick, more steeply lofted than a mashie, used especially for playing from sand and from rough.

1907 *Army & Navy Stores Catalogue* 999: NIBLICKS . . . Ordinary Niblick. Made in three or four several depths of blade. Bunkers have no terrors when one of these is carried.
1912 Harry Vardon *How to Play Golf* 96: Nowadays, a great number of people like to play their approaches with niblicks.
1922 P.G. Wodehouse *The Rough Stuff* (in *The Clicking of Cuthbert* repr. 1956, 151): Ramsden reached for his niblick and plunged into the bushes.
1931 Roger Wethered *The Game of Golf* 72: . . . straight-faced irons down to the most lofted niblick in the bag.

3 Alternate name for the number nine iron.

1941 Patty Berg *Golf* 9: . . . the 'open' stance, as used in playing the no. 9 iron, or 'niblic.'
1961 John Stobbs *Tackle Golf* 80: A niblick can be made to put so much spin on a ball that, on landing, it will actually jump backwards.
1972 *Encyclopaedia Britannica* 10:557: Irons . . . Number Seven (Mashie Niblick), Number Eight (Pitching Niblick), Number Nine (Niblick).

nine *n.* A nine-hole course, or a sequence of nine holes in an eighteen-hole or larger course.

1977 Gordon S. White *New York Times* (July 9) 101: . . . were practically raised on Ridgewood Country Club's three nines.
1977 *Golf Digest* (Aug.) 88: Only nine holes are open, although another nine has been laid out.

nine-iron *n.* An iron club having loft of 45–48 degrees, lie of 62–64 degrees, and length of 35 inches, and giving distance of 105–140 yards (men's clubs). Also, a shot played with a nine-iron. Alternate name, niblick.

nine-iron
Walter Hagen, 1979

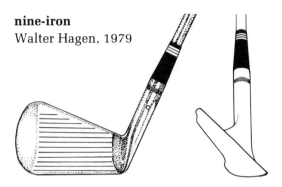

nineteenth hole. The bar of a golf club or course.

1915 A.W. Tillinghast *A Woman's Way* (in *Cobble Valley Golf Yarns* 81): We called Jim Donaldson the "Sage" at Cobble Valley, because in the kingdom of the Nineteenth Hole he was "Philosopher Extraordinary and Authority Unquestioned."
1919 Robert K. Risk *The Golfaiyat of Dufar Hy-yam* in *Songs of the Links* 13:
And softly by the Nineteenth Hole reclined
Make Game of that which maketh Game of thee.
1929 Advertisement (White Star Line) *Golf Illustrated* (Apr.) 79: Think of teeing off in the land where bairns cut their teeth on niblicks and brassies, and the nineteenth hole still thrives—bonny Scotland, the gowfer's paradise!
1974 *The Golfer's Handbook* 557: . . . around every nineteenth hole, legends are recalled of astonishing shots.
1977 *Official Golfers' Joke Book* 126: Whenever show people gather at the 19th hole, this story is sure to crop up about Crosby.

nose *n.* The toe of a wooden club.

1881 Robert Forgan *The Golfer's Handbook* 23: He may hit "off the heel," and so drive to the right hand, or "off the nose," and so "draw" the ball to the left.
1934 *From 102 to 82* . . . 77: The nose of the club . . . should be pointed down.
1973 *Bartlett's World Golf Encyclopedia* 364: Next the woods are sawed and turned at the neck and the nose.

O

odd or **odds** n.   *Obsolete.* A stroke that brings one's score for a hole to one more than that of one's opponent.

1823 James Grierson *Delineations of St. Andrews* 220: A's ball lies farthest behind, and, therefore, by the rules of the game, he is obliged to play again [A and B lying all even]. This is called playing *one more,* or, *the odds.*
1833 George Fullerton Carnegie *The Golfiad* (in *Poems on Golf* 1867, 26):
> Now, near the hole, Sir David plays the
> odds;
> Clan plays the like, and wins it, by the
> gods!

1899 Walter Camp & Lilian Brooks *Drives & Puts* 85: Tom playing the odd, put a ball just this side of the green, and Hugh, on the like, made a beautiful iron . . .
1912 Harry Vardon *How to Play Golf* 16: I happened to be driving rather well, and was generally a little way in front of McEwen from the tee, so that he usually had to play "the odd" in the approaches.
1921 Andrew Kirkaldy *Fifty Years of Golf* 65: . . . the American had the terrible uphill battle to fight, of playing the odd for his second shot all the way round.
1946 Frank Moran *Golfers' Gallery* 98: Fischer had the advantage from the tee . . . because it had the Scot playing the odd.

offset adj.   (Of a club) having a crooked neck or hosel so that the clubhead is set slightly off the line of the shaft.

offset
putter, c. 1915

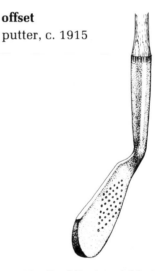

1929 *Spalding's Athletic Library* n.p.: Mashie Niblic (Offset) . . . Pitcher (Offset) . . . Niblic (Offset).
1962 Sam Snead *The Education of a Golfer* 135: I decided on five changes . . . (2) No more offset putters.
1977 Jody Hawkins *Golf Magazine* (June) 76: Players with a dominant right eye should use an offset putter. . . . Players with a dominant left eye should use a straight putter.

on *adv*   On or onto the putting green.

1912 Harry Vardon *How to Play Golf* 23: I managed to get on the green eight times in nine attempts. My opponent . . . did not get on once.

1929 Ralph Trost *Golf Illustrated* (Apr.) 36: The greens at El Paso are . . . unusually small. The very smallness is an asset, for once on, he can be confident of not three-putting.
1968 Buddy Hackett *The Truth About Golf* 51: On the first hole, Arthur and the other finalist . . . were both on in 3.
1977 John S. Radosta *New York Times* (Aug. 22) 34: On the 353-yard 17th North was on in regulation, about 18 feet from the cup.

one-iron *n.* An iron club having loft of about 17 degrees, lie of about 56 degrees, and length of 39 inches, and giving distance of 185–220 yards (men's clubs). Also, a shot played with a one-iron. Alternate name, driving iron.

1937 Abe Mitchell *Essentials of Golf* 116: The No. 1 iron is a club for the expert player.
1951 Dai Rees *Golf My Way* 54: The No. 1 is not an easy club to use and is rarely carried by the average golfer, who finds he can get better results with a spoon or an iron with more loft.
1979 *Golf Illustrated* (Feb. 15) 5: He then took out a one-iron and holed the shot over some 200 yards.

one-putt *v. & n.* **1** *v.trans. & intrans.* To hole (the ball) or play (a green) in one putt.

1956 Herbert Warren Wind *Story of American Golf* 484: . . . had to abandon his thoughts of one-putting that green.
1962 Sam Snead *The Education of a Golfer* 207: . . . his mashie fourth came right through those trees to fall right where he could 1-putt it in.
1977 *Golf Digest* (Aug.) 96: Weiskopf . . . one-putted from six feet for a par.

2 The achievement or fact of holing a green in one putt.

1970 Dick Schaap *The Masters* 136: "Shoo," says Snead, "did he get the ball in the hole! He had twelve oners! Twelve one-putts!"
1975 Mark McCormack *Golf Annual* 179:

. . . as the big Londoner picked him off with one-putt after one-putt.

one-shot *adj.* (Of a hole) requiring one good drive to reach the green.

1901 Findlay S. Douglas *The Outing* (June) 360: A very interesting discussion has been going on in *Golf Illustrated* as to what constitute the best one, two, and three shot holes of the various championship courses.
1913 W. Herbert Fowler *Country Life* (Oct. 4) 467: The next is a "one-shot" hole . . . and is about 150 yards in length.
1931 Bernard Darwin *The Game of Golf* 152: Yet this is a magnificent one-shot hole, demanding the highest golfing qualities.
1954 R. & A. *Decisions on the Rules* (in *The Golfer's Handbook* 1974, 884): A and B were playing a long one-shot hole . . .

one-shotter *n.* A one-shot hole.

1927 Robert T. Jones, Jr. & O.B. Keeler *Down the Fairway* 191: No. 15, a sweet one-shotter of 229 yards over level terrain . . .
1969 Jack Nicklaus *The Greatest Game of All* 161: The sixteenth is a tough one-shotter of 190 yards over a fairway of water.

one up *phr.* **1** In match play, having scored one hole more than one's opponent; also, the score of a player who is one up.

1891 *Golf* magazine (Sept. 18) 13: . . . turned the tables in favour of Andrew and Hugh [Kirkaldy], who started home one up.
1907 Harold Hilton *My Golfing Reminiscences* 24: Twice I was one up, but he always dragged me back again.
1936 H.B. Martin *Fifty Years of American Golf* 375: . . . eliminating him by the very close margin of one up.
1978 Deane McGowen *New York Times* (July 8) 15: The medalists . . . advanced to this afternoon's round with a one-up triumph.

2 Figuratively, being in a position of psychological advantage over an opponent.

1968 Stephen Potter *Golfmanship* 87: . . .

that in golf, one down was one up. The situation appeals to the fighting instinct. The brave horse, the real racer, likes to come up from behind.

1971 Henry Longhurst *My Life and Soft Times* 111: When [Tom Simpson] turned up at Morfontaine for some event after the war and said rather grandly, "Where's the first tee of this place?" I was able to become one up on him by replying, "Just where you put it twenty years ago."

one-wood *n.* Alternate name of the driver.

1961 Tommy Armour *How to Play Your Best Golf All the Time* 48: 1-wood (driver) . . . From the tee into the wind, with the ball well teed-up.

open *adj. & v.* **1** *adj.* (Of a player at address) turned slightly toward the objective; (of a stance) having the near foot (the left, of a right-handed player) placed slightly farther back from the line of play than the other, and turned slightly outward.

1890 Sir Walter Simpson *Badminton Golf* 186: . . . those who stand 'open,' and who have most of their weight on the right leg . . . oftenest commit this fault [slicing].
1912 Harry Vardon *How to Play Golf* 135: In playing for the slice, the stance should be open—the ball about opposite the toes of the left foot, which should be pointing outwards, and the right foot advanced so that the executant feels himself well behind the ball.
1916 P.A. Vaile *The New Golf* 98: The stance which is most generally favored now is what is called the "open" stance.
1929 *Spalding's Athletic Library* 24: The "open" stance. Left foot dropped back, with ball played approximately on a line with left heel.
1950 Sam Snead *How to Hit a Golf Ball* 2: The open stance is the one in which the left foot is drawn farther back from the intended line of flight than the right foot, turning the body slightly toward your objective.
1963 Bob Rosburg *The Putter Book* 33: I play the ball just slightly ahead of stance-center. My hips are open a bit (facing the target) . . .
1967 Mark McCormack *Arnie* 52: As with just about every other good player, Arnold is what the pros call "open," meaning his stance and the position of his body when he addresses the ball are slightly open, turned a little toward the hole.

2 *adj.* (Of a clubface) having the toe turned somewhat back from the line of play.

1978 Ernie Vossler *Golf Magazine* (May) 68: The clubface is considered open when it angles to the right of the swing path at impact.

3 *v.trans.* To turn (a clubface) slightly back from the line of play.

1928 Ned Everhart *Golf Illustrated* (Aug.) 21: With practice, the player will learn just how far he must open the blade of the niblick to get the proper distance desired.
1977 Nick Seitz *New York Times* (Sept. 25) S12: You can heighten the effect of the flange by opening the face of the club at address—pointing it more to the right if you're right-handed.

4 *v.intrans.* (Of a clubface) to turn slightly back from the line of play.

1975 Henry Cotton *History of Golf* 214: . . . allowing the club face to open as the shoulders turned on the way back from the address position.
1977 Ben Crenshaw *Golf Magazine* (Aug.) 32: If you knock it at a point too close to the toe, the blade will open.

out of bounds *phr. & n.* **1** *phr.* (Of a ball) lying out of the area defined as the course, and so not to be played.

1891 *Golf* magazine (Sept. 25) 26: . . . the line of play at various parts lies either alongside or across nooks of cultivated land, which for Golfers is "no man's land," being "out of bounds," and entailing the penalty either of a stroke and distance or dropping and losing two.
1969 Jack Nicklaus *The Greatest Game of All* 155: I started the tournament by hitting three tee-shots out of bounds on the first hole.
1976 *Rules of Golf* 29.1.a: If a ball be lost

outside a water hazard or be out of bounds, the player shall play his next stroke as nearly as possible at the spot from which the original ball was played or moved by him, *adding a penalty stroke* to his score for the hole.

2 out-of-bounds n. An area that is out of bounds.

1926 Joshua Crane *Golf Illustrated* (Dec.) 16: Usually, the out-of-bounds is plainly in sight.
1977 Dave Hill & Nick Seitz *Teed Off* 134: Locke once started a drive to the right, over an out-of-bounds . . .

outside agency. Any object (including a person who is not part of the game) that stops, deflects, or moves a ball in play.

1888 *Rules for the Game of Golf* (in Clapcott 1935, 122): If a player's ball be played away by mistake, or be lifted by any agency outside the match, then the player must drop it, or another ball.
1976 *Rules of Golf* Definition 22: An "outside agency" is any agency not part of the match or, in stroke play, not part of a competitor's side, and includes a referee, marker, an observer, or a forecaddie. . . . Rule 26.1.a. If a ball in motion be stopped or deflected by any outside agency, it is a rub of the green and the ball shall be played as it lies, without penalty.

overclub v. **1** *v.intrans. & reflexive* To select (for oneself) a club giving more distance than required for a particular shot.

1913 Bernard Darwin *Country Life* (Jan. 25) 140: At Muirfield it was the general impression that he was distinctly overclubbing himself.
1956 Herbert Warren Wind *The Story of American Golf* 508: He had overclubbed himself on a couple of approaches.
1975 Mark McCormack *Golf Annual* 29: He overclubbed at the 15th and went over the green.

2 *v.trans.* (Of a caddie) to select (for the player) a club giving too much distance.
1977 Tony Kornheiser *New York Times*

(Aug. 14) S1: But her caddie overclubbed her, and she airmailed her shot 40 yards over the green.

overgolf v., *reflexive.* To subject (oneself) to an excess of golf.

1890 A.J. Balfour *Badminton Golf* 428: Long Willie would say, 'Eh well, Maister So-and-so, I think we've maybe done enough for the day. It's nae a guid thing to over-gowf yersel', ye ken.'
1922 P.G. Wodehouse *Sundered Hearts* (in *The Clicking of Cuthbert* repr. 1956, 67): "One doesn't want to over-golf oneself the first day."
1970 Dick Schaap *The Masters* 44: "I'm getting a little tired," Wright says. "I played twenty-seven holes today, and maybe I'm over-golfed. My edge is gone."

overlap n. An overlapping grip.

1916 P.A. Vaile *The New Golf* 9: I should advise the beginner . . . to try the new overlap.

overlapping *adj.* (Of a grip as used by a right-handed player) having the little finger of the right hand overlapping the space between the forefinger and second finger of the left hand; and the converse for a left-handed player.

1906 Arthur Pottow *Illustrated Outdoor News* (Dec.) 183: For approach work Smith uses the overlapping grip.
1912 Harry Vardon *How to Play Golf* 59: . . . and there is the overlapping grip, which, personally, I think is by far the better and which is now adopted by nearly every professional of note.
1941 Patty Berg *Golf* 3: For myself I prefer the "over-lapping" . . .
1969 Tom Weiskopf *Go For the Flag* 36: The best grip for the average person is the overlapping grip.

overspin n. Forward rotation of the ball in motion.

1948 Ben Hogan *Power Golf* 79: . . . I contend that there is no such thing as overspin on any shot with the possible exception of one that is topped.

1967 Dave Thomas *Modern Golf* 30: People think I tee up the ball so high in order to get the maximum amount of overspin, and run when the ball lands, but this is not so.

1973 Arnold Palmer *Go For Broke* 13: Normally you want to give the ball some overspin when hitting off the tee with a driver.

P

pair n. & v. **1** n. Two golfers playing as partners in a match.

1911 James Braid *Advanced Golf* 290: ... these are important competitions in Scotland. ... Both are by foursome, two pairs representing each club in the one case and one in the other.

2 v.trans. To assign or group (two golfers) to play together as partners in a match.

1899 Walter Camp & Lilian Brooks *Drives and Puts* 37: "Isn't it jolly that you and I are paired together," said Miss Duane, linking her arm in Patty's.
1907 Willie Park in Leach *Great Golfers in the Making* 105: ... my father and I being paired against Old Tom Morris and Jimmie, his son.
1922 P.G. Wodehouse *The Rough Stuff* (in *The Clicking of Cuthbert* repr. 1956, 147): Yet it was with Ramsden that she was paired in ... the annual mixed foursomes.
1962 Sam Snead *The Education of a Golfer* 10: "I'm pairing you with Goodman in a four-ball match against Little and Burke."

3 n. Two golfers playing together in a stroke competition.

1967 George Plimpton *The Bogey Man* 22: We were waiting on the 6th for a pair in front of us.

4 v.trans. To assign or group (golfers) to play together in a stroke competition.

1977 Dan Jenkins *Dead Solid Perfect* (in *Sports Illustrated* (June) 43): ... he was playing with his pal Tom Weiskopf in a pro-am in Cincinnati, and they were paired with none other than Tommy Bolt and his partner.

pairing n. The grouping of two golfers to play together in a stroke competition.

1970 Dick Schaap *The Masters* 92: I really enjoyed that pairing," he said. "Sukree's one of the few people in the tournament I can outdrive."
1977 John S. Radosta *New York Times* (July 9) 11: Today they were in the same pairing, pitted like combatants in a cockfight, matching blow for blow.

par n., adj., & v. **1** n. The standard score in strokes assigned to each hole, and to a round, of a given course; assigned on the basis of one, two, or three strokes through the green according to the length of the hole, plus two putts; and representing the standard of play expected of a first-class player in favorable conditions making no mistakes.

1891 *Golf* magazine (June 10) 291: The result was satisfactory to the handicappers, as the par of the green for gentlemen, viz., 66, was nearly attained by three couples.
1906 Arthur Pottow *Illustrated Outdoor*

News (Nov.) 131: As played now, the course is 6,438 yards in length, the distances and par being: 1, 289, 4; 2, 130, 3; . . .

1911 James Braid *Advanced Golf* 250: The difference between par and bogey is, of course, that the former represents perfect play and the other stands for good play, with a little margin here and there.

1922 P.G. Wodehouse *The Rough Stuff* (in *The Clicking of Cuthbert* repr. 1956, 143): . . . even as early as his seventeenth year, I believe, he was going round difficult courses in par.

1950 Anthony F. Merrill *The Golf Course Guide* 119: New Orleans Country Club. 18 holes, 6538 yards, par 71.

1963 Bob Rosburg *The Putter Book* 61: Par always allows two putts for every green.

2 par-three, par-four, par-five *adj. & n.* (A hole) having a par of three, four, or five.

1977 John S. Radosta *New York Times* (June 17) A17: The meanest hole today was the 18th, a par 4 of 449 yards that all the players considered close to a par 5 today.

1977 George Peper *Golf Magazine* (Aug.) 42: How many times have you come to the tee of a tough par-four hole . . . ?

3 *proper.* An imaginary player who always makes par.

1908 Arnold Haultain *The Mystery of Golf* (repr. 1965) 95: . . . men high up in the handicap have always Bogey; scratch men can compete with Par.

1927 Robert T. Jones, Jr. & O.B. Keeler *Down the Fairway*: After all, it's Old Man Par and you, match or medal. And Old Man Par is a patient soul, who never shoots a birdie and never incurs a buzzard.

1969 Billy Casper in Paul D. Peering *Billy Casper: Winner* viii: . . . the excitement and thrill of the contest with "Mr. Par" and my fellow professionals.

4 *adj.* Of the standard of par.

1899 Willie Tucker *The Outing* (Aug.) 524: The Isle of Woe, or eleventh hole, is 400 yards long and was won in par golf by Macdonald, in 4 to 5.

1915 A.W. Tillinghast *The Spur* (in *Cobble Valley Golf Yarns* 166): "Bill was shaping his life to par figures."

5 *v.trans.* To play (a hole) in par.

1970 Dick Schaap *The Masters* 37: Hogan parred the sixteenth, then parred the seventeenth.

1977 *New York Post* (May 23) 55: The Golden Bear parred all three holes today . . .

park or **parkland** *adj.* (Of a course) laid out in rich grassland with little rough.

1936 H.B. Martin *Fifty Years of American Golf* 65: Our inland type of golf course—or park course—was very much ridiculed by the British.

1975 Henry Cotton *History of Golf* 212: I find very open park courses tedious and boring to play.

1975 Mark McCormack *Golf Annual* 182: Downfield, a superb parkland par-73 of 6,903 yards . . .

partner *n.* **1** A golfer playing in partnership with another in a match.

1976 *Rules of Golf* Definition 23: A "partner" is a player associated with another player on the same side.

2 partner or **playing partner.** A golfer in the same pairing or group as another in a stroke competition.

1890 Horace Hutchinson *Badminton Golf* 230: Upon the medal day, when you play for score, it should be your aim to play without reference to your partner's performance.

1969 Jack Nicklaus *The Greatest Game of All* 22: And then, curiously, I drew Hogan himself as my playing partner for the double round on the last day.

pawky *adj.* [Scottish, from *pawk*="trick, ruse."] Cunning; tricky.

1890 Horace Hutchinson *Badminton Golf* 274: . . . in playing for score the 'pawky' old golfer will defeat the youngster nine times out of ten.

1893 John Thomson *The Auld Golfer's Advice* in *Golfing Poems & Songs* 1:
Your young anes think driving will win them the game,
The auld pawky putter can bring them to shame.

1900 Walter J. Travis *The Outing* (July) 444: Garden City, as it is now, is no place for the pawky player, and furnishes a splendid test of first-class golf.
1929 A.T. Packard *Golf Illustrated* (Apr.) 29: To the average player this elongated putt is worth many an hour of intelligent study. Don't be dissuaded by any claim that it is a pawky stroke.
1975 Geoffrey Cousins *Golf in Britain* 29: [Allan] Robertson was a pawky Scot with business instincts who was able to employ workmen to make clubs and balls.

peg n. A tee.

1946 Percy Boomer *On Learning Golf* 152: "Put me down a peg, will you, and I will take a few swings."
1968 Buddy Hackett *The Truth About Golf* 14: ... picked up the little yellow wooden peg and said, "Here, Milton, don't forget your lucky tee."

penal adj. (Of course architecture) designed primarily to punish poor shots.

1931 T. Simpson *The Game of Golf* 167: Broadly speaking, the penal school follows more or less the methods of Tom Morris and the brothers Dunn, in scattering plenty of bunkers in places most likely to catch inaccurate shots.
1954 Robert Trent Jones in Wind *The Complete Golfer* 298: In the twenties American courses fell into the "penal" pattern of architecture which punishes the golfer for the slightest error.
1975 Henry Cotton *History of Golf* 107: Like myself, Jones objected to the 'penal' system of course design and preferred a 'strategic' layout.

pick up phr.v. To take up (one's ball) without sanction before holing out, thus in match play conceding the hole or in stroke play incurring disqualification.

1890 H.S.C. Everard *Badminton Golf* 350: Tom [Morris] was working away in difficulties ... and still a very long way from the hole. Captain Broughton happening to pass

by, remarked, "Oh, pick up your ball, Tom, it's no use." "Na, na," said he, "I might hole it."
1927 Robert T. Jones, Jr. & O.B. Keeler *Down the Fairway* 106: ... performing one last superbly childish gesture by picking up—that is, withdrawing—in the British Open championship at St. Andrews.
1937 P.G. Wodehouse *The Letter of the Law* (repr. 1976) 95: "I fear that Poskitt has no alternative but to pick up."
1967 George Plimpton *The Bogey Man* 59: Hit another drive out of bounds. Apologized again. Picked up and left Bruno responsible for the hole.
1969 Tom Scott & Geoffrey Cousins *The Golf Immortals* 239: When he would find himself in a really bad lie, he cut his losses, picked up his ball, and incurred the penalty.

pill n. Ball.

1841 William Graham *The Links O' Innerleven* (in Clark *Golf: A Royal & Ancient Game* 1875, 201):
A Gourlay pill's the best of a'
For health at Innerleven.
1910 Grantland Rice *The Winning Shot* 31: Their brassies sweep as they hit the pill ...
1936 H.B. Martin *Fifty Years of American Golf* 372: When the little pill found a resting place it was in tall grass a foot high.
1962 Sam Snead *The Education of a Golfer* 33: ... they couldn't believe it, just stood around the pill, looking first at it and then at me.

pimple n. Bramble.

1912 Harry Vardon *How to Play Golf* 127: During the address, our range of vision ... should end half-way down the ball—on the pimple that is protruding farthest away from the hole (if we are using a ball of pimple marking). (See *also* **bramble** quot. 1916.)

pin n. Flagstick; also the hole as a target.

1893 John Thomson *The Caddie* in *Golfing Poems & Songs* 3:
Tak' a shot at the pin, it whiles helps to win ...

1914 George Duncan *Country Life* (Jan. 17) 103: . . . had a full bang with my mashie, and [the] ball finished 8 yds. from the pin.
1922 P.G. Wodehouse *A Woman Is Only a Woman* (in *The Clicking of Cuthbert* repr. 1956, 34): Our first hole, as you can see, is a bogey four, and James was dead on the pin in seven.
1965 Bob Charles *Left-handed Golf* 67: The sand traps, usually located adjacent to the green, protecting the pin . . .
1977 Dave Hill & Nick Seitz *Teed Off* 195: It is not a hole on which you try to knock your approach shot close to the pin; you just aim for the fat part of the green and hope.

pin-high *adj. & adv.* Level with the pin.

1974 *The Golfer's Handbook* 525: The remaining distance is a steep uphill approach to the green, and his ball finished pin high.
1975 Mark McCormack *Golf Annual* 215: Townsend lashed his ball and it finished pin-high, but in a hollow beside the green.

pin placement *or* **pin position.** The positioning of a hole on a putting green on a given occasion.

1971 Tommy Bolt *The Hole Truth* 150: The pin placements are grotesque. Players joke about them being placed by Hitler or Jack the Ripper.
1975 Jack Nicklaus in McCormack *Golf Annual* 43: The greens were all right and the pin positions were easier than they were on Thursday.

pinsetter *n.* An official responsible for pin placement.

1970 Dick Schaap *The Masters* 163: . . . official pinsetters of the Masters, the men who decide exactly where each pin shall be placed on each green during each round.

pinsetting *n.* Pin placement.

1970 Dick Schaap *The Masters* 163: Clifford Roberts . . . has explained that, over a full seventy-two holes, the pinsetting does not have a great impact on scores.

pitch *v. & n.* **1** *v.trans. & intrans.* To play (the ball) in a steep trajectory, typically with considerable backspin, usually as an approach shot or over difficulty.

1858 *Unidentified newspaper clipping* (in Allan Robertson's album at the R. & A. 90): . . . and here, again, an iron-headed club must be used to 'pitch' or 'loft' the ball over the difficulty.
1890 H.S.C. Everard *Badminton Golf* 363: . . . with what judgment he would pitch a ball up to within a few feet of the hole half a dozen times in succession.
1915 "A Wandering Player" in Revell *Pro & Con of Golf* 47: "As to pitching with the mashie—Taylor's most celebrated and important shot . . ."
1927 Robert T. Jones, Jr. & O.B. Keeler *Down the Fairway*: There was next to no pitching to be done at Sunningdale . . . you needed either iron shots or wood shots or tiny pitches or chip shots to the green.
1945 Arthur Mann *Nelson at His Peak* (in Wind *The Complete Golfer* 1954, 208): He pitched to within four inches of the cup on the fifteenth.
1976 J.C. Jessop *Golf* 72: As the greens in America are well soaked with water, it is comparatively easy to pitch on to the green.

2 *v.intrans.* (Of the ball) to land from a pitched shot.

1896 *Golfer's & Angler's Guide* 149: . . . the approach shot should be played so as to pitch at the top of the green, which slopes downwards.
1912 Harry Vardon *How to Play Golf* 20: I could tell to within two or three yards not only where the ball would pitch, but where it would stop.
1950 Dai Rees *Golf My Way* 55: There is a minimum of backspin, and when it pitches the ball runs forward.

3 *n.* A pitched shot.

1891 *Golf* magazine (Sept. 18) 3: The Kirkaldys got back their lost holes at the road, mainly by a beautiful short pitch by the younger brother.
1919 Robert K. Risk *Songs of the Links* 16:
Where the longest putts get home, dear lass,
And our pitches all run true . . .
1969 Tom Weiskopf *Go For the Flag* 52: A pitch is a high shot that runs little.

pitch-and-putt *adj. & n.* (A diminutive golf course) having holes designed only for approaching and putting.

1936 H.B. Martin *Fifty Years of American Golf* 112: . . . laying out a small pitch and putt course.
1967 George Plimpton *The Bogey Man* 164: "Haven't seen a course, a driving range, pitch 'n' putt, nothing like that for three hundred miles. Must be tennis country."
1974 Advertisement *The Golfer's Handbook* ix: Gleneagles Hotel, Perthshire . . . Pitch and putt course.

pitch-and-run *n.* An approach shot consisting of a short lowish pitch, or chip, followed by considerable run on the ground.

1912 Harry Vardon *How to Play Golf* 90: . . . the most common form of the mashie shot, which is the pitch-and-run.
1933 Alex J. Morrison *A New Way to Better Golf* 148: . . . with the clubhead swinging in a rather flat arc such as is used in playing pitch and run shots.
1946 Byron Nelson *Winning Golf* 144: The chip shot (or pitch-and-run as some call it) . . .
1961 Eric Brown *Knave of Clubs* 45: I played my normal low pitch-and-run shot with the mashie, the old traditional Scottish shot.
1977 George Peper *Scrambling Golf* 108: The basic pitch-and-run is a shot of 20–40 yards that travels about halfway in the air and halfway along the ground.

pitch-in *n.* A pitch that holes out.

1977 *New York Times* (June 11) 14: . . . four consecutive birdies, a pitch-in for an eagle 3.

pitching irons. The short irons.

1941 Patty Berg *Golf* 49: For the 7, 8, or 9 (pitching) irons, stand closer to the ball than in playing the longer irons.
1950 Sam Snead *How to Hit a Golf Ball* 28: The short irons generally are called the pitching irons because that is their chief function.

pitching wedge. An iron club used primarily for playing pitches to the green, having loft of 50–52 degrees, lie of 63–65 degrees, and length of about 35 inches, and having a flange less prominent than that of the sand wedge behind and below the leading edge, to prevent the clubhead from digging into grass. Also, a shot played with this club.

1969 Jack Nicklaus *The Greatest Game of All* 250: I put a pitching wedge about four feet from the pin.
1977 Arnold Palmer *Golf Magazine* (Aug.) 90: Since the pitching wedge has a thinner flange than the sand wedge . . .

pivot *n. & v.* **1** *n.* Rotation of the shoulders, trunk, and pelvis during the swing.

[**1890** Horace Hutchinson *Badminton Golf* 86: . . . the shoulders came swinging round upon the backbone as if it were a pivot on which they revolved.]
1926 Jack Gordon *Golf Illustrated* (Sept.) 25: And the pivot—many players do not pivot enough.
1946 Sam Snead *How to Play Golf* 262: The pivot isn't an artificial action; it is a natural turn of the body.
1954 H.A. Murray *The Golf Secret* (repr. 1976) 30: . . . they allow their heads to be turned to the right during the course of the backswing by the full shoulder pivot.

2 *v.intrans.* To rotate the trunk and pelvis during the swing.

1900 Harry Vardon *The Outing* (May) 147: . . . as the arms go in the upward swing you pivot on your left foot.
1934 *From a Hundred and Two to Eighty-two* . . . 20: Remember the exercise relating to the proper way to turn or pivot.
1969 Tom Scott & Geoffrey Cousins *The Golf Immortals* 34: [Vardon] pivoted much more than any of his contemporaries.

placement *n.* Judgment and accuracy in the targeting of a shot or shots.

1915 A.W. Tillinghast *The Spur* (in *Cobble Valley Golf Yarns* 162): "Did you ever see a

prettier mashie? Why, it had everything—distance, placement, and stop."
1928 A. Linde Fowler *Golf Illustrated* (Sept.) 16: . . . bold pitching for the pins will be precarious. Considerable judgment is needed for proper placement.
1973 Arnold Palmer *Go For Broke* 12: But it was . . . a course that catered more to placement than to power.
1978 Ray Floyd *Boston Globe* (Aug. 11) 35: "With the greens so slow, the key is placement. Get the ball in close."

plate n. See **sole plate**.

plateau n., *often attributive.* A flat-topped hillock, or a putting green situated on one.

1890 Horace Hutchinson *Badminton Golf* 128: One of the features of St. Andrews is that many of the holes are on little plateaux with little banks leading up to them.
1911 James Braid *Advanced Golf* 258: There is the plateau green still to consider, and it is one that generally makes the approach difficult.
1931 Bernard Darwin *The Game of Golf* 147: . . . the plateau greens [at St. Andrews] are not like many of these that are elaborately built up for us by the architects, with the ground rising at the back of them; the St. Andrews plateau generally runs away from the player.
1961 Eric Brown *Knave of Clubs* 15: I hit a weak tee-shot and the ball ran down from the plateau green almost halfway back to the tee.

plateaued adj. Set on a plateau.

1969 Jack Nicklaus *The Greatest Game of All* 115: It was a mildly plateaued green heavily trapped in front.

play v. & n. **1** v.trans. To strike (the ball) with a club.

1744 *Articles & Laws in Playing at Golf* 10: If a Ball be stopp'd by any person, Horse, Dog, or any thing else, the Ball so stopp'd must be played where it lyes.
1976 *Rules of Golf* 12.1.a: A match begins by each side playing a ball from the first teeing ground.

2 v.intrans. To make a stroke.

1744 *Articles & Laws in Playing at Golf* 12: He whose Ball lyes farthest from the Hole is obliged to play first.
1976 *Rules of Golf* 15.2: If a player play when his partner should have played . . .

3 v.trans. To make (a stroke or shot).

1773 *Regulations of the Society of Golfers (Bruntsfield)* (in Clapcott 1935, 23): II. . . . the party who playes first must be allowed to play their second strokes . . .
1833 George Fullerton Carnegie *The Golfiad* (in *Poems on Golf* 1867, 24):
    Full many a stroke is played with heart
        and soul.
1891 *Golf* magazine (March 20) 13: Mr. Dewars for the approach played a three-quarter iron shot.
1921 Andrew Kirkaldy *Fifty Years of Golf* 138: . . . a firmly confident look on his face that means he is going to play the shot as it should be played.
1976 *Rules of Golf* 15.3: If the partners play a stroke or strokes in incorrect order . . .

4 v.trans. To use (a particular club) in making a stroke.

1895 "Calamo Currente" *Half Hours With an Old Golfer* 75: He plays the cleek . . .
1907 George S. Lyon in Leach *Great Golfers in the Making* 199: I, playing an iron, put my ball on the green.
1931 Henry Cotton *Golf* 106: You cannot play the brassie very frequently from the fairway unless you are very accurate or very strong.
1961 Eric Brown *Knave of Clubs* 97: Playing his iron clubs perfectly, he was out in 32.

5 v.intrans. (Of a course) to serve for playing in a particular manner.

1913 Henry Leach *The American Golfer* (Oct.) (in Wind *The Complete Golfer* 1954, 154): . . . the wet weather . . . did vastly less injury to the course than one might have expected; indeed Brookline played very well indeed from start to finish.

1970 Tony Jacklin *Jacklin* 48: The Old Course with its par of seventy-two can never have played easier.
1977 *New York Times* (July 2) 13: "I would say this course played six to eight strokes tougher than normal today."

6 *n.* The action of playing golf.

1976 *Rules of Golf* 21.2.a: When the player and the opponent exchange balls during the play of a hole . . .

7 in play *phr.* (Of a ball) being legitimately on the course during the playing of a hole.

1976 *Rules of Golf* 5.a: A ball is "in play" as soon as the player has made a stroke on the teeing ground. It remains as his ball in play until holed out, except when it is out of bounds, lost or lifted, or another ball has been substituted.

8 *n.* One of the systems of scoring. *See* **match play, medal play, stroke play.**

9 *n.* The making of strokes from the tee and through the green, as distinct from putting.

1970 Dick Schaap *The Masters* 195: "I putted so badly. . . . It was the finest golf I've ever played to lose a tournament," concedes [Gary] Player, differentiating between his "play" and his putting.

playability *n.* (Of a course) the quality of playing satisfactorily.

1977 Charles Price *Golf* 39: No golf course can be said to be truly professionally designed unless it has what the members of the American Society [of Golf Course Architects] call "playability." This esoteric word means that a course should have the ability to accept good shots and reject bad ones. No tricks in short.

playable *adj.* (Of a ball) lying so that it can be played. *See* **unplayable.**

play club. The old name for the straightest-faced, longest-hitting wooden club, later called the driver.

1735 Anon. letter (in Henderson & Stirk *Golf in the Making* 1979, 93): Tell him to provide me in nine clubs viz three play clubs, three scrapers, . . . and three putting clubs.
1823 James Grierson *Delineations of St. Andrews* 218: A set consists of four at least, viz. the common, or play club . . .
1844 William Graham *Songs of the Innerleven Golf Club* (1865) 8:
My play-club capers in my hand,
As supple as an eel.
1897 Price Collier *The Outing* (May) 186: First of all, play all your shots, with the play-club or with the iron, well within your strength.
1921 Andrew Kirkaldy *Fifty Years of Golf* 146: Hitting his hardest with the "play-club," as the driver used to be called . . .

playing partner. *See* **partner** (def. 2)

playing professional. A professional golfer who primarily competes in tournaments.

1928 P.C. Pulver *Golf Illustrated* (Nov.): Leo Diegel, the playing professional of the Fenimore Country Club, White Plains, N.Y. . . .
1948 Ben Hogan *Power Golf* vi: Henry recommended me for the position that he held as the playing professional for the Hershey, Pennsylvania, Country Club.
1974 *The Golfer's Handbook* 434: He was for a period professional to Ardeer Club, but returned to St. Andrews to resume his vocation of playing professional.

play off *phr.v.* **1** *Obsolete.* To drive (a ball) from the tee.

1793 Addendum to Thomas Mathison *The Goff* (3rd edition) 32: . . . he could play off from the tee, at a full stroke, twelve successive balls, and lay every one of them within the space of two or three club lengths from one another.
1823 James Grierson *Delineations of St. Andrews* 221: Thus, suppose A and B to be engaged in a match. A plays off, and then B.
1870 *Rules of the Royal North Devon Club:*

The game commences by each party playing off a ball from a place called the *tee*.

2 To decide (a tie) by playing further holes or a further round.

1870 Charles MacArthur *The Golfer's Annual* 118: On the tie being played off, Sir Robert and Mr. Anderson again tied, which on being played off resulted in a victory for the latter.
1899 Willie Tucker *The Outing* (Aug.) 522: In playing off the tie for the last four places in a qualifying round . . .
1946 Bernard Darwin *British Golf* 18: . . . he was playing off the tie against Willie Fernie.

playoff *n.* Decision of a tie by further play.

1936 H.B. Martin *Fifty Years of American Golf* 365: Roger Wethered, an amateur, upheld the honor of British golf and tied Jock for the seventy-two holes but lost in the play-off.
1970 Dick Schaap *The Masters* 201: The playoff is scheduled to begin in six and a half hours.

plus fours *pl.n.* Voluminous knickerbockers that were in vogue for male golfers (and others) in the 1920s and early 1930s and have been worn by a minority since that period; strictly, knickerbockers cut with four inches more length of cloth than standard sporting breeches, to provide an overhang below the knees that accommodates the golf swing.

1923 A. Herd *Golfing Life* 151: The first time I saw a golfer wearing baggy 'plus 4's' I thought he looked like a lassie.
1933 A.G. Macdonnell *England, Their England* 130: . . . there were the biggest, the baggiest, the brightest plus-fours that ever dulled the lustre of a peacock's tail.
1962 Richard Armour *Golf Is a Four-letter Word* 13: The most important item was the plus fours, a kind of knickers that had to hang exactly right if they were to make the wearer look like Gene Sarazen or Walter Hagen and

not like a guy who put on his mother's bloomers by mistake.
1967 George Plimpton *The Bogey Man* 235: With Hope was Phyllis Diller, the comedienne, outfitted in an outlandish golfing outfit with checked plus fours.
1979 Advertisement *Golf Monthly* (March) 9: PLUS TWOS AND PLUS FOURS Write for details.

plus-man *n.* A man with a handicap better than scratch.

1919 Robert K. Risk *Songs of the Links* 69:
In spring the plus-man's fancy turns
Lightly to Sandwich town . . .
1921 Andrew Kirkaldy *Fifty Years of Golf* 165: . . . a team of twenty-five wholly composed of plus and scratch men was got together for a golfing tournament.

pop *v. & n.* **1** *v.trans.* To play (a ball) in a short shot that comes steeply up very quickly, especially by hitting markedly under it.

1887 Sir Walter Simpson *The Art of Golf* 132: One of these with a face a yard or two in front of it, is a bad ball, which can only either be dunched along the ground a short distance with a brassie, or popped equally far with an iron.
1897 Horace Hutchinson *Country Life* (Jan. 8) 24: The parson put his two shots nicely up to the edge of the bunker, popped the ball over with an iron . . .
1929 A.T. Packard *Golf Illustrated* (Apr.) 69: The loft of a mashie is enough to pop the ball into the air and the backspin is certain to stop it.
1967 Jack Nicklaus *The Best Way to Better Golf* 103: [Buried sand lie] I'm not trying to hit the ball. I want to go under the ball and pop, or "soft" it up.
1970 Dick Schaap *The Masters* 157: Player, often considered the most gifted trap player in golf, pops his ball out to within eight feet of the hole.

2 *n.* A shot played in this manner.

1962 Sam Snead *The Education of a Golfer* 39: An easy 2-wood short of the green, a pop-shot over a bunker, and a 4-foot putt gave me a finishing birdie.

1977 George Peper *Scrambling Golf* 114: To hit the pop chip . . . keep your wrists absolutely rigid.

pot bunker. A deep, usually small bunker with steep sides.

1907 Harold Hilton *My Golfing Reminiscences* 46: . . . from the tee I found a pot bunker.

1927 Robert T. Jones, Jr. & O.B. Keeler *Down the Fairway* 132: . . . pulling my ball off to the left, back of a pot bunker.

power *n., often attributive.* Conspicuous strength in driving.

1899 Walter Camp & Lilian Brooks *Drives & Puts* 160: "A long swing is a vera gude thing, an' so is pooer, but there's mair to it than that."

1931 Joyce & Roger Wethered *The Game of Golf* 45: . . . certain features have been emphasized as being typically American . . . Smoothness, slowness, the economical application of power . . .

1948 Ben Hogan *Power Golf* (title of book).

1962 Sam Snead *The Education of a Golfer* 43: Arnie is a power hitter and a go-for-broke gambler like me.

1964 Julius Boros *How to Win at Weekend Golf* 36: I strongly feel that a swinging swing is much easier for the ordinary golfer to control than is the power swing.

1969 Jack Nicklaus *The Greatest Game of All* 192: It has often been said—and one heard it said continually when Arnold and I won six of the seven Masters between 1960 and 1966—that . . . the Augusta National favors the power golfer.

preferred lies. The practice, under "winter rules," of improving bad lies through the green.

1964 Tony Lema *Golfer's Gold* 16: Playing preferred lies can make a difference of several strokes a round.

1976 Joseph C. Dey *Golf Rules in Pictures*: The U.S.G.A. does not endorse "preferred lies" and "winter rules."

1977 Oscar Fraley *Golf Magazine* (June) 26: . . . most amateurs continually play preferred lies and when they get in a pro-am they have to play the ball as it lies.

president *n.* [Origin unknown.] An iron club, no longer in use, having steep loft equivalent to that of a niblick, with a hole through the face, that was used for playing out of water.

1887 Sir Walter Simpson *The Art of Golf* 23: The 'President' is a niblick with a hole in it.

1895 James P. Lee *Golf in America* 117: Some of these clubs, such as the baffing spoon and the president, are obsolete.

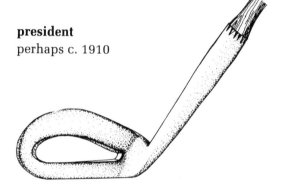

president
perhaps c. 1910

press[1] *v.* **1** *v.intrans.* To strive too hard in making a stroke.

1862 Robert Chambers *A Few Rambling Remarks on Golf* 11: We would also counsel the exercise of caution before attempting to drive a far shot over an intervening hazard, as the chances are, that in pressing for its achievement, the ball is partially missed.

1881 Robert Forgan *The Golfer's Handbook*: . . . never "press" to achieve impossibilities or retrieve disasters.

1890 Horace Hutchinson *Badminton Golf* 95: But directly we begin to force the swing out of its harmony—to over-accelerate the pace—from that instant it loses the character of a swing and becomes a hit, a jerk—and this is 'pressing.' *Festina lente*—Don't press.

1915 Alexander H. Revell *Pro & Con of Golf* 22: Don't press on any shot.

1926 Lucille MacAllister *Golf Illustrated*

(Sept.) 28: It is a notable feature of Miss Collett's game that she seldom presses.
1975 Mark McCormack *Golf Annual* 181: He took an iron off the tee for accuracy ... and then, pressing for length, hooked into the woods.

2 *v.trans.* To put too much effort into (a stroke or shot).

1908 Arnold Haultain *The Mystery of Golf* (repr. 1965) 86: Why should he press or hurry his stroke?
1969 Jack Nicklaus *The Greatest Game of All* 240: ... you try to hit your tee-shots harder and harder. Not very intelligent. You end up pressing every shot.

press[2] *n. & v.* **1** *n.* An additional bet made during a game.

1962 Sam Snead *The Education of a Golfer* 178: Needing something to save the day, I said, "How about a press bet on this one?" "Two hundred suit you?" "Fine."
1975 Dan Jenkins *Dead Solid Perfect* 29: Then he said we'd play Zark and Ruffin a $50 Nassau. Automatic one-down presses ...

2 *v.intrans.* To propose such a bet.

1977 Dave Hill & Nick Seitz *Teed Off* 31: Ford and Goalby were ahead after the first six holes and Snead and Barber pressed—added a bet.

pretty *n.* *Slang, probably obsolete.* Fairway.

1915 H.L. Dobree in Revell *Pro & Con of Golf* 78: If you will take the opportunity of following him across the 'pretty' of such a hole ...
1922 P.G. Wodehouse *The Clicking of Cuthbert* (repr. 1956) Foreword 7: It is the outpouring of a soul as deeply seared by Fate's unkindness as the pretty on the dog-leg hole of the second nine was ever seared by my iron.

pro *n.* A professional golfer.

1893 John Thomson *Golfing Songs & Poems* 21: Yet a pro. at his best, with a card at his back, Would find it hard work a poor eighty to crack.
1908 Arnold Haultain *The Mystery of Golf* (repr. 1965) 143: I am cock-sure my Pro can approach a hole better than he can sign his name.
1936 H.B. Martin *Fifty Years of American Golf* 327: Golf pros are not permitted to enter the clubhouse at Deal, or any of the other British clubhouses, and Hagen and Barnes were no exception to the rule.
1967 Mark McCormack *Arnie* 247: Again and again Arnold has run into the same stumbling block: club pros dictating to playing pros what they can and cannot do with their careers.
1975 Herb Graffis *The P.G.A.* 6: ... it appeared that the misunderstandings and mistakes that later resulted in the split of the P.G.A. into the service-pro and show-pro divisions had already been met and solved.

professional *adj. & n.* **1** *adj.* Playing golf, or practicing any employment based on skill or reputation as a player, as a means of gaining a livelihood.

1857 *Unidentified newspaper clipping* (in Allan Robertson's album at the R. & A. 75): The professionals present were Tom Morris, his brother George, and Park the younger.
1890 Horace Hutchinson *Badminton Golf* 282: One can divide into three classes those who derive a precarious subsistence from the game of golf: professional club-makers, professional players who eke out existence by work in the club-makers' shops, and professional caddies who would be professional players if they played well enough.
1950 Gene Sarazen *Walter Hagen* (in Wind *The Complete Golfer* 1954, 170): Before Hagen broke down the walls of prejudice, a professional golfer had no standing whatever.

2 *n.* A professional golfer.

1863 "J.S." *The Links of St. Rule* (in Clark *Golf: A Royal & Ancient Game* 1875, 136): But the professionals have suffered a loss that cannot be repaired [death of Allan Robertson].
1907 Arthur Pottow *Recreation* (Apr.) 473: The professionals who compete are mostly Scotsmen and Englishmen who have come to

this country to fill positions at golf and country clubs.

1973 *Bartlett's World Golf Encyclopedia* 350: In January, 1970, the P.G.A. outlined a new membership structure for its 7,000 professionals. Three major classifications were designated: Master Professional, Head Professional, and Apprentice Professional.

1976 *R. & A. Rules of Amateur Status* 2.3.a: The professional holds an advantage over the amateur by reason of having devoted himself to the game as his profession.

pronate *v.trans.* [Origin: physiological term, properly meaning "to turn the hand and forearm over from the supine position (palm upward) to the prone position (palm downward) by rotating the radius about the ulna"; from Latin *prōn-āre* = "to make prone," from *prōnus* = "prone, facing downward."] To rotate (the wrist) so that the palm of the hand faces downward. [*Note:* this word is often used loosely or erroneously for the rolling of both wrists together in the backswing; but with any normal grip it is impossible to pronate both wrists simultaneously; typically when one wrist is pronated the other is supinated.]

1928 Johnny Farrell *Golf Illustrated* (July) 23: The mistaken idea seems to prevail that it is necessary to roll or pronate the wrists on the back-swing.

1957 Ben Hogan *Five Lessons* 102: By pronating his left wrist just before impact, a golfer expends his clubhead speed before he strikes the ball.

pronation *n.* Rotation of the wrist so that the palm of the hand faces downward. See *Note* at **pronate.**

1936 H.B. Martin *Fifty Years of American Golf* 325: The "turnover," as Hagen describes pronation, is not conducive to correct or accurate hitting.

1948 Herbert Warren Wind *The Story of American Golf* (repr. 1956) 516: [Hogan] confided . . . what his "secret" was: it boiled down to pronation plus two accompanying adjustments.

1965 Paul Hahn *Shows You How to Play Trouble Shots* (repr. 1975) 21: The hands are turned clockwise on the shaft so that the right hand will subconsciously turn into a hooking pronation during the swing.

1978 *Golf Score* (Oct./Nov.) 31: Your error is unwanted pronation of the left hand.

provisional *adj.* (Of a ball) played to save time, when it seems possible that the regular ball just played is lost or out of bounds.

1974 *The Golfer's Handbook* 551: Mr. Sutherland's first tee shot appeared to go out of bounds and playing a provisional ball he holed in one.

1976 *Rules of Golf* 30.1: If the original ball was played from the teeing ground, the provisional ball may be teed anywhere within the teeing ground; if from through the green or a hazard, it shall be dropped; if on the putting green, it shall be placed.

public links *n., often attributive.* Links open to the public.

1896 C. Turner *The Outing* (Dec.) 45: The example of the public-spirited Park Commissioners of New York . . . in providing public links in Van Cortlandt Park, is bearing good fruit.

1926 *Golf Illustrated* (June) 67: The week of July 5th may see public links golfers in several cities in Kansas trying to qualify for play in the National Public Links Championship.

1977 Gordon S. White *New York Times* (July 12) 23: Four public-links golfers . . . stole the show today of the 25th annual Ike amateur tournament at the North Hills Country Club.

publinx *adj.* Being or related to public links.

1978 Frank Hannigan in *Golf Magazine* (Oct.) 6: "When did you ever see grass like this on a publinx course?"

pull *v. & n.* **1** *v.trans. & intrans.* Of a right-handed player, to play (a ball or shot) that flies in a fairly straight path to the left of the target line; and the converse for a left-handed player.

1867 "H.J.M." *The Golfer at Home* (in Clark *Golf: A Royal & Ancient Game* 1875, 176): . . . Browne varies his partner's entertainment by pulling his ball round with the toe of the club into the whins at the opposite side.
1907 Harold Hilton, *My Golfing Reminiscences* 144: I hit the ground, and pulled the ball round into the sand-hill on the left.
1921 Andrew Kirkaldy *Fifty Years of Golf* 138: . . . he would go through with the shot, without pulling or slicing.
1934 Peter Lawless *Little* (in Wind *The Complete Golfer* 1954, 196): Little pulled his iron shot badly.
1964 Julius Boros *How to Win at Weekend Golf* 125: *Pulling* happens when the clubhead strikes the ball squarely but on an outside-in arc.
1969 Paul D. Peery *Billy Casper: Winner* 88: Goldwater pulled his ball to the left and hit a spectator.

2 *n.* A pulled shot, or a tendency to pull.

1911 James Braid *Advanced Golf* 64: . . . a bad pull is very nearly as bad as anything.
1946 Percy Boomer *On Learning Golf* 125: . . . while an exaggerated in-to-out feel gives *pull*, the correct in-to-out feel gives straightness.
1967 Mark McCormack *Arnie* 65: . . . when he adjusted his swing for the hook, he overcompensated. The result was a horrible pull into the evergreens.

pull cart. A two-wheeled trolley on which a golf bag can be fitted and pulled around a course.

1978 John M. Ross *Golf Magazine* (Oct.) 6: Caddies are provided, but the bulk of the players either tote their own bags or use pull carts.

pull-hook *v. & n.* **1** *v.trans. & intrans.* Of a right-handed player, to play (a ball or shot) that flies to the left of the target line and also curves farther to the left owing to sidespin; and the converse for a left-handed player.

1969 Jack Nicklaus *The Greatest Game of All* 146: In my anxiety, I let my right hand get into my drive too quickly, and I pull-hooked it into the edge of the heavy rough.
1977 Mark Mulvoy *Golf Digest* (Aug.) 52: Hogan missed only one fairway—the third, where he pull hooked his drive into a ravine.

2 *n.* A pull-hooked shot.

1975 Mark McCormack *Golf Annual* 34: I noticed that occasionally a ball would soar off to the left as if Sam had hit a pull hook.

punchbowl *n., often attributive.* [Origin: used from the 19th century to mean "a hollow between hills" in descriptions of landscape and in place names in England.] A putting green in a hollow.

1914 Bernard Darwin *Country Life* (Aug. 1) 173: The putting greens were mainly of the plateau type, and I can recall only one of the old-fashioned punch-bowls so beloved of an earlier generation of architects.
1963 Bob Rosburg *The Putter Book* 55: Then there are rarities which . . . have a "punchbowl" depression.
1969 Jack Nicklaus *The Greatest Game of All* 89: . . . all even coming up to the 35th, 513 yards to a punch-bowl type of green.

push *v. & n.* **1** *v.trans. & intrans.* Of a right-handed player, to play (a ball or shot) that flies in a fairly straight path to the right of the target line; and the converse for a left-handed player.

1962 Sam Snead *The Education of a Golfer* 44: Palmer pushed his drive into the woods.
1977 Gordon S. White *New York Times* (July 13) A14: Mattwell, who had been pushing his drives most of the day, went to the practice range after lunch.

2 *n.* A pushed shot.

1978 Steve Werner *Golf Score* (Oct./Nov.) 14: Pushes and pulls are straight shots which start in the wrong direction and stay in the wrong direction.

putt *v. & n.* [Origin: Scottish, from *put* or *putt* = "to push gently, nudge"; a Scottish form of the same verb that in standard southern English became *put* (Old English *putian* = "to push, place"). In golf, whether spelled *put* or *putt*, the word was always pronounced to rhyme with *but*. The alternate spelling *put* survived into the 20th century (see quots.) but is now obsolete.]

1 *v.intrans.* To play one of the relatively gentle strokes characteristic of the final stage of the play of a hole, either on the putting green or on smooth ground near it; almost always using a putter; usually playing the ball along the ground; and always aiming either to hole out or to leave the ball close enough to be holed out with the next stroke.

1776 *Rules of the Company of Golfers* (Bruntsfield) (in Clapcott 1935, 29): . . . nor must any person whatever stand at the hole to point it out or to do any other thing to assist you in putting.
1783 *Laws of Golf* (Aberdeen) (in Clapcott, 34): No Stones, loose Sand, or other impediments shall be removed with putting at the Hole.
1834 *Rules of the Musselburgh Golf Club* (in Clapcott, 65): . . . while the first party are putting at the hole, the second shall not play upon them.
1881 Robert Forgan *The Golfer's Handbook* 61: PUT.—To play the delicate game close to the hole. (Pronounce u as in *but*).
1898 M. Gertrude Cundill *The Outing* (Oct.) 19: "And I really don't put badly, do I?"
1912 Harry Vardon *How to Play Golf* 100: I do not intend to tell anybody how to putt.
1923 John E. Baxter *Locker Room Ballads* 3:
And with good distance still might be
Upon the green to put for three.
1961 Eric Brown *Knave of Clubs* 113: . . . the South African, putting in almost uncanny fashion on the saturated greens while I kept leaving my ball short.

2 *n.* A stroke or shot in putting.

1793 Anon *Song in Praise of Golf* (in Thomas Mathison *The Goff*, 3rd edition, 25):
While with long strokes and short
strokes we tend to the goal,
And with *put* well directed plump into
the hole.
1863 "Ned" (a caddie) in *The Links of St.*

Rule (in Clark *Golf: A Royal & Ancient Game* 1875, 137): "The first hole was halved—Drumwhalloch holin' a lang *putt*."
1893 John Thomson *Golfing Songs & Poems* 18:
Then the drives grow mighty,
Longest puts go in;
1900 Harry Vardon *The Outing* (May) 147: . . . a missed put counts as much as a topped drive.
1908 Arnold Haultain *The Mystery of Golf* (repr. 1965, 56): Not even an expert dare be careless of his stance or his stroke for even the shortest of Puts.
1937 Henry Longhurst *Golf* 157: Furthermore, when a putt is missed, the stroke has been lost for ever.
1968 Buddy Hackett *The Truth About Golf* 51: His opponent had a putt of 40 feet and Park had a 12 footer.

3 *v.intrans.* (Of a putting green) to be in condition for putting of a stated kind.

1969 Jack Nicklaus *The Greatest Game of All* 83: We didn't have a drop of rain . . . so . . . the greens putted very fast.

putter *n.* **1** A club designed for putting, generally straight-faced or nearly so, of upright lie, and short-shafted. Up to the 1850s the putter was always a wooden club; then iron putters were introduced and became prevalent; and from the turn of the century numerous innovative designs such as the center-shafted putter were also introduced.

1783 *Laws of Golf* (Aberdeen) (in Clapcott 1935, 34): If any of the Players or their Club-bearers, by standing at or near the hole, stop a Ball, whether from a Putter or any other Club, the Hole shall be lost to the Party so stopping.
1841 William Graham *The Links of Innerleven* (in Clark *Golf: A Royal & Ancient Game* 1875, 201):
I'd cast aside my tackit shoon,
And crack o'putter, cleek, and spoon . . .
1857 H.B. Farnie *The Golfer's Manual* 21: Sometimes an iron-headed putter is used for the short game, instead of the more common kind.
1881 Robert Forgan *The Golfer's Handbook* 15: . . . the "Iron Putter," which differs from

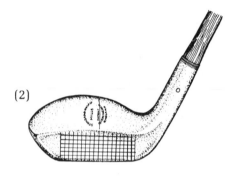

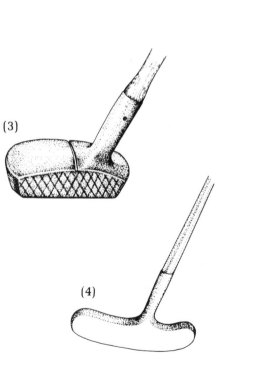

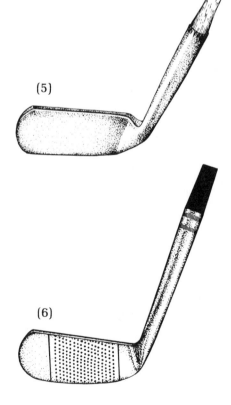

putter

(1) wooden putter, Auchterlonie Special (modern reproduction of putter, c. 1880)
(2) aluminum putter, Braid-Mills, 1915
(3) Schenectady putter
(4) center-shafted putter, brass-headed P.G.A. model
(5) putting cleek, R.W. Kirk, Liverpool (1845–86)
(6) blade putter

the "Putting Cleek" in being *double-faced*. . . . This "Iron Putter" . . . rather in vogue at present; but, in face of the fashion, we strongly counsel the retention of the good old wooden weapon.

1890 Horace Hutchinson *Badminton Golf* 60: In the old days of baffy spoons, golfers used to putt almost exclusively with wooden putters. These are now very generally superseded by iron putters.

1911 James Braid *Advanced Golf* 150: I am sure that true hitting is easier with the aluminum and wooden putters than with putting cleeks.

1915 Alexander H. Revell *Pro & Con of Golf* 9: There are two kinds of putters in general use in this country. One is the ordinary steel-blade putter, and the other is the wood or the flat metal-head putter.

1963 Bob Rosburg *The Putter Book* 18: Virtually every putter ever made falls into two categories—the mallet and the blade.

2 See **driving putter.**

3 A player rated in terms of putting ability.

1842 *Chambers' Edinburgh Journal* (Oct. 8) 298: Some men are good putters without being good drivers.

1893 John Thomson *Golfing Poems & Songs* 1:

> Your young anes think driving will win
>   them the game,
> The auld pawky putter will bring them
>   to shame.

1906 Arthur Pottow *Illustrated Outdoor News* (Nov.) 131: To such a perfect putter as Mr. Travis, who would putt if need were with an umbrella or walking-stick, doubtless there are no difficulties.

1921 Andrew Kirkaldy *Fifty Years of Golf* 64: He [Travis] was the greatest putter, amateur or professional, I have met in my fifty years of golf.

1953 Bobby Locke (in Wind *The Complete Golfer* 1954, 268): I am recognized as a good, consistent putter.

1963 Bob Rosburg *The Putter Book* 151: However, most putters on the circuit fall into two basic types: (1) the "strokers"; and (2) the "jabbers." The stroker has a relatively long backswing. The jabber has a shorter backswing and he taps the ball harder.

putting cleek. *See* **cleek** (def. 1, quot. 1881) *and* **putter** (def. 1, quot. 1911).

putting green. *See* **green** (def. 2).

putt out *phr.v.* To hole out (the ball) with a putt.

1875 "J.F.McL." *A Golf Song* (in Clark *Golf: A Royal & Ancient Game* 192):

> "Halved hole," says the foe; but "No"—I
>   say—"No;
> Putt it out, mine enemie!"

1890 Horace Hutchinson *Badminton Golf* 135: Putting is commonly and conveniently divided into two heads—'approach putting,' and 'putting out,' or 'holing the ball.'

1919 Robert K. Risk *Songs of the Links* 19:

> And therefore, in a future state,
>   When we shall all putt out in two . . .

1963 Bob Rosburg *The Putter Book* 141: Don't leave your golf ball in the hole after putting out.

putty *n.* *Slang, obsolete.* The Eclipse ball.

1890 Horace Hutchinson *Badminton Golf* 70: Finally, there is the ball called the 'Eclipse,' but more commonly known among golfers as the 'putty,' because it is of softer substance than the gutta-percha ball, and because 'putty' rhymes with 'gutty.'

Q

quail-high *adv. & adj.* (Of a shot) hit on a low and flattish trajectory.

1948 Ben Hogan *Power Golf* 58: When the wind is blowing, a low shot, or quail high as we say in Texas, will bite right into the wind and cover more ground than you would ordinarily get under the same conditions with a normal flight of the ball. . . . 157: Keep the ball quail high . . .
1962 Sam Snead *The Education of a Golfer* 43: I hit a quail-high hook under a tree.

quarter shot. A shot made with a greatly reduced swing, less than that for a half shot.

[**1842** George Fullerton Carnegie *Another Peep at the Links* (in *Golfiana* 20):
Alike correct, whatever may befal,
Swipe, iron, putter, quarter-stroke and all.]
1875 Robert Clark *Golf: A Royal & Ancient Game* 270: . . . we will stake our belief on ALLAN's short game, especially in quarter shots.
1901 R.H. Lyttelton *Cricket & Golf* 148: Some of the strokes are given with scarcely an effort, such as all putts and little quarter shots.

R

rabbit n. **1** An amateur golfer of little accomplishment.

1931 T. Simpson *The Game of Golf* 167:
. . . a rabbit ought to feel sincerely grateful for the comparatively comfortable journey which a strategic course gives him from start to finish, except, of course, at the shorter holes, where he shares and shares alike with the tiger.
1979 John Stobbs *Par Golf* (March) 11: Result, a handicap of less than 18. A Golfer, no longer a Rabbit!

2 A touring professional who has won no exemptions and must compete in qualifying rounds for chances to play in tournaments.

1964 Tony Lema *Golfer's Gold* 28: "Every rabbit on the tour is going to come rushing."
1971 Tommy Bolt *The Hole Truth* 106: There are a bunch of rabbits out there who can hit the ball as good as the guy who wins on Sunday.
1977 John S. Radosta *New York Times Magazine* (Aug. 21): In the official jargon, he is a "qualifier" but in real life he is a "rabbit," a term that the late Tony Lema coined some years ago, evoking the image of a hungry rabbit nibbling at lettuce.

rake n. A lofted iron club, no longer in use, having vertical slots through the

rake
"Thistle" water
iron, Thomas
Brown, c. 1895

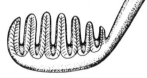

face, used for playing out of water and from sand.

1913 Bernard Darwin *Country Life* (Jan. 11) 69: . . . the curious iron weapon which he calls his rake. This is an implement having a number of prongs where its face ought to be, and not only is it very effective in getting the ball out of a bunker, but it will pitch the ball over a bunker.

rap v.trans. To hit (a putt, or the ball in putting) firmly and rather hard.

1946 Frank Moran *Golfers' Gallery* 42: . . . even the last putt was rapped firmly in.
1969 Jack Nicklaus *The Greatest Game of All* 20: My best chance would be to rap the ball so firmly that neither the left or right break could really take effect.
1977 John S. Radosta *New York Times* (Aug. 15) 38: . . . he rapped in the putt smartly for the winning par.

read *v.trans.* To scrutinize and interpret the contour and texture of (a putting green).

1948 Ben Hogan *Power Golf* 132: Bobby [Locke] has a great putting stroke but more than that he has an uncanny ability to read greens.
1970 Dick Schaap *The Masters* 50: "Every day, every minute," says Frank Beard, explaining the psychological impact of the Masters, "the greens get a little more difficult to read."

readable *adj.* (Of a putting green or aspect of a putt) that can be read.

1969 Jack Nicklaus *The Greatest Game of All* 161: The putt had a clearly readable break to the left of about a foot.

recover *v.intrans.* To play from rough, from a hazard, or from any undesirable place, to a satisfactory position back on the line or onto the green.

1890 H.S.C. Everard *Badminton Golf* 359: The recovering shots he used to make were sometimes deadly.
1912 Harry Vardon *How to Play Golf* 117: We are not all so strong as Braid, who can recover from anything.
1931 Henry Cotton *Golf* 129: The niblick has always been reckoned as a club for recovering from bad places.
1977 Frank Hannigan *Reader's Digest* (July) 149: Jones played some dreadful shots, often in critical situations. But he could recover gloriously.

recovery *n.* A shot played from rough, from a hazard, or from any undesirable place, to a satisfactory position back on the line or onto the green.

1896 *Baily's Magazine* (Nov.) 408: ... when anything amiss happened, there was always a good recovery and a tight fight on the putting green.
1908 Pentland Peile *Clanbrae* 35: ... found himself twice trapped. The first time he was lucky in making an unexpected recovery.

1929 Archie Compston *Golf Illustrated* (May) 37: ... the Hagen who has endeared himself to the golfing gallery is the Hagen of the recoveries.
1937 Henry Longhurst *Golf* 196: An ideal club for recovery shots is the old-fashioned jigger.
1969 Jack Nicklaus *The Greatest Game of All* 167: From that lie I had no option but to wedge the ball back to the fairway, almost laterally. My recovery actually rolled through the fairway into light rough on the right.
1975 Henry Cotton *History of Golf* 210: The day of the recovery player, down in two from anywhere, had dawned.

regulation *n., often attributive.* Par scoring.

1928 *Golf Illustrated* (June) 70: ... par fours, all of them sporty, requiring excellent shotmaking to obtain the regulation figures.
1969 Paul D. Peery *Billy Casper: Winner* 95: He used only 112 putts for the 72 holes, 32 under regulation.
1977 Barbara Romack *Woman Golfer* (July) 20: The U.S.G.A. sets a golf course so long that even King Kong would have a tough time reaching the greens in regulation.

relief *n.* Permission under the Rules to lift and drop the ball, generally without penalty, in certain situations.

1976 *Rules of Golf* 32.1: Interference by casual water, ground under repair, or a hole, cast or runway made by a burrowing animal, a reptile or a bird occurs when a ball lies in or touches any of these conditions or when the condition interferes with the player's stance or the area of his intended swing. If interference exists, the player may either play the ball as it lies or take relief as provided in Clause 2 of this Rule.
1978 Neil Amdur *New York Times* (July 17) C6: Later that day, Nicklaus would receive relief on the seventh and eighth holes from the referee for ground under repair on the green.

reverse overlap. A grip in which (for a right-handed player) the forefinger of the left hand overlaps the little finger of the right hand; and the converse for a left-handed player; widely used in putting.

1941 Patty Berg *Golf* 72: Use what is commonly called the "reverse overlap" grip.
1963 Bob Rosburg *The Putter Book* 30: Even more common is the reverse overlap.

ribbed *adj.* (Of an iron club) marked with prominently scored ribs and grooves on the face; a feature now banned (*see* Rules of Golf, App. III).

1921 Andrew Kirkaldy *Fifty Years of Golf* 67: I have seen the ribbed iron clubs, and I don't like them.
1946 Frank Moran *Golfers' Gallery* 147: He afterwards admitted that he was helped by the ribbed mashie which was barred eventually.

ribbed
The "Deadstop,"
Arthur Andrews, 1920

rifle *v.trans.* To play (a shot) far and very accurately.

1956 Herbert Warren Wind *The Story of American Golf* 178: At the 17th he rifled a masterful two-iron through the narrow opening to the green and 8 feet from the cup.
1969 Tom Scott & Geoffrey Cousins *The Golf Immortals* 99: Armour was a tremendous iron player, rifling his shots on to the target with almost monotonous regularity.
1978 Denis J. Harington *Golf Score* (Oct./Nov.) 53: From a tight lie he rifled a 190-yard approach to the putting surface.

rim *v.trans.* To run round the edge of (the cup).

1899 Walter Camp & Lilian Brooks *Drives & Puts* 134: The ball ran true, then, rimming the cup a little, it gave a lurch and dropped in.
1916 P.A. Vaile *The New Golf* 42: ... the topped put, which often "rims" or "lips" the hole and runs out again.
1979 *Florida Times-Union* (Feb. 5) D8: Bradley's putt ... rimmed the cup and came out. ... "Pat's shot came out, but mine rimmed the cup and fell in," [said JoAnne Carner].

rim out *phr.v.* To rim the cup and fail to hole.

1962 Sam Snead *The Education of a Golfer* 95: ... after a short putt rimmed out.
1975 Mark McCormack *Golf Annual* 80: Player stepped up to oblige—and again rimmed out the putt.

roll[1] *n. & v.* **1** *n.* The run of a ball along the ground after landing.

1895 "Calamo Currente" *Half Hours with an Old Golfer* 82: ... he's a stunner at judging the roll. [*Footnote:*] run or travel.
1963 Arnold Palmer *My Game and Yours* 74: ... California, where the fairway grass stays alive all winter and provides very little roll.

2 *v.trans.* To play (a putt) so that it travels along the ground smoothly and with minimum spin.

1931 Joyce Wethered *The Game of Golf* 93: "Rolling" the ball quite smoothly in putting —to turn it, as it were, on an even keel—is not quite as simple a matter as it looks.
1977 Larry Dennis *Golf Digest* (July) 52: For years a lot of good putters, from Bobby Jones to Jack Nicklaus, have been telling us to roll out putts at a speed which allows the ball to die into the hole.

roll[2] *v.* **1** *v.intrans.* (Of the wrists) to turn over during the swing.

1931 Joyce & Roger Wethered *The Game of Golf* 52: In the back-swing do not let the wrists roll and turn away the face of the club.

2 *v.trans.* To turn over (the wrists) during the swing.

1946 Byron Nelson *Winning Golf* 54: ... the common and disastrous fault of rolling your wrists (turning the left under and the right over, as the club-head progresses into the follow-through of the swing).

roll in *phr.v.* To sink (a putt).

1977 *New York Times* (June 13) 43: ... Geiberger ... rolled in a 10–12-footer.

rough *n.* Ground on a course where the grass and other vegetation is considerably heavier than on the fairway.

1907 Frank H. Scroggie in Leach *Great Golfers in the Making* 229: McFarlane had been driving rather wildly, having repeatedly left Tait in the rough.
1909 Garden G. Smith *Golf Illustrated* (May 14) 233: ... when [pot-bunkers] are used to guard the edges of the course so as to take the place of the universal gorse or "rough" which used to be there.
1952 Henry Cotton *History of Golf in Britain* (in Wind *The Complete Golfer* 1954, 252): ... when the war ended in 1945 so many golfers had got used to playing "around the park" that the days of rough as we used to know it were ended.
1970 Charles Price *Golf* 16: Rough, on the other hand, is turf that has been allowed to grow to a coarse consistency, often several inches in height.
1977 Mike Bartlett *Golf Magazine* (June) 46: The first six inches of rough will be 1½ to two inches and the rest three to 3½ inches.

round *n. & adv.* **1** *n.* (The playing of) an entire circuit of the holes of a course, formerly consisting of various numbers of holes, now stipulated by the rules as consisting of eighteen holes.

1744 *Act of the Town Council of Edinburgh* (in *Badminton Golf* 1890, 22): ... and if two or more shall have won an equal number, that they play a round by themselves in order to determine the match.

1841 William Graham *The Links O' Innerleven* (in *Poems on Golf* 1967. 62):
I and my caddie would be found,
Describing still another round
On thy links, sweet Innerleven!
1862 Robert Chambers *A Few Rambling Remarks on Golf* 7: But, whether the direction taken be from the starting-hole once round a course somewhat circular, or from the starting-hole to the end and back again on a straight course, the term invariably applied to each series of holes played is a *round*.
1913 Bernard Darwin *Country Life* (June 28) 966: In the morning there were two very fine rounds of 73 and 74 by Vardon and Mr. Blackwell.
1931 Henry Cotton *Golf* 81: ... to my greatest satisfaction I finished the round in seventy-three.
1974 *The Golfer's Handbook* 458: Blackheath had seven holes, and the usual match there was three rounds to make twenty-one holes. ... The accidental incident that 18 was the most convenient number of holes at St. Andrews ... operated in the direction of 18 holes being accepted as the standard round of golf.
1976 *Rules of Golf* Definition 29: The "stipulated round" consists of playing the holes of the course in their correct sequence. ... The number of holes in a stipulated round is 18.
1977 *New York Times* (June 12): Al Geiberger, the leader since his record round of 59 ...

2 *adv.* Having completed a round.

1897 *Country Life* (Jan. 23) 82: Mr. Glover, playing from scratch, was round in 86.
1907 Harold Hilton *My Golfing Reminiscences* 23: On both occasions he was round in a score comfortably under 80.

royal and ancient. [Origin: chiefly after *The Royal and Ancient Golf Club of St. Andrews*, which was so entitled by permission of King William IV in 1834, in recognition of the fact that golf had then been played in Scotland continuously for about 400 years, and that among its devotees were Kings and Queens of Scots from James IV (reigned 1488–

1513) onward.] The traditional epithet of the game of golf.

1857 H.B. Farnie *The Golfer's Manual* 14: . . . that in such a region the royal and ancient game of Golf is in imminent danger of dying a natural death.
1875 Robert Clark *Golf: A Royal & Ancient Game* (title of book.)
1890 Horace Hutchinson *Badminton Golf* 53: The present writer, when an undergraduate at Oxford, had the privilege of introducing his logic tutor to the royal and ancient game of golf.
1907 Arthur Pottow *Recreation* (May) 540: The golf critics had all agreed that the Royal and Ancient game was of such a nature that ages must elapse before an American would be able to meet a British golfer with any prospect of success.
1929 *Golf Illustrated* (Apr.) 46: We sincerely believe that airplanes are to become as important as motor cars in connection with the royal and ancient game.
1957 George Houghton *The Truth About Golf Addicts* 7: As an important item in the design for happy living, the Royal and Ancient pursuit must be treated with the respect it merits.
1977 William Price *Golf Digest* (Dec.) 89: Had dinner under the Tiffany glass. Toasted the Royal and Ancient Game.

rub *n.* [*Origin:* borrowed from the old bowls (lawn bowling) term *rub* = "an obstacle on the bowling green that affects the running of a bowl in play"; recorded in bowls from the 16th century, the rule being that such an occurrence must be accepted without compensation. Golf and bowls were played in Scotland on the same tracts of common ground (links) from an early date; thus both the term *rub* and the principle of the rule were taken over into golf. (Outside golf, the bowls term was also taken up as a metaphor of trouble in general, as in Hamlet's "Ay, there's the rub.") Note that *green* in the phrase *rub of the green* means the whole course, not the putting green; see **green** (def. 1).]

1 *n.* *Obsolete.* An accident, good or bad.

1793 Anon *The Goffers* (in Thomas Mathison *The Goff*, 3rd edition, 26):
While round the Links our Balls we
    play,
What tho' with *rubs* we sometimes meet,
We still push on, all brisk and gay,
Such chances make the game more
    sweet.
1833 George Fullerton Carnegie *Golfiana* (in Clark *Golf: A Royal & Ancient Game* 1875, 141): The green has its bunkers, its hazards, and rubs.
1881 Robert Forgan *The Golfer's Handbook* 32: You may attempt [in stymie play] to run your ball close past that of your adversary with a chance of getting a lucky "rub" to turn yours into the hole.
1890 Horace Hutchinson *Badminton Golf* 292: [The caddie] should be ever ready to run forward to the hole, to stand at it for your opponent, and thus prevent any possibility of his getting a good 'rub' by striking the staff of the flag.

2 rub of the green *phr.* Any mere accident, not caused by a player or caddie, that moves or stops a ball in play; for which no relief is given under the rules.

1812 *Regulations* (St. Andrews): Whatever happens to a ball by accident must be reckoned a Rub of the green.
1857 *Rules of Golf:* Whatever happens to a ball by accident, such as striking any person, or [being] touched with the foot by a third party, or by the forecaddie, must be reckoned a rub of the green, and submitted to.
1890 *Badminton Golf* 448: *Rub on the green.* —A favourable or unfavourable knock to the ball, for which no penalty is imposed, and which must be submitted to.
1961 John Stobbs *Tackle Golf* (repr. 1977) 105: It is in the nature of golf that rubs of the green daunt the player in his happiest as well as his most wretched moments.
1968 Chick Evans (in J.S. Martin *The Curious History of the Golf Ball*, 12): But even with the elimination of most hazards, "rubs" of the green remain to cause crazy bounces and cranky lies.
1976 *Rules of Golf* Definition 27: A "rub of the green" occurs when a ball in motion is stopped or deflected by any outside agency. Rule 26.1.a: If a ball in motion be accidentally stopped or deflected by any outside agency,

it is a rub of the green and the ball shall be played where it lies, without penalty.

rubbercore n.   A rubber-cored ball.

1905   W. Whytock *Golf Illustrated* (July) 87: If trial matches were played between some of our best professionals, one using the rubber-core, the other the old gutty ball, it would be seen what a very small margin, if any, there lies between the two.
1913   R.E. Howard *Country Life* (Apr. 26) 612:   ... watching the feverish efforts of errant players to rescue rubber-cores from the water.
1968   J.S. Martin *The Curious History of the Golf Ball* 58:   Beginning in 1901 when the first rubbercores began reaching Great Britain ...

rubber-cored adj.   (Of a ball) having a core of rubber; specifically, having an interior formed of strip rubber wound around some center, with a cover of balata or similar material; first achieved as a manufacturable proposition by Coburn Haskell and J.R. Gammeter in 1898–1900.

1902   Horace Hutchinson *Country Life* (Dec. 13) 767:   ... the rubber-cored balls can be bought freely at 25 s. or so the dozen.
1912   Harry Vardon *How to Play Golf* 14: There has been no period in the history of the game so pregnant with evolution as the past seven or eight years, since golfers began to understand the possibilities of the rubber-cored ball.
1936   W.B. Martin *Fifty Years of American Golf* 169:   ... when the new rubber-cored ball took the place of the old guttie.

run n. & v.   **1** n. The onward roll of a ball after pitching, due to topspin or to relative lack of backspin.

1889   Alexander Lawson *Letters on Golf* 24: The iron likewise leaves a ball with less run on it, a result of its lofting it more.
1895   "Calamo Currente" *Half Hours With an Old Golfer* 74:   Eighty yards of run, never

fear! [*Footnote:*] The distance the ball runs after it has come to the ground.
1931   Roger Wethered *The Game of Golf* 58: ... that the art of iron play, as opposed to wooden club play, consists in reducing the run of the ball, or at least bringing it under more exact control.
1941   Patty Berg *Golf* 51:   Learn how to put "stop" (with "bite" or back-spin) or "run" (with "over-spin") on the ball.
1950   Dai Rees *Golf My Way* 57:   Because of the high trajectory of the ball's flight, and the backspin imparted on impact, there is very little run after pitching.

2 v.trans.   To play (a ball) along the ground.

1895   James P. Lee *Golf in America* 181: Run—To run a ball along the ground in approaching the hole instead of lofting it.
1900   Harry Vardon *The Outing* (Apr.) 86: I always run a ball in preference to pitching it, if the nature of the ground permits.

3 n.   A shot played along the ground.

1946   Bernard Darwin *British Golf* 25:   He was a great iron player, and a versatile one wedded neither to the pitch nor to the run.

run down phr.v.   To hole (a putt).

1900   Walter J. Travis *The Outing* (July) 418:   It is so easy to run a putt down in one when you have two for the hole.
1928   Bernard Darwin *Hagen at Hoylake* (in Wind *The Complete Golfer* 1954, 173):   But Hagen took a good long look, pitched beautifully out of the bunker and ran down a five-foot putt.
1963   Bob Rosburg *The Putter Book* 64:   I managed to run down a 50-foot putt for another birdie.

run in phr.v.   To hole (a putt).

1977   *New York Times* (June 13) 43:   He ran in a 30–35-foot birdie putt.
1978   *Boston Globe* (Aug. 7) 21:   Meanwhile, Mahaffey ran in a 45-foot putt.

run up phr.v.   To play (the ball) with a run-up.

1890 Horace Hutchinson *Badminton Golf* 129: ... the stroke termed 'running up with the iron' ... The ball thus struck will be sent skimming close above the ground for the early part of its journey, and will then run on up the slope on to the putting green.
1921 Andrew Kirkaldy *Fifty Years of Golf* 130: Instead of running the ball up as I did ... he tried his favourite pitching shot.
1946 Percy Boomer *On Learning Golf* 15: ... in fact, she runs up better than do many players with handicaps lower than her own 15.
1962 Sam Snead *The Education of a Golfer* 204: I know sixty-year-old women who can chip and pitch and run up with almost a pro's ability.

run-up *n.* A short low approach shot that bounces and runs uphill to the green.

1899 Willie Tucker *The Outing* (Aug.) 524: ... Douglas used his iron playing the Musselburgh run-up shot.
1919 Robert K. Risk *Songs of the Links* 22: When run-ups check and falter on their way ...

1962 Sam Snead *The Education of a Golfer* 203: I was getting placement to the greens that I had been missing for months by playing the old Scottish-British run-up approach game with the lower-lofted irons.
1977 George Peper *Scrambling Golf* 114: ... the run-up takes several small bounces, enabling it to cover ground quickly and climb hills without being deterred.

rut iron or **rutter** or **rutting iron** or **rutting niblick.** Alternate names for the track iron or iron niblick, referring to its use in playing out of ruts left by cartwheels. [These names, handed down by club-making firms, are used by golf historians and museums, but no early printed citations for them have so far been found.] *See* **track iron, niblick,** and **iron.**

(1979) captions of early clubs in the Museum of the R. & A.: rutting iron, rutting niblick.
1979 Ian T. Henderson & David I. Stirk *Golf in The Making* 176: The 'rutter' or rut-iron or track-iron ...

S

sammy n. [Origin: see quotation.] An iron club, no longer in use, similar to the jigger but having a rounded back, used for approaching.

1909 H. Fulford letter to *Golf Illustrated* (May 7) 211: Mr. Geoffrey Hoffman and myself first brought out the "Sammy," by twisting an old cleek head. And more in jest than anything else, called it "Sammy" after a man who works in my shop. Mr. T. Stewart, of St. Andrews, made the first batch of these heads.

sand n., *often attributive.* The sand in a bunker or bunkers; of or related to playing from bunkers.

1970 Tony Jacklin *Jacklin* 25: I had been in sand three times in four holes.

1970 Dick Schaap *The Masters* 188: Then Billy Casper, who is considered more skilled at putting and chipping than sand play, blasts to within four feet of the pin.

1977 Raymond Schuessler *Golf Illustrated* (Summer) 23: Reading about sand techniques doesn't help them much either, because not too many golfers can learn from a book.

1977 Gene Sarazen in *Golf Magazine* (Aug.) 20: "Ken did [give] one tip about when you're in the sand to swing as if you were clipping the ball off the living room rug. I tried it and I'm back on my sand game."

Sammy

c. 1910

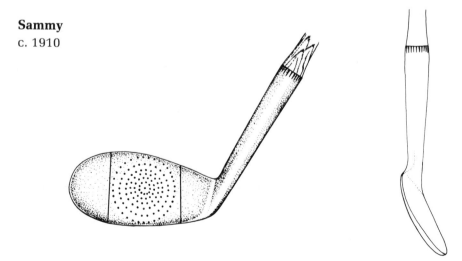

sand-blaster *n.* A sand wedge.

1941 Patty Berg *Golf* 2: . . . all irons from numbers 2 through 9, putter, "sand-blaster."
1946 Byron Nelson *Winning Golf* 18: . . . a sand-blaster or double duty iron.

sand iron. **1** A heavy, lofted, stiff-shafted iron club, no longer in use, that was used for playing from bunkers.

1858 *Unidentified newspaper clipping* (in Allan Robertson's album at the R. & A. 88): . . . he seizes his sand-iron—a short stout club, with a scooped iron face.
1881 Robert Forgan *The Golfer's Handbook* 16: The "Sand Iron," as may be at once inferred from its name, is mainly employed to extricate a ball from sandy ruts and bunkers.
1890 Horace Hutchinson *Badminton Golf* 66: The sand iron is practically a heavy driving iron with the face very much laid back. Its use has, however, been of late almost entirely superseded by that of the niblick and mashie.

2 Sand wedge.

1950 Gene Sarazen *Thirty Years of Championship Golf* (in Wind *The Complete Golfer* 1954, 274): The sand-iron . . . is the greatest stroke-saver in the game. I'm proud to have invented it.

sand trap. See **trap.**

sand wedge. An iron club used primarily for playing explosion shots from sand, having loft of 54–58 degrees, lie of 63–65 degrees, and length of about 35 inches, and having a substantial flange behind and below the leading edge to prevent the clubhead from digging into sand. Also, a shot played with this club.

1928 U.S. Patent Office. Edwin Kerr MacClain, of Houston, Texas: Sand wedge. . . . It is an object of my invention to provide a wing or guide . . . underneath and back of the face.
1937 Henry Longhurst *Golf* 196: . . . that invaluable weapon known variously as the

sand iron
Carrick sand iron or bunker iron, c. 1860

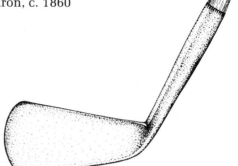

blaster, iron man, sand wedge, sand iron, and so forth.
1945 Arthur Mann *Nelson at His Peak* (in Wind *The Complete Golfer* 1954, 208): It's a deep-faced niblick, devised in 1929 and actually the only new club introduced in more than a quarter-century. It's called a dynamiter and a sand wedge.
1962 Sam Snead *The Education of a Golfer* 163: It was Sarazen who invented the sand wedge in 1931, which revolutionized trap play.
1977 George Peper *Scrambling Golf* 125: Ever since 1932, when Gene Sarazen invented the strange club with the wide-open face and heavy flange . . . the sand wedge has been virtually the only club to hit from a trap.

scare *n.* [Origin: Scottish *scare* or *skair* ="spliced or notched joint in wood," from Old Norse *skor*="joint in ship's planking."] The spliced joint by which wooden clubheads were fixed to shafts before the drilled socket was introduced at the end of the 19th century.

1857 H.B. Farnie *The Golfer's Manual* 80: SCARE—The point of junction between head and shaft.
1881 Robert Forgan *The Golfer's Handbook* 61: SCARE—The narrow part of the clubhead by which it is glued to the handle.
1899 J.H. Taylor *Practical Club-making* (in Henderson & Stirk *Golf in the Making* 1979, 322): The scare should be about six inches long, and should be made very thin at the end.

scared *adj.* (Of a wooden club) having the head joined to the shaft with a scare.

1907 Willie Auchterlonie in Leach *Great Golfers in the Making* 224: I prefer decidedly the old-fashioned scared pattern of wooden club to the newer socket variety.
1915 *New York Sun* (quoted in Alexander H. Revell *Pro & Con of Golf* 34): In considering scared or socket clubs, Ray prefers the scared, believing that there is less give in the neck.

Schenectady or **Schenectady putter.** A center-shafted putter with an aluminum head, patented by Arthur F. Knight of Schenectady, New York, in 1903, used by Walter J. Travis in winning the British amateur championship in 1904, and shortly thereafter banned by the R. & A.

1907 Walter J. Travis in Leach *Great Golfers in the Making* 93: One of my compatriots suggested my trying his Schenectady putter.
1919 Robert K. Risk *Songs of the Links* 60:
Schenectadies erstwhile stood over par;
They have vanished from our view . . .

Schenectady
Harry C. Lee, New York

sclaff, *also* **schlaff,** *v. & n.* [Origin: Scottish, from *sclaff* = "to slap"; said to be onomatopoeic, imitating the sound of a flat blow or slap.] **1** *v.intrans.* To hit or graze the ground unintentionally with the clubhead before hitting the ball.

1887 Sir Walter Simpson *The Art of Golf* 91: There is no reserve force in him if he sclaffs. His club sticks in the mud, or is twisted out of his hand.
1890 *Badminton Golf* 445: *Sclaff*—Almost synonymous with *Baff*, which see. The distinction is so subtle as almost to defy definition.
1892 R. Whyte Gibson *The Caddies of St. Andrews* (in Andrew Lang *Golfing Papers*, 86): "Sur, you're no playin' the day ava. Haud up your shouthers; dinna sclaf!"
1912 Harry Vardon *How to Play Golf* 153: Schlaffing is caused by throwing the weight on to the right leg at the moment of hitting, and therefore dropping the right shoulder too quickly.
1933 John Ressich *Thir Braw Days* 90: . . . kicked aff his buits an' flyped aff his socks an' stood up bare-fitted. He had twa-three swings an' then Sandy askit him: 'Hoo dae ye feel wi' it, Dougie?' 'Fine,' says Dougie, 'fine. Ye get a graun' grip wi' your big tae, but I'm sclaffin' a bit.'
1947 Jim Dante & Leo Diegel *The Nine Bad Shots of Golf* 115: Sclaffing—This is not too common a fault. . . . If you want to hit the ground behind the ball, this is an excellent position to be in.

2 *v.trans.* To hit (the ball or a shot) with a stroke that sclaffs.

1899 Willie Tucker *The Outing* (Aug.) 523: Macdonald was dazed at Holabird's shot and sclaffed his second into the bunker guarding the green.
1921 Andrew Kirkaldy *Fifty Years of Golf* 116: [Tom Morris] was rather bad at short putts, and he would say when he missed one about a foot and a half, "Man, Andra, I schlaffed it," laughing as he said it.

3 *n.* A stroke that sclaffs.

1886 David Jackson *Golfing Songs & Recitations* 5:
The *sclaff*, the *foozle*, the *weel sent hame*,
The *ups* and *downs* of this dear game.
1890 Horace Hutchinson *Badminton Golf* 93: . . . a 'top' or 'sclaff' will be the almost certain result.
1961 John Stobbs *Tackle Golf* (repr. 1977) 24: Hence the flying divots, the sclaffs . . . [Footnote:] A foozle resulting from hitting the ground behind the ball, or digging under it.

scoop *v.trans.* To pull (the ball) upward with the clubhead at the moment of striking.

1931 Henry Cotton *Golf* 117: Another thing to guard against in striking the ball is the tendency to scoop the ball to get it into the air.

1969 Jack Nicklaus *The Greatest Game of All* 52: Let's say he was working on getting us not to scoop the ball on the upswing, one of his basic tenets.

scorecard. See **card.**

score play. Stroke play.

1897 *Country Life* (May 29) 588: Always stronger in score play than in match play, he has twice won the Open competition, which is a scoring competition open to the world.

1907 John L. Low in Leach *Great Golfers in the Making* 9: ... score play should be discouraged, as tending to destroy the idea which is at the right root of all good games, namely, that *one side* plays *the other*.

1930 Bernard Darwin *Golfer's Year Book* 55: ... to be played for by score play over thirty-six holes.

scoring n. The marking of a clubface with grooves, punch marks, etc.

1976 *Rules of Golf* Appendix III: In general a definite area of the surface is reserved for scoring.

Scotch foursome. A foursome match.

1974 *The Golfer's Handbook* 87: There has been a tendency to use the word [foursome] to cover a four-ball match, and so the term

"SCOTCH FOURSOME" has been used in some cases to distinguish between the two.

1977 John S. Radosta *New York Times* (Sept. 15) B25: In tomorrow's play [Ryder Cup] the format is formally called "foursomes," known in the United States as "Scotch foursomes." Each two-man team plays one ball, with the two players alternating on the shots from drive to holed-out putt.

scramble *v.trans. & intrans.* To play erratic golf; also, to obtain some satisfactory result by playing erratic but effective golf.

1907 Harold Hilton *My Golfing Reminiscences* 69: ... I scrambled a five.

1919 Robert K. Risk *Songs of the Links* 77:
When it grows warmer, it is heavy odds
That I shall scramble round in 99.

1931 Joyce & Roger Wethered *The Game of Golf* 40: Scrambling near the hole may be well enough, but scrambling off the tee, especially where heather abounds, is apt to start a vicious circle.

1975 Dan Jenkins *Dead Solid Perfect* 228: I managed to scramble three pars out of the rough and the sand, dropping some idiot putts.

1977 Ben Crenshaw (in George Peper *Scrambling Golf* 7): I guess the perfect golfer is the one who never has to scramble at all ... what it boils down to is that we're *all* scramblers.

scrambler n. A player who plays some erratic golf but can achieve good results by bold recovery play.

1967 Mark McCormack *Arnie* 168: He is a

scoring

(1) multiple scorings (now illegal), Burke Rotary Special Mashie-Niblick, 1915

(2) standard modern scoring, five-iron, Walter Hagen, 1979

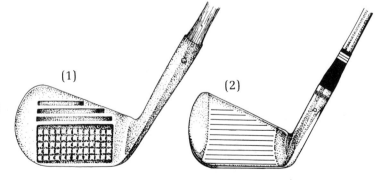

(1)

(2)

master scrambler . . . and . . . can cut through the dense vegetation.

1977 Dave Hill *Golf Digest* (July) 110: But he recognizes his deficiencies and has the guts to play around them. He never quits. He's a great scrambler—he can get it up and down out of a ballwasher.

scrambling *adj.* (Of a stroke) seeking to recover from erratic play; (of a score) achieved despite erratic play.

1961 Tommy Armour *How to Play Your Best Golf All the Time* 159: I think that the delicate techniques of some "scrambling" shots, such as a gentle pitch over a bunker, show thrilling artistry.
1970 Dick Schaap *The Masters* 99: Jack Nicklaus . . . comes in with a scrambling 71. He missed nine of eighteen greens, but made six putts from more than seven feet to preserve his sub-par round.
1977 George Peper *Scrambling Golf* 69: From there he sank a 30-footer for the scramblingest par you'd ever want to see.

scraper *n.* *Obsolete.* A presumably lofted wooden club.

1735 Anon. letter in Henderson & Stirk *Golf in the Making* 1979, 93: Tell him to provide me in nine clubs viz three play clubs, three scrapers, one of which a half scraper or spoon and three putting clubs.
1790 *Hoyle's Games* 288: . . . there are six sorts used by good Players; namely . . . the Scraper and Half Scraper, [used] when [the ball lies] in long grass . . .

scratch *n. & adj.* [Origin: in 19th-century athletics, the *scratch* was a line marked or scratched on the ground, as a starting line for a race. In some handicap races, the competitor(s) who had a handicap of zero "started from scratch," while those receiving handicaps started from points farther ahead. Thus *scratch* came to mean "a zero handicap" in the various sports, including golf, in which handicapping was adopted.] **1** *n.* A zero handicap.

1897 *Country Life* (Jan. 23) 82: Mr. Glover, playing from scratch, was round in 86.
1973 *Bartlett's World Golf Encyclopedia* 423: If we all played from scratch, those friendly foursomes would seldom develop.

2 *adj.* Having a zero handicap.

1889 Alexander Lawson *Letters on Golf* 12: . . . to fix the odds necessary to give him a fair chance with scratch players.
1915 Alexander H. Revell *Pro & Con of Golf* vii: Not being in the "scratch class" myself, but an average player . . .
1963 Arnold Palmer *My Game and Yours* 14: . . . scratch player, hacker or beginner who has never yet held a golf club.
1971 Henry Longhurst *My Life and Soft Times* 38: I suppose I must have been scratch for about twenty years.

3 scratch score. A par for a course for a scratch player.

1897 *The Outing* (March) 617: Distance, 5,821 yards; scratch score, 84.
1928 *Golf Illustrated* (June) 64: The scratch score of Royal Melbourne is 75.
1974 *The Golfer's Handbook* 100: The Standard Scratch Score is the score in which a scratch player is expected to go round the course, playing from the medal tees, in summer conditions.

scruff *v.intrans.* *Obsolete.* To graze the turf with the clubhead.

1857 H.B. Farnie *The Golfer's Manual* 80: SCRUFF—Slightly razing the grass in striking.

scuff *v.trans.* To misplay (a stroke) by grazing or hitting the ground with the clubhead before hitting the ball.

1950 Sam Snead *How to Hit a Golf Ball* 72: The common cause for scuffing is an attempt—conscious or otherwise—to scoop the ball up into the air. The result is a striking of the ground behind the ball first and then hitting the ball.
1977 Mark Mulvoy *Golf Digest* (Aug.) 60: . . . missed his first putt, then, unbelievably, scuffed the tap-in past the hole and took a 7.

scull. See **skull.**

second n.   The shot after the tee shot.

1890   Lord Wellwood *Badminton Golf* 36: 'Have they played their second?' 'No, only one of them.'
1922   P.G. Wodehouse *The Heel of Achilles* (in *The Clicking of Cuthbert*, repr. 1956, 138):   The latter played a good second to within a few feet of the green.
1931   Joyce & Roger Wethered *The Game of Golf* 54:   . . . the first and foremost object of the drive is to keep the ball in play, so that the second may be played off the fairway.
1969   Jack Nicklaus *The Greatest Game of All* 152:   I hit a pretty bad second.
1974   *The Golfer's Handbook* 463:   Unknown to each other, both players hit their seconds (chip shots) at the same time.

setup n.   A player's positioning for the address.

1975   Mark McCormack *Golf Annual* 72: Cole missed eight fairways in the first twelve holes before changing his set-up at address, moving the ball back in his stance and his hands forward.
1977   Tom Kite *Golf Magazine* (Aug.) 52: Jack Nicklaus has said that setting up to the ball is the most important single maneuver in golf. . . . Yet, important as the setup is to professional golfers, it is doubly important to amateurs.

set up phr.v.   To position oneself for the address.

1961   John Stobbs *Tackle Golf* (repr. 1977) 17:   . . . the right approach to the shot ('setting-up' as the professional will probably call it).

seven-iron n.   An iron club having loft of 38–40 degrees, lie of 61–63 degrees, and length of 36 inches, and giving distance of 125–160 yards (men's clubs). Also, a shot played with a seven-iron. Alternate name, mashie-niblick.

seven-iron
Walter Hagen 1979

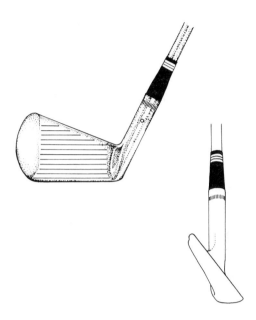

1961   John Stobbs *Tackle Golf* (repr. 1977) 118:   Much easier to play a 5-iron to an open green, than to play a 7-iron at an awkward—and frightening—angle.

shaft n., *also* **clubshaft.**   The long thin part of a club by which it is wielded, enclosed by the grip at the top and fixed to the neck or socket of the head at the bottom; made of various woods until the 20th century, and since the 1920s made predominantly of tubular steel.

1687   Thomas Kincaid *Diary* (Jan. 20) (in *Book of the Old Edinburgh Club* XXVII, 1949, 131):   The shaft of your club most be of hazel.
1743   Thomas Mathison *The Goff* 5:
  Of finest ash Castalio's shaft was made . . .
1890   Horace Hutchinson *Badminton Golf* 65:   On the whole, however, no improvement can be made upon split hickory for shafts.
1930   Advertisement *The Golfer's Year Book* ii: . . . the first irons and the only irons to combine the advantages of the steel shaft with the sweet feel of the finest hickory!

1964 Julius Boros *How to Win at Weekend Golf* 44: The clubshaft should appear to be an extension of the left arm.

1973 *Bartlett's World Golf Encyclopedia* 360: A further advance toward more distance and accuracy was the development of the aluminum shaft in 1967.

1976 *Rules of Golf* Appendix II.c.: The shaft shall be designed to be straight from the top to a point not more than 5 inches above the sole. The shaft, including any inserted plug, shall be generally circular in cross-section and shall extend to the upper end of the grip.

shallow *adj.* (Of a clubface) relatively narrow from top to bottom.

1907 *Army & Navy Stores Catalogue* 999: Gibson's shallow-faced or "Gem" putter, narrow blade, with thick sole.

1916 P.A. Vaile *The New Golf* 38: Vardon's putter was so shallow in its face that he was actually able sometimes to hit the ball beneath the centre of its height.

1931 Henry Cotton *Golf* 105: . . . a cleek, the head of which is generally smaller and the face more shallow than the iron.

1977 Tom Watson *Golf Magazine* (July) 104: . . . you continue teeing the ball at the same height even though the new driver may have a shallower or deeper face.

shank *v. & n.* **1** *v.intrans.* To hit the ball with the hosel of an iron club.

1931 Roger Wethered *The Game of Golf* 65: Of all the golfing diseases, shanking is by far the most outrageous in its devastating results.

1948 Ben Hogan *Power Golf* 139: Crossing over the hands or closing the face of the club during this shot will cause you to shank.

1977 Johnny Miller *Golf Magazine* (Aug.) 73: . . . I've only shanked once since I turned pro.

2 *v.trans.* To hit (the ball or a shot) with the hosel of an iron club.

1969 Jack Nicklaus *The Greatest Game of All* 174: I was making a run at him until I shanked my 8-iron on the short twelfth into deep right field.

1977 Gordon S. White *New York Times*

(June 11): Mrs. Carner, however, shanked the ball hitting it hard right directly at the people lined up to the right of the green.

3 *n.* A shanked shot.

1947 Jim Dante & Leo Diegel *The Nine Bad Shots of Golf* 121: Another reason the shank is so dreaded is that it strikes without warning.

1962 Sam Snead *The Education of a Golfer* 216: Shanks are so contagious that even watching them is risky, and that includes the pro player.

1977 Dave Hill & Nick Seitz *Teed Off* 181: We've always heard that a shank—that awful-looking shot that squirts right off the hosel—is the closest thing to a perfect shot.

4 *n.* A tendency to shank the ball.

1967 Michael Green *The Art of Coarse Golf* 48: . . . he went to the club pro and asked for an hour's tuition to cure his shank.

shoot *v.trans.* To play (golf of a stated standard); make (a stated score); play (a hole or course) in a stated score.

1910 Grantland Rice *The Winning Shot* 33: . . . a golfer who averages around ninety-five for the eighteen holes will some day lose control of himself and shoot an eighty-four.

1927 Robert T. Jones, Jr. & O.B. Keeler *Down the Fairway*: I was shooting some hot golf and enjoying myself immensely.

1934 Grantland Rice *The Fabulous Commodore Heard* (in Wind *The Complete Golfer* 1954, 115): Twenty years later at the age of 65 he was shooting his age. That means at the age of 65 he shot a 65.

1946 Frank Moran *Golfers' Gallery* 26: He "shot" a 70 in the first round.

1968 Buddy Hackett *The Truth About Golf* 19: . . . the shoemaker won't ask "What kind of game do you shoot?"

1977 Dwayne Netland *Golf Digest* (Aug.) 27: Starting out on the 10th tee, Geiberger shot the back nine in 30.

short *adj. & adv.* **1** *adj.* Not getting as far as the objective.

1890 Horace Hutchinson *Badminton Golf* 110: . . . With regard to approach shots . . .

the failing of the great majority of players is being short.

1916 P.A. Vaile *The New Golf* 66: The golfer's cardinal sin on the green is being short, not "giving the hole a chance."

1931 Bernard Darwin *The Game of Golf* 116: If we walk about on a medal day . . . we shall see man after man miserably short—short with his approach, short with his approach putt, short often with his holing-out putt.

2 *adv.* Not far enough.

1977 John S. Radosta *New York Times* (Sept. 6) 55: Weiskopf . . . chipped 10 feet short and missed the putt.

3 *adj.* (Of a player) not far-hitting.

1977 Dave Hill & Nick Seitz *Teed Off* 125: [Nicklaus] can afford to let out because he's stronger out of the rough. Long grass doesn't bother him the way it does us shorter players.

4 *adj.* (Of a club) hitting a relatively small distance.

1915 Alexander H. Revell *Pro & Con of Golf* 7: . . . the easiest clubs to play with are the shorter ones, the putter coming first.

1977 Davis Love *Golf Digest* (July) 42: When a driver and a shorter club to the green gives you little advantage . . .

5 *adv.* (Of a course) as if it were shorter, owing to weather conditions.

1969 Jack Nicklaus *The Greatest Game of All* 83: Muirfield measured 6806 yards but it played fairly short.

short course. A course of less than full length, typically having mostly par-three holes, some par-fours, and no par-fives.

1977 *New York Times* (June 11) 14: Gary Player . . . had a 59 on a short course in the Brazilian Open three years ago . . .

short hole. A par-three hole.

1911 James Braid *Advanced Golf* 251: The longest of the short holes must, of course, still be a [par] 3, though it may be a bogey 4.

1971 Henry Longhurst *My Life and Soft Times* 264: This turned out to be a long short-hole of some 210-odd yards.

short irons. The highly lofted irons.

1946 Byron Nelson *Winning Golf* 30: . . . short irons (numbers 7, 8, 9).

1950 Gene Sarazen *Walter Hagen* (in Wind *The Complete Golfer* 1954, 171): He was the finest short-iron player the game has ever known.

1965 Bob Charles *Left-handed Golf* 54: . . . short irons, the pin-splitting eight, nine, pitching wedge and sand wedge.

1978 *Boston Globe* (July 29) 19: In his 63, he had eight birdies. "And I was weak with my short irons."

short spoon. *See* **spoon.**

shot *n.* A stroke and the resulting movement or journey of the ball; a particular type of stroke; also the score of a stroke.

1857 H.B. Farnie *The Golfer's Manual* 33: . . . elevation of the ball is of primary importance in a spoon shot.

1890 Tom Morris *Badminton Golf* 431: I gaed roon' in a single wi' Mr. H. in 81. . . . it'll tak' the best of the young ones, I reckon, to be mony shots better than *that*.

1899 Findlay S. Douglas *The Outing* (June) 221: . . . playing shots at all distances and marking the carry and run.

1912 Harry Vardon *How to Play Golf* 171: I spent nearly all my spare hours in learning new shots.

1922 P.G. Wodehouse *Sundered Hearts* (in *The Clicking of Cuthbert*, repr. 1956, 71): He had never shown much indication of becoming anything in the nature of a first-class golfer, but he had managed to acquire one or two decent shots.

1931 Joyce & Roger Wethered *The Game of Golf* 41: . . . the perfectly played shot is infinitely more difficult than it appears to be.

1977 Mike Bartlett *Golf Magazine* (June) 46: In short it's tough and you'll have to play every shot in the bag.

shotmaker *n.* A player who can play a great array of different shots.

1926 P.C. Pulver *Golf Illustrated* (June) 21: . . . as more has been done for the golfer, so much less has been the demand made upon his skill as a shot-maker.

1927 Robert T. Jones, Jr. & O.B. Keeler *Down the Fairway* 128: I could hit the shots well; I couldn't help knowing that. But was I a golfer, or one of those hapless mechanical excellencies known as a shot-maker, who cannot connect the great shots in sufficient numbers to win anything?

1950 Gene Sarazen *Thirty Years of Championship Golf* (in Wind *The Complete Golfer* 1954, 273): I think a principal reason why we developed such solid shotmakers in the early days was that golfers played with only eight or nine clubs and got to know them all.

1969 Tom Weiskopf *Go For the Flag* 4: Tommy Bolt . . . always has been regarded as one of the finest shotmakers in the game.

1977 Ben Crenshaw (in George Peper *Scrambling Golf* 8): In order to progress from a mere golfer to a shot-maker, you have to know how to hit it from right to left, left to right, high in the air, and low to the ground.

shotmaking n. The ability to play a great array of different shots.

1928 A.T. Packard *Golf Illustrated* (Apr.) 29: Absolute perfection in shot-making may be imagined but not attained.

1977 Dave Hill & Nick Seitz *Teed Off* 188: By shotmaking I mean the ability to bring off all types of shots under all types of conditions. I admire the man who can hit a low fade when he has to or a high fade. . . . There aren't ten good shotmakers on the tour today.

shut adj. (Of a club) having the face turned somewhat forward relative to the line of play.

1928 Johnny Farrell *Golf Illustrated* (July) 23: The shut face is the method I advocate in iron play.

1962 Sam Snead *The Education of a Golfer* 19: Then I saw that the clubface was tilted slightly forward at that stage of my windup where I was coiled to strike. . . . I was looking at what pros call a "shut face"—which term I didn't know at the time.

1969 Tom Scott & Geoffrey Cousins *The Golf Immortals* 61: Sarazen's secret was his perfection of the low-flying approach with backspin played with a shut face.

1975 Henry Cotton *History of Golf* 212:

Since 1941 there has been a general trend to use and recommend a more shut club face *at the top of the swing,* and this fashion has been in vogue ever since.

shut-faced adj. Having a shut face.

1931 Joyce Wethered *The Game of Golf* 96: If the shut-faced principle of putting is adopted . . .

1975 Henry Cotton *History of Golf* 207: I am sure that they had all tried out this shut-face method. . . . The shut-to-open-face player can, of course, play very straight shots . . . shut-face golf is young man's golf.

side n. **1** In match play, one of the two competing entities, each consisting of one or two players (occasionally more) playing as partners.

1842 *Chambers' Edinburgh Journal* (Oct. 8) 297: . . . the first thing to be done is to tee the balls, of which each party or side has one.

1888 *Rules of Golf:* The game of golf is generally played by two sides. . . . it may also be played by three or more sides.

1976 *Rules of Golf* Definition 28: *Foursome:* A match in which two play against two, and each side plays one ball.

2 A half round of a course; the first or the last nine holes.

1967 Mark McCormack *Arnie* 59: . . . if there is a nine-hole stretch anywhere in the world on which a gambling golfer can make up ground, it is the back side of Augusta.

1977 *Golf Digest* (Aug.) 101: Schroeder, second, was disappointed but philosophical: "I played the back side two over."

sidehill adj. Situated on the side of a hill, from the viewpoint of a player facing toward the hole.

1948 Ben Hogan *Power Golf* 150: When you have a sidehill lie and the ball is higher than your feet you play it farther away from the feet at address.

1977 Johnny Miller *Golf Magazine* 42: Those in the field who fall short to either side will face a long sidehill bunker shot into the wind.

sidehiller n.   A ball in a sidehill lie.

1956 Herbert Warren Wind *The Story of American Golf* 170:   Walter tapped his sidehiller into the corner of the cup, only to have it twist out again and linger on the lip.

sidesaddle *adv. & adj.*   (Of an unorthodox style of putting) standing and facing directly toward the hole and holding the putter at the side of the body with the hands far apart.

1975 Mark McCormack *Golf Annual* 207:   The old boy uses that side-saddle approach, a yip-fighting sweep of the ball from beside his right foot.

single n.   A match between two players.

1857 H.B. Farnie *The Golfer's Manual* 65:   In playing a single, the novice should neither select for his antagonist one very much worse or very much better than himself.
1896 *Baily's Magazine* (Oct.) 329:   . . . the great majority preferring friendly matches in singles and foursomes.
1946 Frank Moran *Golfers' Gallery* 116:   Only three of the eight singles were won by the British team.
1977 Joseph C. Dey *Golf Digest* (Aug.) 18:   The 1969 Ryder Cup at Birkdale was all square as the last singles came to the home green—Jack Nicklaus vs. Tony Jacklin—and *they* were all square.

sink *v.trans.*   To hole (a putt).

1921 Andrew Kirkaldy *Fifty Years of Golf* 129:   I was in no hurry or flurry, but just looked and sank the ball.
1928 Glenna Collett *Golf Illustrated* (Oct.) 19:   I won the match by sinking a forty-foot putt.
1970 Dick Schaap *The Masters* 91:   On the eighth hole, Gene Littler sinks a four-foot putt for a birdie.
1977 *New York Times* (June 11) 14:   Miss Higuchi sank five birdies for her five-under-par round.

sinker n.   **1** *Obsolete.* A golf ball that would sink in water.

1913 H.B. Martin *Golf Yarns* 59:   When he came to this pond hole he tossed the boy a ball and said: "Boy, will you find out if this is a sinker?"
1968 J.S. Martin *The Curious History of the Golf Ball* 88:   Ladies and light hitters would do better with large floaters, strong men with smaller, denser sinkers.

2 A well-holed putt.

1963 Bob Rosburg *The Putter Book* 30:   . . . the tremendous feeling of confidence a couple of early "sinkers" create.

sit down *phr.v.*   (Of a pitched ball) to bite the green and stop.

1941 Patty Berg *Golf* 35:   . . . the imparting of backspin to the ball so that it will have a true flight and "sit down" abruptly when it lights on the green.
1975 Mark McCormack *Golf Annual* 12:   You may have seen it on television—a nine-iron on the 17th hole that sat down inches from the pin.

sit up *phr.v.*   (Of a ball at rest through the green) to lie conveniently supported by grass.

1912 Harry Vardon *How to Play Golf* 166:   So long as the golfer keeps to the fairway, the ball generally sits up for him with some nobleness of bearing.
1921 Andrew Kirkaldy *Fifty Years of Golf* 164:   . . . the straight player . . . will always find his ball "sitting up" for the use of the wooden club if required.
1950 Sam Snead *How to Hit a Golf Ball* 3:   [The driver] is used only from the tee except when extra distance is demanded from the fairway and the ball is sitting up pertly.
1969 Jack Nicklaus *The Greatest Game of All* 245:   The fairways were easily the best I've ever played in this country. The ball was always sitting up for you.
1977 William Price Fox *Golf Digest* (Dec.) 72:   No such thing as a bad lie in the fairway. Ball sits up like its on [A]stroturf and you can come down hard.

six-iron *n.* An iron club having loft of 33–36 degrees, lie of 60–61 degrees, and length of 36½ inches, and giving distance of 135–170 yards (men's clubs). Also, a shot played with a six-iron. Alternate name, spade or spade-mashie.

1970 Dan Jenkins *The Dogged Victims of Inexorable Fate* 158: He splintered the flag with a six-iron at the 12th.

skull *also* **scull** *v.trans.* To hit (the ball) at or above its center with the leading edge of an iron club.

1962 Sam Snead *The Education of a Golfer* 167: If the wet sand is packed very hard, look out for the club bouncing up and out fast, which can make you skull the ball.
1968 Buddy Hackett *The Truth About Golf* 39: He took his wedge and sculled the ball.
1977 Raymond Schuessler *Golf Illustrated* (Summer) 23: Aside from the general fears of a sand shot, many golfers fear they might "skull" the ball and send it a mile over the green, perhaps into another trap.

six-iron
Walter Hagen, 1979

sky *v.trans.* To hit (the ball or a shot) very high.

1881 Robert Forgan *The Golfer's Handbook* 9: By the peculiarity of its construction, [the play club] does not *sky* the ball too much, so as to waste its velocity "in the desert air."
1921 Andrew Kirkaldy *Fifty Years of Golf* 81: I skied my tee shot at the sixteenth hole.
1939 William D. Richardson (in Wind *The Complete Golfer* 206): Guldahl's tee-shot was none too long. In fact it was "skied" a bit and on the short side.
1950 Sam Snead *How to Hit a Golf Ball* 72: SKYING—If you're losing too much distance to height, chances are you're teeing the ball too high or using a club with too shallow a face.
1974 *The Golfer's Handbook* 490: In 1921, at Kettering, a drive, badly skied, killed a sparrowhawk.

slice *v. & n.* **1** *v.trans. & intrans.* Of a right-handed player, to play (a ball or shot) so that it curves strongly from left to right owing to sidespin, often having started in a path to the left of the target line; and the converse for a left-handed player.

1890 Horace Hutchinson *Badminton Golf* 105: It is not, of course, very easy to slice the ball just when and how desired.
1912 Harry Vardon *How to Play Golf* 97: At the eighteenth hole, I sliced my second shot.
1931 Joyce & Roger Wethered *The Game of Golf* 54: The art of pulling and slicing at will consists, with every club alike, in altering the angle of the swing with reference to the line of play.
1969 Jack Nicklaus *The Greatest Game of All* 197: I . . . succeeded only in slicing the ball into the creek.

2 *n.* A sliced shot, or a tendency to slice.

1916 P.A. Vaile *The New Golf* 165: In playing for an intentional slice the stance is much more open than for an ordinary drive.
1946 Byron Nelson *Winning Golf* 180: The first step in playing a deliberate slice (flight of ball curves to the right) is to take an *open stance.*

1948 Ben Hogan *Power Golf* 84: Many golfers are plagued with a slice or hook while trying to play a straight shot, but you're not a finished golfer until you control slices and hooks to your own advantage on the golf course.

1971 Henry Longhurst *My Life and Soft Times* 41: . . . this golfing baptism left me with a slice that lasted to the end of my days.

slicer *n.* A player who habitually slices.

1890 Sir Walter Simpson *Badminton Golf* 189: If the slicer of the old school is not prepared to change his stance entirely . . .

1912 Harry Vardon *How to Play Golf* 150: Ten or twelve years ago, the natural slicer was more common than the natural puller; nowadays, the latter predominates.

1963 Bob Rosburg *The Putter Book* 147: I'm a slicer so I just go ahead and allow for it. . . . I hope this gives heart to some weekend slicers. Sure, we should try to hit the ball as straight as possible—perhaps to cut the slice down to a gentle fade.

slump *n. & v.* **1** *n.* A period of bad play.

1927 Robert T. Jones, Jr. & O.B. Keeler *Down the Fairway* 44: . . . he has spent many hours, most of them profane, coaching me when I was in a slump with one club or another.

1975 Henry Cotton *History of Golf* 55: . . . strangely enough this great 9-stroke victory heralded a tragic slump in Vardon's game. He became subject to putting jitters.

2 *v.intrans.* To suffer a decline in play.

1970 Dick Schaap *The Masters* 29: In the final round, Player's touch deserted him. He slumped to a 74.

smother *v. & n.* **1** *v.trans.* To hit down on (the ball or a shot) so that it goes a short distance along the ground.

1927 Robert T. Jones, Jr. & O.B. Keeler *Down the Fairway* 205: . . . a persistent attack of smothering the ball caused me to change after a couple of rounds to a more conservative model [of driver].

1941 Patty Berg *Golf* 79: Some players put a "hook" on the ball by "rolling" their wrists over at impact, but there is a danger of exaggerating this action so much that the club face will be "closed" (turned in) at impact, and "smother" the ball.

1962 Sam Snead *The Education of a Golfer* 18: And sometimes I smothered the shot entirely, driving the ball into the ground just beyond the tee for no reason I could explain.

2 *n.* A smothered shot.

1947 Jim Dante & Leo Diegel *The Nine Bad Shots of Golf* 7: When you come down to the ball from that position, the face also will be closed, or even hooded, and you will get a bad hook or a smother.

snake *n.* *slang* A serpentine putt.

1962 Sam Snead *The Education of a Golfer* 226: . . . it gave me a worse case of the yips than when I'm looking down an old snake of a 6-foot putt with first place at stake.

1969 Jack Nicklaus *The Greatest Game of All* 177: . . . rolled in a 50-foot snake to birdie the 71st.

1971 Tommy Bolt *The Hole Truth* 141: He pitched up on the green, holed one of those caged snakes of his for a birdie.

snap-hook *v.trans.* To hit (the ball or a shot) with an acute hook.

1966 Gary Player *Grand Slam Golf* 69: In fact I hit a bad tee-shot and snap-hooked the ball to the left.

1975 Mark McCormack *Golf Annual* 194: . . . picked his drive clean off the tee and snap-hooked it into the barranca.

socket *n. & v.* **1** *n.* The hosel of an iron clubhead.

1887 Sir Walter Simpson *The Art of Golf* 20: They [irons] have sockets instead of necks.

1907 *Army & Navy Stores Catalogue* 998: Diamond-backed Mashie . . . Blade, 3⅛ in. Socket, 2¾ in.

1976 *Rules of Golf* Appendix II: . . . and

neck or socket shall not be more than 5 inches in length measured from the top of the neck or socket to the sole.

2 *v.trans. & intrans.* To hit (the ball or a shot) with the socket; shank.

1905 Advertisement *Golf Illustrated* (July 21) 77: J.H. Taylor's Mashie prevents that fell and painful disease known as "socketing."
1928 Robert T. Jones, Jr. *Golf Illustrated* (Oct.) 14: . . . a tendency for the left elbow to stray outward and cause the heel of the club to be presented to the ball, a common cause of "socketing."
1971 Henry Longhurst *My Life and Soft Times* 111: . . . he socketed his tee-shot into some impenetrable bracken beside the tee.

3 *n.* A socketed shot.

1971 Henry Longhurst op. cit. 206: Some people have only to read about that other ridiculous golf shot, the socket, in which the ball shoots off, knee high, almost at right angles, to start doing it themselves.

sole *n. & v.* **1** *n.* The bottom surface of an iron or wooden clubhead, which generally rests on the ground at address.

1881 Robert Forgan *The Golfer's Handbook* 11: The "Wooden" and the "Brassy" Niblicks are in every respect the same, except that the latter has a "brass sole."
1913 Horace Hutchinson *Country Life* 248: The piece of brass which is screwed on the sole of a brassey . . . is . . . a worse than useless piece of metal.
1937 Henry Longhurst *Golf* 105: He said that the secret of successful brassie play was to imagine yourself slapping the flat sole of the club on the ground immediately behind the ball.
1952 Henry Cotton *History of Golf in Britain:* He had to use . . . ordinary niblicks with "thin" soles.
1977 Davis Love *Golf Digest* (July) 47: . . . the blade will turn and misdirect the shot. This won't happen with a wood because it has a curved sole.

2 *v.trans.* To ground (a club) at address.

1910 Walter J. Travis (in Wind *The Complete Golfer* 1954, 147): Mr. Holden's tee-

shot found a pot bunker. . . . He unwittingly soled his club.
1916 P.A. Vaile *The New Golf* 11: Many quite good players handicap themselves by their faulty method of soling the club.
1948 Ben Hogan *Power Golf* 139: Of course, there is a penalty for touching the sand or *soling* the club at address [in a hazard].
1977 John Jacobs *Golf Magazine* (July) 56: If you sole the club correctly and aim the leading edge of an iron, or the face of a wood, at the target . . .

sole plate. A metal plate screwed to the sole of a wooden clubhead.

1973 *Bartlett's World Golf Encyclopedia* 364: The first operation is the insertion of the sole plate, which is done by stamping and forming the clubhead to receive the plate. Aluminum plates go into drivers and brassies, brass plates into the fairway woods.

spade *or* **spade-mashie** *n.* **1** A deep-faced iron club, no longer in use, somewhat more lofted than a mashie.

1927 Robert T. Jones, Jr & O.B. Keeler *Down the Fairway* 180: I used either a

sole plate
three-wood, MacGregor Tourney

spade mashie

D. & W. Auchterlonia,
1912

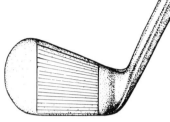

mashie-niblick or its slightly stronger companion, a spade.

1956 Herbert Warren Wind *The Story of American Golf* 168: [Walter Hagen's] mashie-niblick and spade-mashie play, from 70 to 165 yards, was without peer.

2 Alternate name for the number six iron.

spare *v.trans.* To play (a shot or club) with considerably less power than usual.

1898 H.L. Fitzpatrick *The Outing* (Nov.) 140: ... the true golfer should play short, either by sparing the wooden club or by using a cleek.
1908 W.W. Tulloch *Life of Tom Morris* 10: He [Allan Robertson] would, quite unknown to his adversary, pretend to spare a ball, or put extra power into his shot, so as to deceive his opponent as to what the shot required.
1926 P.C. Pulver *Golf Illustrated* (June) 21: The spared shot, calling for the acme of judgment and delicacy of touch, has become little more than a memory.
1929 Charles Herndon *Golf Illustrated* (Apr.) 37: If you must use a club that is too long for the shot, don't spare the shot with it —but grip a little lower.... "Spare the stroke and spoil the shot."

splash *v. & n.* **1** *v.trans. & intrans.* To play (the ball) with an explosion shot, or a similar shot from rough.

1961 Tommy Armour *How to Play Your Best Golf All the Time* 152: Instead of swinging the club smoothly, and splashing the ball out of the sand, the unfortunate fellow scuffed it over the green.

1975 Mark McCormack *Golf Annual* 58: ... dropped the ball into a greenside bunker 180 yards away. Gary was now, of course, on familiar ground, splashed out to ten feet and holed the putt.

2 *n.* A splashed shot.

1977 Davis Love *Golf Digest* (July) 45: From thick rough, you can play a "splash" shot with a wood, just as from a bunker.... You can "splash" the ball out of high grass by making a more descending swing into the grass two to four inches behind the ball.

spoon *n. & v.* [Origin: the loft on early clubfaces, both wood and iron, was most often concave, and sometimes therefore literally resembled the bowl of a spoon.] **1** *n.* Any of a group of early wooden clubs having graduated lofts greater than that of the grassed driver, and correspondingly shorter shafts.

1790 *Hoyle's Games* 288: ... there are six sorts used by good Players; namely ... the Spoon, [used] when [the ball lies] in a Hollow ...
1837 *Encyclopaedia Edinensis* (in Donald Walker *Sports & Games* 179): Another kind is called the Spoon, and differs from the first [grassed driver] chiefly in having the straight edge scooped out so as to form a hollow accommodated to the spherical shape of the ball. This is used for striking the ball out from among long grass.
1857 H.B. Farnie *The Golfer's Manual* 18: Spoons derive their very suggestive name from the great slope in the face of the club head ... various lengths, viz.: —LONG SPOON; MIDDLE SPOON; SHORT SPOON; and BAFFING SPOON.
1881 Robert Forgan *The Golfer's Handbook* 10: Spoons are a rather numerous family. They are employed in a similar way to the Grassed Driver, but do not send the ball so far.... The "Long Spoon" comes into play when the "bad lie" is too much for the Grassed Driver to overcome.... The Long Spoon handle is an inch shorter and considerably stiffer than that of the Grassed Driver, while the head is also heavier and more sloped in the face. The "Middle Spoon" is a very strong club, and is especially useful in "forcing" a ball out of a grassy rut, and in

playing a three-quarters stroke. It is shorter, stiffer, and heavier than its elder brother. The "Short Spoon" . . . is still more sloped in the face, and is employed in similar predicaments when the distance required is not so great.
1902 Advertisement *Golf Illustrated* (Dec. 5) 199: The Mills Aluminium Clubs . . . Driver, Brassie, Long Spoon, Mid Spoon, Short Spoon, Baffy Spoon.

2 *n.* A wooden club of the early 20th century, somewhat more lofted than the brassie.

1912 Harry Vardon *How to Play Golf* 162: Alexander Herd is a master of the spoon.
1921 Andrew Kirkaldy *Fifty Years Of Golf* 153: . . . he has always the courage to take his "spoon" when others take irons.

3 *n.* Alternate name for the number three wood.

1927 Robert T. Jones, Jr. & O.B. Keeler *Down the Fairway* 202: The conventional clubs, according to Victor East, a great designer, are lofted in the following degrees: driver, 79 degrees; brassie, 75; spoon, 71.
1946 Byron Nelson *Winning Golf* 62: The spoon is a highly important club to the average player.
1966 Gary Player *Grand Slam Golf* 28: I hit a drive, a spoon and a wedge.

4 *n.* *Obsolete*. Loft on a clubface.

1857 H.B. Farnie *The Golfer's Manual* 32: The spoon or slope in the face of the head should be greater than that of the grassed driver.
1881 Robert Forgan *The Golfer's Handbook* 16: Many players . . . carry only one Iron for driving and lofting, finding a weapon of medium weight and "spoon" quite equal to the performance of both functions.
[**1895** James P. Lee *Golf in America* 132: It is here that the great value of a spoon-faced club is seen.]

5 *v.trans.* To hit (the ball) with an upward scooping motion.

1887 Sir Walter Simpson *The Art of Golf* 149: Out of a cup one's natural instinct is to try to spoon the ball.
1976 *Rules of Golf* 19.1: The ball shall be fairly struck at with the head of the club and must not be pushed, scraped or spooned.

spooned *adj.* *Obsolete*. (Of a clubface) lofted.

1857 H.B. Farnie *The Golfer's Manual* 34: The head [of an iron] should be deep in the face, . . . it should also be well spooned, curving a little in the centre.
1881 Robert Forgan *The Golfer's Handbook*

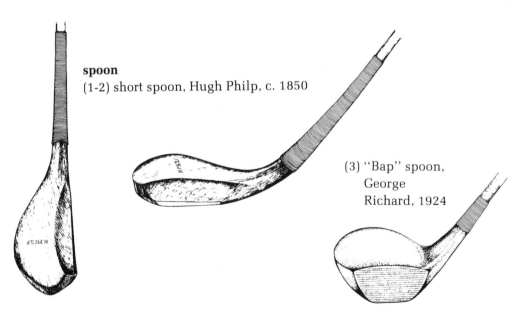

spoon
(1-2) short spoon, Hugh Philp, c. 1850

(3) "Bap" spoon, George Richard, 1924

11: The "Baffing Spoon" . . . is very much spooned out in the face.
1890 Horace Hutchinson *Badminton Golf* 107: Take a club spooned at such an angle that the inclination of the face will compensate for the angle of the hill . . .

spray *v.trans.* To play (a shot or shots) very erratically as to direction.

1954 Robert Trent Jones (in Wind *The Complete Golfer* 310): After playing the circuit layouts where a sprayed tee-shot followed by a wedge left them putting for birdies . . .
1969 Jack Nicklaus *The Greatest Game of All* 92: I started spraying my drives.
1975 Mark McCormack *Golf Annual* 166: . . . his new driver betrayed him by spraying a shot into the trees.

spread-eagle *v.trans.* [Origin: in earlier use in horse-racing meaning "to beat the field utterly"; originally from British army term *spread eagle* = a man tied up to be flogged.] To defeat (a field of golfers in stroke play) utterly.

1890 Horace Hutchinson *Badminton Golf* 356: The following year (1869) he absolutely spread-eagled the field, winning with 157 at Prestwick, no less than 11 strokes better than Bob Kirk, 168.
1926 A.T. Packard *Golf Illustrated* (Oct.) 25: [Hagen] simply spread-eagled a field of golfers including a dozen, yes, a score, any one of whom has a chance of winning any tournament he enters.
[**1961** Eric Brown *Knave of Clubs* 10: At the 551-yard seventeenth Mangrum really had us spreadeagled, for he hit a No. 3 wood to five feet from the pin, and Snead holed the putt for the eagle three.]

spring *n.* Flexibility of a clubshaft.

1881 Robert Forgan *The Golfer's Handbook* 9: The handle or shaft . . . is carefully tapered . . . in order to give it the proper "spring" or degree of suppleness.
1913 Horace Hutchinson *Country Life* (Jan.

11) 69: It [Hugh Philp's baffy] is, indeed, quite rigid, with no spring in it at all, and such as we like in our modern mashies.
1929 *Spalding Athletic Library* 123: Spring—The degree of suppleness in the shaft. Also "whip."
1976 J.C. Jessop *Golf* 17: He will choose shafts that have some spring or whip; the older you are, the whippier shaft you will need.

square[1] *adj. & v.* **1** *adj.*, or **all square** (Of a match) standing even, both sides having won the same number of holes.

1833 George Fullerton Carnegie *The Golfiad* (in *Poems on Golf* 1867, 26):
  Baird plays a trump—we hole at three—
    they stare,
  And miss their putt—so now the match
    is square.
1855 *Unidentified newspaper clipping* (in Allan Robertson's album at the R. & A. 65): After going three rounds, it was found that there was no advantage on either side, the result being all square on the day's play.
1907 Arthur Pottow *Recreation* (Sept.) 123: Travis was 1 up at the eighteenth; they were all square at the twenty-seventh and all square at the thirty-sixth.
1921 Andrew Kirkaldy *Fifty Years of Golf* 91: They were all square and one hole to go.
1970 R. & A. *Decisions on the Rules* (in *The Golfer's Handbook* 1974, 913): Two ladies were playing a Club Championship match and were all square coming to the 18th tee . . .

2 *v.trans.* To bring (a match) to the position of being all square.

1881 Robert Forgan *The Golfer's Handbook* 58: Allan and his companion had managed to square the match at the second last hole.
1907 Arthur Pottow *Recreation* (Sept.) 123: In the morning round Byers finished 2 up and it was only at the thirtieth hole that the match was squared.
1969 Jack Nicklaus *The Greatest Game of All* 17: I managed to settle down and won two of the next four holes to square the match.
1978 Deane McGowen *New York Times* (July 9) S4: The Yuan brothers . . . were 2 up going into the last two holes but lost both as the Merion team squared the match.

square[2] *adj.* **1** (Of a stance) having both feet level with a line parallel to the intended line of play; neither open nor closed.

1887 Sir Walter Simpson *The Art of Golf* 99: . . . the straightness which a 'square' stance gives.
1916 P.A. Vaile *The New Golf* 98: In the square stance, still used by many good golfers, the player stands so that a line across his toes would be nearly parallel to the line from the ball to the hole.
1931 Joyce & Roger Wethered *The Game of Golf* 51: A square stance, or nearly square, is to be recommended in preference to an open . . .
1964 Julius Boros *How to Win at Weekend Golf* 32: The square stance is assumed by placing your feet squarely along the intended line of flight of the ball.
1969 Tom Weiskopf *Go for the Flag* 42: As you can see, I have a square stance.

2 (Of a clubface) aligned at right angles to its swing path, or to the target line; neither open nor closed.

1961 John Stobbs *Tackle Golf* (repr. 1977) 83: In both of them [the hook and the cut] the face is square to the target at impact, but not square to the line of flight of the club-face.
1978 John Jacobs *Golf Magazine* (July) 50: The clubface is square to the swing path (facing in the same direction) but closed to the target line (facing to the left of it).

Stableford *n., usually attributive* [Origin: invented in 1931 by Dr. Frank Stableford of the Wallasey and Royal Liverpool Golf Clubs.] *Chiefly British.* A form of stroke competition in which points are won for scores in relation to a fixed score (or par) at each hole of a round; 1 point for a hole done in one over the fixed score, 2 points for a hole done in the fixed score, 3 for a hole done in one under, 4 for two under, and 5 for three under.

1937 Henry Longhurst *Golf* 273: The Stableford system gains yearly in popularity.
1979 *Golf Illustrated* (Feb. 15) 5: They came up with six sub-par net scores in a heart-warming round that totalled 41 Stableford points which earned them first place in the 18-hole fourball competition.

stance *n.* The standing position assumed by a golfer at address; with particular reference to the position of the feet in relation to the ball and to the intended line of play.

1783 *Laws of Golf* (Aberdeen) (in Clapcott 1935, 32): No person shall be at Liberty to vary or better his Stance in playing, by breaking the Surface of the Green, by placing or removing Stones, Sand or and other Substance; damping his feet with Water excepted.
1858 *Unidentified newspaper clipping* (in Allan Robertson's album at the R. & A. 90): It is thus important to learn the proper 'stance,' or space to keep between the player and the ball.
1890 Sir Walter Simpson *The Art of Golf* 189: If the slicer of the old school is not prepared to change his stance entirely . . .
1911 James Braid *Advanced Golf* 48: There is the question of the square stance or the open one.
1931 Joyce & Roger Wethered *The Game of Golf* 51: It is difficult to prescribe in the matter, as one man's stance may be another man's poison.
1969 Tom Weiskopf *Go For the Flag* 26: There are three basic types of stances—the open . . . the square . . . and the closed.
1976 *Rules of Golf* Definition 29: Taking the "stance" consists in a player placing his feet in position for and preparatory to making a stroke.

steal *n.* *Obsolete.* A long improbable putt that just holes out.

1833 George Fullerton Carnegie *The Golfiad* (in *Poems on Golf* 1867, 23):
Clan plays the like, and wins it, by the gods!
A most disgusting *steal;* . . .
[*Footnote:*] *Steal,* the act of holing the ball contrary to probability.
1857 H.B. Farnie *The Golfer's Manual* 80: STEAL—An unlikely put holed from a distance, but not by a gobble.

1862 Robert Chambers *A Few Rambling Remarks on Golf* 25: . . . in a very few months you will be able to hole in five too, with an occasional 'steal' in four.
1891 *Golf* magazine (Sept. 18) 3: . . . lost their advantage at the tenth hole, owing to Sayers getting down a long steal of twenty yards, and holing in three.

stick[1] *n. Slang.* A golf club. [*Note:* resented by golfers when used by beginners or nongolfers; but long used among themselves as slang.]

1857 H.B. Farnie *The Golfer's Manual* 27: We shall, therefore, take the clubs *seriatim* in this chapter, and explain, in each case, what constitutes a good *stick.* . . . The club makers . . . always aim at turning out good "sticks."
1898 W.G. Van T. Sutphen *The Peripatetic Hazard* (in *The Golficide* 136): Jones simply didn't care to play golf, and he certainly knew nothing about the game. He spoke of the clubs as "sticks."
1921 Andrew Kirkaldy *Fifty Years of Golf* 51: . . . my son Davie put his sticks together to try his fortunes across the water.
1929 *Spalding Athletic Library* 75: Replacing these shafts each spring costs the members far more than the nominal charge of a dollar a month made at most clubs for the care of one's golf sticks.
1934 Grantland Rice *The Fabulous Commodore Heard* (in Wind *The Complete Golfer* 1954, 115): "I swung three times and missed," the Commodore relates, "and so I went back to town and asked at the store for a sack of sticks. 'You mean a bag of golf clubs,' the clerk said. I bought one of every kind of club he had."
1936 H.B. Martin *Fifty Years of American Golf* 348: . . . a golf club [is often] erroneously called a stick.
1953 Jimmy Demaret *My Partner, Ben Hogan* (in Wind *The Complete Golfer* 1954, 258): Watching Hogan pick his club amounts to watching one of the greatest club selectors in golf. He knows precisely what each stick in the bag will do for him.
1968 Buddy Hackett *The Truth About Golf* 38: Irving Mansfield plays a nice stick, as the saying goes.
1969 Jack Nicklaus *The Greatest Game of All* 201: I felt a 9-iron was the right stick.

1971 Tommy Bolt *The Hole Truth* 16: . . . he was signed by Kroydon for very little money, but with the assurance that he would be supplied with golf clubs. "That was my only thought. I needed sticks."

stick[2] *n.* Flagstick.

1969 Jack Nicklaus *The Greatest Game of All* 158: . . . hit a beautiful shot four feet from the stick.
1978 Gordon S. White *New York Times* (July 24) C11: Mrs. Carner, however, began throwing iron shots right at the sticks to move into the lead.

stiff *adv.* So close to the hole that the ensuing putt seems unmissable; dead (def. 1).

1962 Sam Snead *The Education of a Golfer* 88: . . . on the par-5 fourteenth I chipped stiff for a birdie.
1967 Mark McCormack *Arnie* 184: Winnie said, "Well, at least he'll birdie this one." And sure enough Arnold knocked his second shot stiff for a birdie.
1972 Michael Murphy *Golf in the Kingdom* 28: I had always tried for spectacular shots —long drives, approaches stiff to the pin . . .
1978 Lee Trevino *Golf Magazine* (Oct.) 81: "Ain't nothin' going to foul up a golfer's game faster than the other guy hitting it stiff to the pin and slam-dunking ten-footers."

stipulated round. (The playing of) eighteen holes of a course in their correct sequence.

1976 *Rules of Golf* Definition 30: The number of holes in a stipulated round is 18 unless a smaller number is authorised by the Committee. In match play only, the Committee may, for the purpose of settling a tie, extend the stipulated round to as many holes as are required for a match to be won.

stop *n.* Backspin, causing a pitched ball to stop dead or nearly so on impact.

1912 Harry Vardon *How to Play Golf* 161:

He introduces an enormous amount of "stop" into his lofted shots.

1941 Patty Berg *Golf* 51: Learn how to put "stop" (with "bite" or backspin) or "run" (with "over-spin") on the ball.

1962 Sam Snead *The Education of a Golfer* 156: The pin was 40 feet away, with little putting surface between the trap exit and cup. I needed quick altitude. Then I needed fast "stop," or backspin.

straight *adj.*   Able to hit consistently straight drives.

1894 *Baily's Magazine* (Apr.) 282: Rolland . . . has always been regarded solely as a powerful and straight driver.

1913 Bernard Darwin *Country Life* (May 10) 684: The straightest drivers . . . come from genuine links whereon they have had plenty of room to slash out boldly in their youth.

1967 Dave Thomas *Modern Golf* 9: Rightly or wrongly, I have earned a reputation for being the longest, straightest driver in the world today.

1975 Mark McCormack *Golf Annual* 82: Player was almost monotonously straight.

straightaway *adj. & n.*   (A hole) having a straight fairway.

1956 Herbert Warren Wind *The Story of American Golf* 363: Tony teed up nervously on the 16th hole, a straightaway 439-yard four.

1973 *Bartlett's World Golf Encyclopedia* 265: There are straightaways, like the par-4 10th, a 345-yarder that narrows at one point like an hourglass.

straight-faced *adj.*   (Of a club) having no loft on the face, or relatively little loft.

1862 Robert Chambers *A Few Rambling Remarks on Golf* 15: . . . but some players prefer putting with a straight-faced iron club, called a putting-iron.

1912 Harry Vardon *How to Play Golf* 99: My own running-up mashie is my mongrel club. It is nearly straight-faced.

1931 Roger Wethered *The Game of Golf* 58: In a lesser degree the straighter-faced clubs

cannot prevent the ball spinning backwards.

1948 Ben Hogan *Power Golf* 155: Furthermore, on a wet day you can throw away your brassie and one-iron. It is almost impossible to get the proper flight on the ball with such straight-faced clubs.

1961 Eric Brown *Knave of Clubs* 88: I had decided to discard my centre-shafted putter on the last day, for I thought it was too straight-faced to suit the greens.

strategic *adj.*   (Of golf course architecture) designed to challenge a thinking response from the player rather than merely to punish bad shots.

1926 A. Mackenzie letter to *Golf Illustrated* (Dec.) 35: In regard to my reference to a "penal" and [a] "strategic" school of golf architecture . . .

1931 T. Simpson *The Game of Golf* 166: The strategic architect, in a word, hides his hand as much as he possibly can, and likes to keep the scratch player guessing.

1954 Robert Trent Jones (in Wind *The Complete Golfer* 1954, 300): This is the essence of strategic architecture: to encourage initiative, reward a well-played, daring stroke more than a cautious stroke, and yet to insist that there must be planning and honest self-appraisal behind the daring.

1969 Jack Nicklaus *The Greatest Game of All* 190: [Augusta National] . . . one of the most testing and interesting inland courses in the world, strategic golf at its finest.

1977 Tom Watson *Golf Magazine* (Aug.) 32: . . . the trapping is both beautiful and strategic.

strike off *phr.v.*   To drive off from the tee.

1744 *Articles & Laws in Playing at Golf*: 3. You are not to change the ball which you strike off the tee.

1783 *Laws* (in Clapcott 1935, 31): III. The party gaining a Hole shall have the Privilege of striking off first.

1833 George Fullerton Carnegie *The Golfiad* (in *Poems on Golf* 1867, 24):

Reader, attend! And learn to play at Goff;
The lord of Saddell and myself strike off!

1899 *Golf Illustrated* (June 16) 11: Harry Vardon . . . drew a gallery of two or three hundred spectators when he struck off at half-past eleven.

1976 Joseph C. Dey *Golf Rules in Pictures* 32: In a threesome or a foursome, the partners strike off alternately from the teeing grounds . . .

stroke *n. & v.* **1** *n.* A player's action in striking at the ball with a club, counted to the player's score whether successful or not.

1744 *Articles & Laws in Playing at Golf* 11: If you draw your Club, in order to Strike and proceed so far in the Stroke, as to be bringing down your Club; if then, your Club shall break, in any way, it is to be accounted a Stroke.
1790 *Hoyle's Games* 289: . . . the Party who gets their Ball in by the fewest Number of Strokes are the Victors.
1890 Horace Hutchinson *Badminton Golf* 236: Each stroke must be calculated with a view to its effect on the next stroke.
1915 Alexander H. Revell *Pro & Con of Golf* 2: He should first become well acquainted with the brassie, cleek, mid-iron, mashie, and putter, and as expert as possible with all the strokes made with these clubs.
1976 *Rules of Golf* Definition 31: A "stroke" is the forward movement of the club made with the intention of fairly striking at and moving the ball.

2 *n.* The score of a stroke added to a player's score as a penalty or deducted from it as a handicap allowance.

1744 *Articles & Laws in Playing at Golf* 8: If you should lose your Ball, by its being taken up, or any other way, you are to go back to the spot, where you struck last, and drop another Ball, And allow your adversary a Stroke for the Misfortune.
1824 *Rules of the Thistle Golf Club* 48: . . . the player is entitled to drop it behind the hole, and play with an Iron, without losing a stroke.
1976 *Rules of Golf* Definition 24: A "penalty stroke" is one added to the score of a side under certain Rules.

3 *v.trans.* To play (the ball) with a smooth, fluid motion, especially in putting.

1931 Joyce Wethered *The Game of Golf* 94: The older players [in putting] . . . had peculiar difficulties to contend with, which entailed considerable skill in cutting, pulling, imparting top or drag, or the like to the ball. As a rule, they definitely struck the ball rather than stroked it.
1970 Dick Schaap *The Masters* 116: Knowing he must charge now to get in contention, he strokes his iron boldly for the pin.
1977 Larry Dennis *Golf Digest* (July) 55: Determining how hard to stroke a putt to roll it a given distance comes only with practice.

strokemaker *n.* A shotmaker.

1946 Frank Moran *Golfers' Gallery* 160: . . . illustrates just how wonderfully consistent a stroke-maker Vardon was in his heyday.

stroke play. Golf in which the score is by the total of strokes for the round or rounds, and in which numerous players can compete together.

1907 Alexander Herd in Leach *Great Golfers in The Making* 121: I won two first prizes of £20 each, one for stroke and one for match play.
1926 A. Linde Fowler *Golf Illustrated* (Oct.) 13: It is significant that the Atlanta marvel has won the British and American Open championships this year and has been beaten in the British and American amateurs. He is still more the supreme master of stroke play than he is of match.
1977 George Peper *Golf Magazine* (Aug.) 42: But stroke play is usually limited to tournaments and club-wide events. Most weekend golfers compete at match play.

stylist *n.* A golfer whose swing is admired as correct, consistent, and esthetically pleasing.

1896 *Baily's Magazine* (July) 78: [Vardon] is young—somewhere about twenty-four—small in stature, with a neat, clean style, suggestive of that great stylist of his day, Bob Pringle.
1936 H.B. Martin *Fifty Years of American*

Golf 360: Jones was a stylist, with scarcely a blemish in a swing that appeared to the onlookers to be absolutely perfect.

1946 Percy Boomer *On Learning Golf* 196: It is an excellent thing to be a stylist, if your style is supported and molded by a good golfing temperament.

stymie *n. & v.* [Origin: Scottish *stymie, stimy,* or *steimy,* probably a special usage of *stymie* = "short-sighted person." The exact nature of the usage poses difficulties. Jamieson (1808) records a slang expression *a blind stymie* = "an awkwardly peering half-blind person." It seems probable that the reference is to the blocked ball, which (figuratively) is "blind," i.e., "cannot see" the hole; or to the blocked player, who would often have got down near the balls and peered from side to side looking for a line to the hole.] **1** *n.* *Obsolete.* A situation in match play on the putting green in which one side's ball blocks the line of the other side's ball to the hole, and the latter must attempt to play past, around, or over the blocking ball. The stymie was abolished in 1951 (see Rule 35).

1834 *Rules of the Musselburgh Golf Club* (in Clapcott 1935, 66): XIII. With regard to stimies the ball nearest the hole if within six inches shall be lifted.
1842 *Chambers' Edinburgh Journal* (Oct. 8) 298: He plays like an adept, and places his ball right between the other and the hole—in the language of the links, a *stymie.*
1858 *Rules* (R. & A.) (in Clapcott 1935, 107): All holes must be played out on medal days, and no stimies allowed.
1862 Robert Chambers *A Few Rambling Remarks on Golf* 17: It is not considered quite fair to play *intentionally* so as to lay a steimy.
1881 Robert Forgan *The Golfer's Handbook* 32: . . . if your opponent's ball lies in the line of your "put" at a distance of more than six inches from your ball, you are obliged to play without it being removed. This predicament is called a "stimy."
1897 Horace Hutchinson *Country Life* (Apr. 10) 388: "I tell you, sir," the colonel con-

cluded, in a perfect paroxysm, "that the man who would abolish the stimy would willingly break any law, either human or divine."
1926 William D. Richardson *Golf Illustrated* (Oct.) 38: Bobby squared the match by virtue of laying Von Elm a stymie for the second time. This was no partial one and George had to try to jump it and failed.
1941 Henry Longhurst *Failure of a Mission* (in Wind *The Complete Golfer* 1954, 202): . . . hacked their ball onto the green and followed it up by lofting it into the hole from seven feet over a stymie.
1962 Sam Snead *The Education of a Golfer* 45: In 1938 at Shawnee-on-the-Delaware, Jimmy Hines had me the next thing to whipped when we reached the fourteenth green, where I laid him a stymie. In those days we played all stymies.

2 *v.trans.* *Obsolete.* To block (a player) with a stymie.

1851 *Unidentified newspaper clipping* (in Allan Robertson's album at the R. & A. 40): Tom having retained his hole a-head all the time, and indeed, but for being *stimied* by Dunn's ball, he would have been further above his opponent.
1892 Andrew Lang *A Song of Life and Golf* in *Golfing Papers* 28:
And aye, where'er my ba' may row
Some limmer stimies me!
1916 P.A. Vaile *The New Golf* 59: . . . even when one is stymied, in the great majority of cases one can get some assistance from the green and so get into the hole around the obstructing ball.
1926 Joshua Crane *Sports Illustrated* 16: . . . four times out of five it is the outcome of bad play on the part of the one who is or who persuades himself that he is stymied.
1962 Sam Snead *The Education of a Golfer* 207: Another time, I stymied Runyon, and what did he do but pitch over me with a wedge.

3 *v.trans.* *Informal.* To block (a player) with an obstacle such as a tree.

1964 Tony Lema *Golfer's Gold* 50: I was partially stymied by a tree.
1969 Jack Nicklaus *The Greatest Game of All* 203: . . . a 2-iron which I had to hook around the pine tree on the left side of the fairway which stymied my direct route to the green.

1975 Mark McCormack *Golf Annual* 77: It was a hook, not vicious, but wide enough to stymie him behind a bush in the rough.

sudden death. A form of playoff in which the tied players play further holes, the winner being the one who first wins a hole.

1971 Tommy Bolt *The Hole Truth* 165: I know that the guys out there would rather play an eighteen-hole playoff for some of that big prize money than a sudden-death playoff. **1977** John S. Radosta *New York Times* (Aug. 15) 37: Lanny Wadkins ... won the Professional Golfers' Association championship today on the third hole of a sudden-death playoff with Gene Littler.
Note. There have been suggestions that the term be changed to "sudden victory."

superintendent *n.* An official in charge of the maintenance of a course.

1978 Jolee Edmondson *Golf Magazine* (Oct.) 53: Superintendent Paul Ortiz ... a zealous sculptor of grass, sand, wind and trees who studied under Robert Trent Jones, chatters on about the woes and ecstasy of golf course maintenance.

supinate *v.trans.* [*Origin:* physiological term, properly meaning "to turn the hand and forearm over from the prone position (palm downward) to the supine position (palm upward) by rotating the radius about the ulna"; from Latin *supīnāre* = "to make supine," from *supīnus* = "supine, facing upward."] To rotate (the wrist) so that the palm of the hand faces upward.

1957 Ben Hogan *Five Lessons* 101: Every good golfer supinates his left wrist [at the moment of impact]. **1968** Alastair Cochran & John Stobbs *The Search for the Perfect Swing* 58: First the 90-degree turn of the forearm continues freely through impact, so that the forearm begins to roll the other way, with the back of the hand turning now towards the ground ('supinating').

supination *n.* Rotation of the wrist so that the palm of the hand faces upward.

1957 Ben Hogan *Five Lessons* 104: Supination [of the left wrist at the moment of impact] builds distance and accuracy in other ways.

swale *n.* [*Origin:* an old dialectal word in various parts of both Britain and North America, originally meaning a cool hollow place; probably brought into golf in the United States.] A gently contoured depression or hollow on a fairway.

1929 A.W. Tillinghast *Golf Illustrated* (June) 43: However a slight swale in front may deceive the player to the belief that a shorter club may reach. **1978** Roland Rudosky in *Golf Magazine* (Oct.) 53: "You know, that little course of yours is all carry. Swales all over it."

sweet *adj.* Esthetically satisfying. Applied to various golfing experiences and phenomena, especially the feel of a perfectly hit shot.

1890 Lord Wellwood *Badminton Golf* 38: Again, what sweeter sound is there to the golfer's ear than the metallic ring of the iron which accompanies a well-played approach shot! **1919** Robert K. Risk *Songs of the Links* 12: "How sweet a well-hit Second Shot!" think some ... **1929** Advertisement *Golf Illustrated* (Apr.) 8: Perhaps, like thousands of golfers, you have found that the steel shaft has a very sweet feel in a wooden club—and a very sour feel in an iron. **1975** Henry Cotton *History of Golf* 126: Sam Snead ... The sweetest swinger of a club that has ever been seen.

sweet spot *or* **sweetspot** *n.* The perfect hitting spot on a clubface.

1929 *Spalding's Athletic Library* n.p.: Every golf club has a "Sweet Spot." It is that one spot on the face of the club which gives greatest distance to the ball and sweetest feel to the shot.

1977 Bruce Devlin *Golf Magazine* (July) 22: "Because the weight was so low on these clubs it was hard to tell whether I had hit the ball on the sweetspot or to the toe or heel side of the sweetspot."

swing *n. & v.* **1** *n.* The characteristic movement of the body and arms by which a golf stroke is made, commencing with the backswing and proceeding to the downswing and the follow-through.

[**1687** Thomas Kincaid *Diary* (Jan. 26) (in *Book of the Old Edinburgh Club* XXVII, 1949, 136): I found that seeing the swinge of your body by the turning it upon your legge is the largest and strongest motion, therfor it most begin first and the turning at the small of the back most only second it, and then most follow the motion at the shoulders.]

1823 James Grierson *Delineations of St. Andrews* 221: But an idea of its difficulty may be formed by considering the smallness of the object struck compared with the largeness of the circle described in the swing round with the club.

1867 *The First Hole at St. Andrews* (in *Poems on Golf* 32):
He whirls his club to catch the proper
    swing . . .

1881 Robert Forgan *The Golfer's Handbook* 24: A truly scientific swing is very difficult of attainment, but, once acquired, it is the distinctive mark of the accomplished golfer.

1895 James P. Lee *Golf in America* 126: The upward swing, when compared with the force of the downward swing, should be more deliberate.

1896 *Baily's Magazine* (March) 237: Fernie teaches "the perfect swing," not "the perfect hit." His system has reference to style rather than to play itself.

1912 Harry Vardon *How to Play Golf* 161: Taylor can always be watched with advantage; his swing is beautifully under control.

1919 Robert K. Risk *Songs of The Links* 13:
Myself when young did eagerly frequent
Club-makers' shops, and heard great
    Argument
Of Grip and Stance and Swing . . .

1931 Joyce & Roger Wethered *The Game of Golf* 40: The full swing is the most artistic movement in the whole field of golf.

1952 Henry Cotton *History of Golf in Britain:* . . . the steel shaft had made golf an easier game. Only one swing was necessary, and I had to find out as soon as possible the swing which would suit me.

1969 Jack Nicklaus *The Greatest Game of All* 21: It is an inexhaustible subject, the golf swing.

2 *v.trans. & intrans.* To move (the body, the arms, and the club) in the swing.

swinger *n.* **1** A performer of the swing; a golfer.

1890 Horace Hutchinson *Badminton Golf* 56: A slow swinger will incline to compensate for the want of velocity by the increase in weight.

1977 Gordon S. White *New York Times* (June): There were 244 good and bad swingers who played in a pouring rain yesterday.

2 A golfer whose fluid coordination and consistency of swing is the essence of his or her game.

1931 Roger Wethered *The Game of Golf* 60: With all the greatest swingers in the history of golf—taking Harry Vardon and Mr. Bobby Jones as supreme examples . . .

1946 Bernard Darwin *British Golf* 48: [Women] are essentially swingers rather than hitters and that is a virtue.

1964 Julius Boros *How to Win at Weekend Golf* 35: . . . the most popular and successful golf swings were those of Sam Snead and Ben Hogan. Both were "swingers." They moved the club back from and through the ball with little or no apparent effort, yet drove the shots farther than have most professional golfers before or since.

swingweight *n.* A measurement of the weight of a club, in which the weight of the shaft (including the grip) and that of the head are correlated, and which is generally specified as a constant for all the clubs in a particular set.

[**1929** Advertisement *Golf Illustrated* (Apr.) 67: For some time it has been noticed that

swingweight

The Lorhythmic swinging weight scale

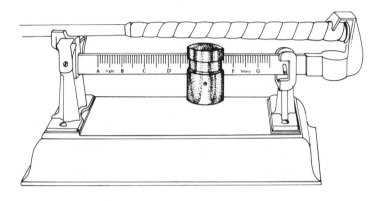

Golf Clubs should be built in related *balance* and *swinging weight* one with another.]

1977 *Golf Illustrated* (Summer) 36: Swingweight is the relationship of weight of the club components, grip, shaft, and head, to one another, and is measured on a scale for that particular purpose. Designations of swingweight range from A–O, the lightest, to E–9, the heaviest. Most golfers fall into the C and D categories.

1977 *Golf Magazine* (Aug.) 25: Kenneth Smith, the man who pioneered the swing-weight scale and the manufacture of custom-made golf clubs, died July 12 in Austin, Tex. at age 76. . . . In 1926 Smith was the first to employ the Lorhythmic Swingweight Scale to match clubs, advancing the process from guesswork to precise measurement.

swipe *v. & n.* [*Origin:* probably a variant of *sweep* = "to make a swinging, sweeping blow."] *Obsolete?* **1** *v.trans. & intrans.* To play (the ball) a full shot, especially a powerful one, and especially from the tee.

1833 George Fullerton Carnegie *The Golfiad* (in *Poems on Golf* 1867, 23): Sir David swipes sublime! Into the quarry!

1842 *Chambers' Edinburgh Journal* (Oct. 8) 297: Some are so great in driving, or *swiping*, as this feat is variously called, as to make the ball go to a distance not easily credited.

1891 J.C. Fraser *Golf* magazine (Mar. 26) 19: The rival ba' is swipit frae the tee.

2 *n.* A full shot, especially a powerful one, and especially from the tee.

1881 Robert Forgan *The Golfer's Handbook* 61: SWIPE.—A full driving stroke.

1908 W.W. Tulloch *Life of Tom Morris* 12: It was Allan's honour—a lovely swipe from the tee.

1921 Hugh Bennett in Andrew Kirkaldy *Fifty Years of Golf* 5:
Andra sune came to fame
As a dab at the game,
His swipe was a swift daisy-cutter; . . .

T

takeaway n.   Backswing.

1961 John Stobbs *Tackle Golf* (repr. 1977)
41:   Many professionals will tell you that the
take-away of the club, the back-swing should
be straight back from the ball with the clubface kept 'square.'
1969 Jack Nicklaus *The Greatest Game of
All* 260:   The harder I want to hit the ball,
the slower I start my takeaway.

tap in *phr.v.*   To hole a very short putt.

1970 Dick Schaap *The Masters* 186:   . . .
Billy Casper putts to within a foot of the hole
and taps in for his par.

tap-in n.   A very short putt.

1964 Julius Boros *How to Win at Weekend
Golf* 11:   Some people will remember a 28-
putt round I had at Augusta, but most of these
were tap-ins—my chips were close to the
cup, and I didn't have long putts to make.
1977 *Woman Golfer* (Nov.) 28:   You can afford to laugh when you have a two-stroke
lead in the U.S. Open and only a tap-in remaining.

tee n. & v.   [Origin: Old Scottish *teaz*
(noun and verb) and *tie* (verb); further
origin unknown.]   **1 (a)** n.   A small
heap of sand used to elevate a ball for
driving.

1673 *Wedderburn's Vocabulary* [(in O.E.D.)
giving Latin equivalents for golfing terms]:
Statumen, the Teaz [Latin *statumen* = a support or prop].
1744 *Articles & Laws in Playing at Golf:*   2.
Your Tee must be upon the Ground.   3. You
are not to change the Ball which you strike
off from the Tee.
1776 *Rules* (in Clapcott 1935, 28):   2.—
Your Tee must be upon the ground and un-
connected with any conductor or leader to
the ball.
1815 *Regulations* (Aberdeen) (in Clapcott,
50):   1. . . . The Tee must be placed on the
ground, not nearer than 4 yards of the hole.
1819 *Blackwood's Edinburgh Magazine*
(Sept.) (in Clark *Golf: A Royal & Ancient
Game* 1875, 126):
> Whilst trotting club-man follows fast
>   behind,
> Prepared with ready hand the "tees" to
>   lay . . .

1823 James Grierson *Delineations of St. Andrews* 224:   Their business is to carry clubs
and balls, and to place the ball upon the *tee,*
as it is called, or in the best position for making a good stroke at the first setting off from a
hole.
1834 *Rules* (Musselburgh) (in Clapcott, 65):
II. . . . The turf of the putting green shall not
be raised up for a tee . . . And no Cady shall
be employed who does not carry a bag with
moist sand or clay for the tees.
1890 *Badminton Golf* 449:   *Tee* the pat of
sand on which the ball is placed for the first
stroke at each hole.

1912 Harry Vardon *How to Play Golf* 46: Very few caddies make good tees. The ball should be just perched on the sand so that none of the latter can be seen; . . .
1922 P.G. Wodehouse *The Rough Stuff* (in *The Clicking of Cuthbert* repr. 1956, 155): Silently Ramsden Waters made a tee and placed thereon a new ball.

(b) n. *Obsolete*. Mud on the course regarded as a hazard.

1773 *Regulations* (in Clapcott, 23): III. To prevent Disputes in taking up Balls from water, every Ball taken from water or Tee, either upon the Green or a hazard, such ball shall be teed behind and lose one.
1775 *Laws* (in Clapcott, 25): 5. If your Ball is half covered or more with water, you are at liberty to take it out, tee it behind the Hazard, and play it with any Club, allowing your adversary a stroke; And if on Tee, you may take it up, and tee it behind the Tee, losing one, or play it off the Tee, in the option of the Player.

2 n. Any of various reusable or disposable devices on which a ball is placed for driving.

tee

1895 W. Dalrymple *Handbook to Golf* 97: You have india-rubber tees, made captive by a cord, and others anchored by an iron pin; others of paper, of card-board, of goodness knows what.
1907 *Army & Navy Stores Catalogue* 1003: India-rubber Golf Tees. . . . Paper Golf Tees. Will be found very serviceable in places where sand is not easily obtainable.
1926 Advertisement *Golf Illustrated* (Sept.) 46: "Yes sir, the team I captained in England all used the MORLEY YELLO TEE." Signed, Walter Hagen.
1970 Charles Price *Golf* 14: The golf ball

is usually placed upon a "tee," a wooden peg about the size of a toothpick.

3 v.trans. & intrans. To place (a ball) on a tee.

1673 *Wedderburn's Vocabulary* [see 1 (a) above]: *Statumina pilam arena*, Teaz your ball on the sand. [Latin *statuminā* = "you should support," imperative of *statumināre* = "to support"; *pila* = "ball"; *arena* = "sand."]
1687 Thomas Kincaid *Diary* (Jan. 20) (in *Book of the Old Edinburgh Club* XXVII, 1949, 133): The way to learn this [i.e., hitting the ball cleanly, without letting the clubhead touch the ground] is to tie your ball at first pretty high from the ground.
1744 *Articles & Laws in Playing at Golf*: 1. You must Tee your Ball, within a Club's length of the Hole. . . . 5. If your Ball comes among Watter, or any Wattery filth, you are at liberty to take out your Ball and bringing it behind the hazard and Teeing it, you may play it with any Club, and allow your Adversary a stroke.
1773, 1775 See quots. in **1(b)** above.
1815 *Regulations* (Aberdeen) (in Clapcott, 50): 1. No sand to be taken for teeing within 10 yards of the hole.
1867 *Golfing Song* (in *Poems on Golf*) 78:
    But, laddie, tak a club in han',
      Then tee and drive the ba'; . . .
1888 *Chambers's Journal* (May 26): . . . he tapped with the handle of his driver the spot he wished to tee on.
1933 A.G. Macdonnell *England, Their England* 137: He teed his ball on a pinch of sand with a dexterous twist of his fingers and thumb.
1975 Mark McCormack *Golf Annual* 194: Panasiuk, who tees his ball higher than most professionals . . .
1976 *Rules of Golf* Definition 32: In "teeing," the ball may be placed on the ground or on sand or other substance in order to raise it off the ground.

4 n. Teeing ground.

1842 *Rules* (R. & A.) (in Clapcott, 77): The game commences by each party playing off a ball from a place called the *tee*, near the first hole.
1897 *Country Life* (June 19) 656: The tees were put back to their extremest limits.
1931 T. Simpson *The Game of Golf* 207: I have never yet seen a course where the tees

were kept in really good condition—no doubt on the ground of expense.

1954 Robert Trent Jones (in Wind *The Complete Golfer*, 1954, 299): Another feature of Peachtree is exceptional flexibility, brought about through the extreme length of the tees. ... In some cases the tees are as much as eighty yards long.

1977 *Golf Magazine* (June) 96: It measures 6,615 yards from the back tees and 5,361 from the ladies' tees.

5 off (*or* **from**) **the tee(s)** *phr.* In making tee shots.

1901 Findlay S. Douglas *The Outing* (June) 360: Vardon excels off the tee and through the green, but Taylor offsets this advantage with his superior short game.

1948 Gene Sarazen (in Ben Hogan *Power Golf* 55): "In my prime I was extremely wild off the tee."

1977 Deane McGowen *New York Times* (June 17) A18: Mrs. Bower, a steady player, won because her rival was often erratic off the tees or with second shots.

1978 Neil Singelais *Boston Globe* (July 29) 19: ... combined an outstanding round from the tees along with a solid putting game to put it all together.

tee-box n. A box containing sand for making tees, formerly placed at a teeing-ground.

1907 Harold Hilton *My Golfing Reminiscences* 143: I relieved the tension by throwing my putter at the teeing-box.

1922 P.G. Wodehouse *Sundered Hearts* (in *The Clicking of Cuthbert* repr. 1956, 70): Mortimer sat down on the tee-box, and buried his face in his hands.

1951 S.L. McKinley *Francis Drives Himself In* (in Wind *The Complete Golfer* 1954, 122): ... at the teebox a microphone had been placed to pick up the click of club meeting ball.

teed *adj.* or **teed up.** (Of a ball at rest through the green) lying supported and accessible.

1887 Sir Walter Simpson *The Art of Golf* 139: Be cautious with a teed ball in a shallow sand bunker.

1931 Roger Wethered *The Game of Golf* 79: If it is well teed up, either on the fairway or on a tuft of grass ...

1952 Henry Cotton *History of Golf in Britain*: Even from a very teed-up lie in sand, the modern professional will blast the ball on to the green.

1971 Henry Longhurst *My Life and Soft Times* 204: ... you can find yourself tee-ed up on the fairway with a quite impossible shot to follow.

teeing ground. The place from which the play of a hole is begun, now defined under the rules (*see* quot. 1976).

1867 R.H. Smith *The Golfer's Year Book* 79: ... the luck of the Champion in holing the Station hole in a single stroke from the teeing-ground of the "green hollow" ...

1912 Harry Vardon *How to Play Golf* 32: Gorse, bracken, and other flora of the heath or common, stretching from teeing-ground to green, constitute good guards for short holes.

1946 Bernard Darwin *British Golf* 32: ... how he disdained a tee and would throw his ball down on the teeing-ground with a noble gesture and drive it from where it lay.

1976 *Rules of Golf* Definition 33: The "teeing ground" is the starting place for the hole to be played. It is a rectangular area two club-lengths in depth, the front and the sides of which are defined by the outside limits of two tee-markers.

tee off *phr.v.* To play a tee shot.

1891 *Golf* magazine (Sept. 25) 20: The opening ceremony was performed by Lady Egerton of Tatton teeing off the ball from the Knutsford end of the park, and declaring the links open.

1977 Dave Anderson *New York Times* (May 26) D15: He was about to tee off in a celebrity tournament ...

tee-shot n. A shot played from a tee, or from a teeing ground.

1858 *Unidentified newspaper clipping* (in Allan Robertson's album at the R. & A. 88): Brown places himself opposite his ball, grasps his play-club . . . swings the club slowly back and sharply down, and has 'struck off his tee-shot.'

1890 Lord Wellwood *Badminton Golf* 38: We have already touched on the topped tee-shot.

1915 Alexander H. Revell *Pro & Con of Golf* 17: Of course, the drive is what is termed a "tee shot"; that is, one can use a "pinch of sand" as the Scotchman said, to lift his ball from the ground.

1931 Joyce & Roger Wethered *The Game of Golf* 45: The ideal tee shot aims at gaining good direction, plenty of run, and the full application of the player's power.

1946 Sam Snead *How to Play Golf* n.p.: The tee-shot is probably the most important in golf, for a good start is half the battle.

1977 George Peper *Scrambling Golf* 41: . . . discovered that his teeshot had come to rest on top of a coiled-up snake.

tee up *phr.v.* To place a ball on a tee; start a game.

1902 Horace Hutchinson *Country Life* (Nov. 15) 615: . . . teed up his ball and drove it gallantly towards the faces of a couple approaching.

1946 Frank Moran *Golfers' Gallery* 22: Hagen himself told me that he never teed-up in a big event with less confidence.

1977 *Golf Magazine* (Aug.) 49: Mark Lye is a 24-year-old Californian who will tee it up in this year's World Series because he won the Australian P.G.A. Order of Merit.

tempo *n.* Control of timing in the swing.

1969 Jack Nicklaus *The Greatest Game of All* 182: I think of tempo as the rate of speed throughout the golf swing.

Texas wedge. [*Origin:* said to be from its use by Ben Hogan and other Texans.] A shot played with a putter from outside the putting green.

1969 Tom Scott & Geoffrey Cousins *The Golf Immortals* 255: . . . so confident in fact that on not a few occasions he [Nicklaus] uses his putter from off the green. This shot used

to be referred to and is still referred to in some quarters as the "Texas wedge."

1977 John P. May *Golf Digest* (Aug.) 101: Menne used only 99 putts for 72 holes . . . Texas wedges, putts from the fringe, were not counted.

thin *adv. & adj.* (Hitting the ball) with the clubhead traveling on too high a line, catching the ball above center.

1969 R. & A. *Decisions on the Rules* (in *The Golfer's Handbook* 1974, 957): A player plays a 'thin' shot from a bunker, walks up to his ball to see if he has cut it . . .

1977 Hubert Green *Golf Magazine* (July) 37: The only way I can mishit the shot is to catch it a little thin, and that kind of shot—sort of a half-top—isn't too harmful.

three-putt *v.trans. & intrans.* To take three putts on (a green or hole).

1970 Tony Jacklin *Jacklin* 27: I bogied the fifth, three putting from no more than six yards.

1977 *New York Times* (June 27) 37: But he three-putted the 18th for a bogey.

three-ball match. **1** A match in which three players play one ball each, and each is playing a match against each of the other two.

1839 *Rules* (Hon. Company of Edinburgh Golfers) (in Clapcott 1935, 69): In a Three-ball match, the Ball nearest the hole, and within the prescribed distance, must be lifted, if the third party require it, whether the Player does so or not.

1921 Andrew Kirkaldy *Fifty Years of Golf* 153: Herd was playing a three-ball match with Mr. John Ball, of Hoylake, and me.

1976 *Rules of Golf* 40.2: In a three-ball match, each player is playing two distinct matches.

2 A best-ball match between one player and two playing as partners.

1890 Horace Hutchinson *Badminton Golf* 229: . . . the three-ball match. These matches are of two kinds, that wherein each plays each, and that wherein two are in combination against a third, though each play his individual ball. . . . The latter plays against the best ball, as it is called, of the other two.

three-iron n.   An iron club having loft of 23–25 degrees, lie of 57–59 degrees, and length of 38 inches, and giving distance of 165–200 yards (men's clubs). Also, a shot played with a three-iron. Alternate name, mid-mashie.

1967 Dave Thomas *Modern Golf* 15:   It was very wet and cold, and when I played a three iron shot from a steeply angled uphill lie the club struck in the ground, although the shot was perfect, and I felt my back being wrenched.

three-quarter shot.   A shot made with a reduced swing, somewhat less than that for a full shot.

1889 Alexander Lawson *Letters on Golf* 26: The approach shot is ordinarily a three-quarter, or half, or wrist shot.

three-iron

Walter Hagen, 1979

1915 "A Wandering Player" in Revell *Pro & Con of Golf* 45:   "I had a strong feeling that he won his fourth championship at Deal a few years ago as much on his half and three-quarter iron shots as anything else."

1954 H.A. Murray *The Golf Secret* (repr. 1976) 81:   . . . if you wish to play a three-quarter, half, or quarter shot, do not try to do so by limiting the distance that your hands or the club head travel.

1977 Dave Hill *Golf Digest* (July) 107:   He is very weak pitching the ball with a three-quarter swing. The three-quarter shot is a feel shot.

threesome n.   A match in which one player plays against a side consisting of two players who play one ball with alternate strokes.

1976 *Rules of Golf* Definitions 28:   Threesome: A match in which one plays against two, and each side plays one ball.

three-wood n.   A wood club having loft of 15–17 degrees, lie of 55–57 degrees, and length of 42 inches, and giving dis-

three-wood

Ben Hogan, 1979

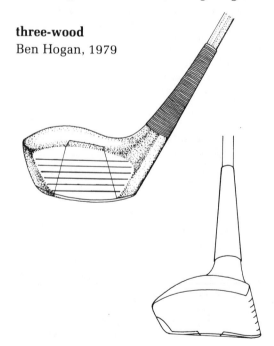

tance of 210–250 yards (men's clubs). Also, a shot played with a three-wood. Alternate name, spoon.

1970 Dick Schaap *The Masters* 94: Jack Nicklaus . . . takes a three-wood to go for the green with his second shot.
1975 Henry Cotton *History of Golf* 146: His second stroke, a three-wood over the water, came down 18 feet from the pin.

through the green *phr.* **1** *Obsolete.* (Playing or lying) anywhere on the generally clear part of the links other than the teeing ground and putting green; generally not including "hazards" in the original sense, e.g., areas where gorse bushes grew, which would now be classified as "rough." See *green* (def. 1), *fair green*, and *hazard* (def. 1).

1783 *Laws* (in Clapcott 1935, 33): XV. If a Ball, in playing thro' the Green, be stopt by the Player's partner or their Club-bearers, it shall be played where it chance to ly.
1807 *Regulations* (Clapcott, 40): That if a ball goes into the whins or is lost in playing through the Green . . .
1828 *Laws* (Clapcott, 53): VII.—If the Player by mistake strikes his Opponent's Ball in playing through the Green, the Stroke shall not be reckoned against either.
1857 H.B. Farnie *The Golfer's Manual* 57: Respecting open swiping through the long green we have few remarks to offer.
1890 Horace Hutchinson *Badminton Golf* 320: The lies through the green are execrable—but then there practically is no 'through the green.'
1893 *Rules for the Game of Golf* (R. & A.): 11. In playing through the green, all *loose* impediments, within a club length of a ball which is not lying in or touching a hazard, may be removed.

2 (Playing or lying) anywhere on the fairway or in the rough.

1912 Harry Vardon *How to Play Golf* 67: . . . and the brassie, when he takes it for a shot through the green, will be an old friend.
1931 Henry Cotton *Golf* 104: . . . [the brassie] is also one of the most difficult shots through the green to play really well.
1950 Sam Snead *How to Hit a Golf Ball* 57:

If the ball is lying in casual water through the green or on the green . . .
1967 Mark McCormack *Arnie* 56: Arnold was angry because he knew the imbedded-ball rule applied "through the green," which included the rough.
1970 Charles Price *Golf* 16: Although not spelled out in the Rules of Golf, "through the green" is universally accepted to consist of two separate areas: "fairway" and "rough."
1976 *Rules of Golf* Definition 35: "Through the green" is the whole area of the course except:—a. Teeing ground and putting green of the hole being played; b. All hazards on the course.

tiger *n.* A strong player.

1937 P.G. Wodehouse *There's Always Golf* (repr. 1976) 126: "Plinlimmon's playing a nice game," he said. "Nice and steady. Now that the tigers are off the map, I'm backing him."
1946 Percy Boomer *On Learning Golf* 40: Now my own observations of many thousands of golfers from neophytes to tigers . . .
1978 Alistair Cooke *Golf Journal* (Mar./Apr.) 7: . . . not every delegate to the U.S.G.A. Annual Meeting is a tiger who plays scratch golf.

tiger country. Heavy rough.

1962 Sam Snead *The Education of a Golfer* 171: A little later, Clayt drove into "tiger country."
1968 J.S. Martin *The Curious History of the Golf Ball* 21: For those of us who began our golf as caddies, and between rounds as urchin ball-hunters in deep hay and rank thickets—the untamed "tiger country" of yesteryear . . .

tight *adj.* **1** (Of a fairway) narrow; (of a course) having narrow fairways.

1950 Anthony F. Merrill *The Golf Course Guide* 139: It's a good tight course with good fairways and greens.
1975 Mark McCormack *Golf Annual* 262: Huntingdale is an excellent course but very, very tight. "This is the tightest course I have seen for years and you are dead if you stray from the fairway," Vines said.

2 (Of a lie) sitting down close to the ground.

1963 Arnold Palmer *My Game and Yours* 74: You're used to tight lies, where the ball sits right down against the ground as if it were lying on a tabletop.
1969 Jack Nicklaus *The Greatest Game of All* 251: ... with a tight lie on crusty ground I decided that the intelligent shot was to lay up.

toe n. & v. **1** n. The end of the clubhead; the point farthest from the shaft.

1862 Robert Chambers *A Few Rambling Remarks on Golf* 22: ... he is apt, when standing too far from his ball, to fall in to it, and run the chance of striking with the point or 'toe' of the club.
1931 Roger Wethered *The Game of Golf* 69: ... and the toe of the club ought to turn on to the ball a little sooner.
1977 Davis Love *Golf Digest* (July) 47: If the ball is above your feet, the toe of the iron will catch.

2 *v.trans.* To hit (the ball or a shot) with the toe of the clubhead.

1890 Lord Wellwood *Badminton Golf* 33: ... either 'heeling' or 'toeing' the ball instead of hitting it with the middle of the face.
1911 James Braid *Advanced Golf* 149: The ball is either toed or heeled, and it is sent off in the wrong way.

3 *v.trans.* To turn (the clubhead) in toward the player's feet.

1941 Patty Berg *Golf* 81: Don't "toe" (turn in) the club-head. This results in a "smothered" hook or pulled shot (to the left).

toed in. (Of a clubhead) having a specially prominent toe, with the face turned slightly in.

1975 Herb Graffis *The P.G.A.* 67: ... the pull head, which was toed in, was for the players who habitually sliced.

top v. & n. **1** *v.trans. & intrans.* To hit (the ball) above its center.

1862 Robert Chambers *A Few Rambling Remarks on Golf* 21: ... if too much force be applied, the chances are, that instead of hitting the ball fair, it is topped, and so driven a comparatively short distance.
1915 Alexander H. Revell *Pro & Con of Golf* 13: Or you may do just the reverse, top the ball.
1931 Bernard Darwin *The Game of Golf* 109: A moment later he had topped into the bunker at his feet.
1968 Buddy Hackett *The Truth About Golf* 64: Mantle topped his ball and it went in the creek.

2 n. A shot in which the ball is topped.

1890 Horace Hutchinson *Badminton Golf* 314: As long as we do not make an egregious top into the burn ...
1977 Jim Hardy *Golf Magazine* (Aug.) 38: There is more than one way to top a ball. There are in fact three separate and distinct kinds of tops. ... The three kinds of tops are the "shallow top," the "steep top" and the "missed-radius top."

topspin n. Forward rotation of the ball in motion.

1953 Bobby Locke (in Wind *The Complete Golfer* 1954, 268): It is so necessary to put topspin on the ball when putting, as it makes the ball run through on the line to the hole.

torque n. & v. **1** n. The tendency of a clubshaft to twist under the impact of a shot; torsion.
2 *v.intrans.* (Of a clubshaft) to twist under the impact of a shot.

1977 Advertisement *Golf Digest* (July) 23: ... torsional stability of steel to stop excessive torquing.

torsion n. The tendency of a clubshaft to twist under the impact of a shot.

1952 Henry Cotton *History of Golf in Britain*: Then it was realized that a shaft with no torsion was nearer to the ideal one.

touch *n*. Delicate accuracy, especially in putting.

1857 H.B. Farnie *The Golfer's Manual* 62: . . . its [wooden putter's] heavy head and stiff shaft . . . do not preclude the delicate touch, which is the chief feature in the handling of an iron.
1898 Charles B. Macdonald *Golf* magazine (Jan.) 20: Golf requires the delicacy of touch and nicety of judgment incident to billiards.
1913 Bernard Darwin *Country Life* (Mar. 15) 397: And there is no doubt that the fine delicacy of his touch which makes him so great at billiards is the quality that makes his putting great also.
1926 Francis Ouimet *Golf Illustrated* (Nov.) 45: Unless they have lost their putting touch altogether they will certainly need no more than two putts.
1946 Frank Moran *Golfers' Gallery* 42: Lawson Little, who, finding his putting touch in the last round, turned in a 69 which made an amateur record for the course.
1977 Bob Hope *Golf Digest* (Dec.) 21: "I think he [Bing Crosby] got that putting touch of his shooting pool as a kid."

touch shot. A very delicately hit shot.

1969 Jack Nicklaus *The Greatest Game of All* 160: . . . I played one of the best touch shots of my life, a little low pitch into the bank with my 7-iron.

tour *n*. A scheduled series of tournaments in which card-carrying professionals compete.

1967 Mark McCormack *Arnie* 257: It was not until 1929 that the P.G.A. came up with the idea of bringing some organization to the tournament structure and having a "tour."
1970 Tony Jacklin *Jacklin* 143: I have played only occasionally on the home tour in the last two years but remember being shocked at the small crowds.
1977 John P. May *Golf Digest* (July) 122: Deane Beman, the commissioner of the P.G.A. Tour, has announced that a firmed-up 1977 schedule will offer a record total purse of $9,688,977, including pro-ams and second-tour events as well as the 45 regular tournaments.

touring *adj*. Playing or working in a tour.

1967 George Plimpton *The Bogey Man* 254: There are about forty professional caddies—touring caddies, they're called . . .
1977 Tom Kelly letter to *Golf Magazine* (Aug.) 88: I'm 17 years old and I plan to become a touring professional.

tournament *n*. A public competition in which a number of golfers compete; formerly often played in the form of a series of elimination matches; now most usually played by stroke play, with four rounds played on consecutive days.

1857 *Unidentified newspaper clipping* (in Allan Robertson's album at the R. & A. 74): PRESTWICK GOLF CLUB . . . The most important business transacted was undoubtedly that relating to the contemplated Golf Tournament. This competition is to be open to all clubs.
1977 *New York Times* (June 27) 37: Tom Watson fired a 69 today and won the Western golf tournament.

track iron. Alternate name for the rut iron or earliest iron niblick; by later writers, as the niblick evolved, regarded as a separate and more "primitive" club.

1858 *Unidentified newspaper clipping* (in Allan Robertson's album at the R. & A. 90): At St. Andrews [the iron niblick] is termed a *track-iron*.
1862 Robert Chambers *A Few Rambling Remarks on Golf* 18: The NIBLICK, or

track iron
track iron or iron niblick,
c. 1860

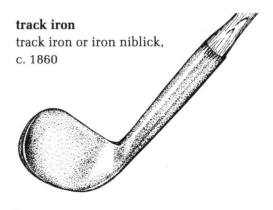

TRACK-IRON, is of very important service when the ball lies in a narrow cart-rut, horseshoe, or other print in sand, thick and stiff whins, or in any round deep hollow.

1881 Robert Forgan *The Golfer's Handbook* 55: . . . is ready with . . . the cleek, or the niblick, or the track iron.

1907 Robert Ferguson in Leach *Great Golfers in the Making* 188: The track iron took its name from the fact that it was used for getting the ball out of the cartwheel tracks which crossed the links. . . . It was the forerunner of the niblick.

trap n., or **sand trap.** Bunker (def. 1)

1899 Van Tassel Sutphen *Golf Illustrated* (July) 199: At the twenty-sixth hole Douglas found the trap-bunker in his drive.

1905 Frederick Upham Adams *John Henry Smith* 16: "I pitched it out of that trap a moment ago," . . .

1906 Arthur Pottow *Illustrated Outdoor News* (Nov.) 131: It is quite a common feature of our courses to see sand traps placed to catch pulled or sliced shots.

1913 Bernard Darwin *Country Life* (Sept. 20) 401: It takes a day or two for the English onlooker [in the U.S.] to grow accustomed to hear the hole called a cup and a bunker a trap.

1928 A.T. Packard *Golf Illustrated* (Nov.) 51: . . . his second seemed to roll into a sand-trap guarding the green.

1936 Willie Dunn (in H.B. Martin *Fifty Years of American Golf* 34): The place was dotted with Indian burial mounds, and we left some of them intact as bunkers in front of greens. We scraped out some of the mounds and made sand traps.

1961 Tommy Armour *How to Play Your Best Golf All The Time* 151: . . . the shot from the guarding sandtrap often is preferred.

1962 Sam Snead *The Education of a Golfer* 6: . . . he pointed to a bunker 270 yards away. "Can you drive into that trap?"

trapped adj. **1** Caught in a trap.

1907 Harold Hilton *My Golfing Reminiscences* 180: I have a rooted dislike to hitting a ball right down the middle of the course and finding it trapped.

2 Furnished with traps.

1926 *Golf Illustrated* (June) 43: [Evian, France] It is cleverly trapped and has a par 73.

1969 Jack Nicklaus *The Greatest Game of All* 115: It was a mildly plateaued green, heavily trapped in front.

trapping n. Arrangement of traps.

1954 Robert Trent Jones (in Wind *The Complete Golfer*, 1954, 299): At the right side of the fairway we devised a long Sahara-like maze of trapping . . .

1977 Tom Watson *Golf Magazine* (Aug.) 32: . . . the trapping is both beautiful and strategic.

trolley n. *Chiefly British.* A two-wheeled pull cart on which a golf bag can be fitted and pulled around a course.

1961 John Stobbs *Tackle Golf* (repr. 1977) 105: . . . breaking all your clubs across your trolley and jumping on your umbrella.

1975 Geoffrey Cousins *Golf in Britain* 102: Named caddie-cart at first and now universally known as the trolley.

trouble n., *often attributive.* Rough, hazards, obstacles, bad lies, or any encounter with any of them.

1897 Horace Hutchinson *Country Life* (Jan. 23) 80: . . . then you had a difficult loft, over all sorts of broken trouble, to the green.

1912 Harry Vardon *How to Play Golf* 117: I have not infrequently made my way into them [bunkers] in order to have the chance of laying the next shot dead. . . . Under certain conditions, there is something to be gained by considering whether the "trouble," as it is called, can be used to advantage.

1921 Andrew Kirkaldy *Fifty Years of Golf* 154: I don't like the way [the rubber-cored ball] jumps trouble and runs bunkers.

1962 Sam Snead *The Education of a Golfer* 215: In heavy grass, sand, or loose dirt, for instance, you won't use a 4-iron, but one of the trouble clubs.

1971 Tommy Bolt *The Hole Truth* 77: It's good to know you can smack the five-iron up and over all the trouble around a green.

1977 George Peper *Scrambling Golf* 21: In hitting trouble shots there is no repeating swing, no list of checkpoints involved, because each unusual situation calls for a different type of swipe.

turn *n.* The halfway point in a round, after nine holes have been played.

1870 Charles MacArthur *The Golfer's Annual* 135: [At St. Andrews] . . . Fergusson and Park being 1 ahead at the turn . . .
1895 "Calamo Currente" *Half Hours With an Old Golfer* 170: *Turn.* "The turn," when half the match is played the players are said to be "at the turn."
1907 Arthur Pottow *Recreation* (Feb.) 339: Everybody thought the match was over at the ninth hole for Travis was 3 up at the turn.
1922 P.G. Wodehouse *The Heel of Achilles* (in *The Clicking of Cuthbert* repr. 1956, 126): "Robinson won in a walk, after being three down at the turn."
1969 Jack Nicklaus *The Greatest Game of All* 23: I moved ahead of him with an eagle 3 on the long fifth and made the turn in 32.
1977 *New York Times* (June 13) 43: . . . was two shots down at the turn but rallied with a back nine four-under-par 32.

twitch *n. & v.* *Chiefly British.* **1** *n.* Putting nerves.

1895 "Calamo Currente" *Half Hours With an Old Golfer* 106:
O'Conor's put, by nervous twitch
    restrained,
Drew up too soon, and three feet short
    remained.
1971 Henry Longhurst *My Life and Soft Times* 205: What settled the problem for me was what we call the twitch and the Americans the "yips." . . . You then become totally incapable of moving a piece of ironmongery to and fro without giving at the critical moment a convulsive twitch.

2 *v.trans.* To mishit (a putt) from an attack of the twitch.

1967 Dave Thomas *Modern Golf* 73: Many golfers who start to twitch their short putts do so because in their lack of confidence they try to strike the ball too soon.

two-iron *n.* An iron club having loft of 20−22 degrees, lie of 57−59 degrees, and length of 38½ inches, and giving distance of 175−210 yards (men's clubs). Also, a shot played with a two-iron. Alternate name, mid-iron.

1951 Dai Rees *Golf My Way* 55: The No. 2 iron, with which most matched sets start these days, is the swinging equivalent of the brassie.
1970 Dan Jenkins *The Dogged Victims of Inexorable Fate* 112: "I really let that two-iron go at the thirteenth. I put the hands to it."

two-iron
Walter Hagen, 1979

two-putt *v.trans. & intrans.* To hole (the ball) or play (a green) in one putt.

1967 Mark McCormack *Arnie* 60: He two-putted for his birdie.
1970 Dick Schaap *The Masters* 41: . . . hits his tee shot fifteen feet short of the pin and two-putts for a par.

two-shot *adj.* (Of a hole) requiring a drive and another full shot to reach the green.

1908 Horace Hutchinson *Country Life* (Jan. 25) 141: With a "dog-leg" to the right it will make this seventeenth a two-shot hole.
1931 Joyce Wethered *The Game of Golf* 136: Convert the two-shot holes of 384 yards into 433 . . .

two-shotter n. A two-shot hole.

1913 W. Herbert Fowler *Country Life* (Oct. 4) 467: There are two short holes and several fine "two-shotters."
1927 Robert T. Jones, Jr. & O.B. Keeler *Down the Fairway* 38: . . . most of them were long two-shotters, the hardest type of hole on which to keep scoring par.
1956 Herbert Warren Wind *The Story of American Golf* 484: Jones had a violent distaste for drive-and-pitch par fours, gift birdie holes. He believed that a two-shotter should demand two good shots.

twosome n. A pair of golfers playing together in a stroke competition.

1970 Dick Schaap *The Masters* 90: Gary Player and his playing partner, Michael Bonallack . . . find another twosome still waiting to hit.
1974 *The Golfer's Handbook* 87: "TWOSOME" is not a golf term. If one man plays against another, the match is a "SINGLE." In stroke play, two players competing together are a "COUPLE."

two-wood n. A wood club having loft of 13–14 degrees, lie of 54–56 degrees, and length of 42½ inches, and giving distance of 220–270 yards (men's clubs). Also, a shot played with a two-wood. Alternate name, brassie.

1969 Tom Weiskopf *Go for the Flag* 10: I recommend the two wood instead of the driver.

U

uncock *v.trans. & intrans.* To straighten (the wrists) in the downswing; (of the wrists) to straighten themselves.

1928 Robert T. Jones, Jr. *Golf Illustrated* (June) 21: ... the power has been spent too soon, the wrists have been uncocked before the stored-up energy could be expended upon the ball.... Coming down the arms supply the initial acceleration, but there is little force exerted, until just before impact when the wrists uncock.
1948 Ben Hogan *Power Golf* 49: Wrists are fully uncocked. Right arm is straightening.
1976 J.C. Jessop *Golf* 39: It is at this point that the right hand comes into play, when the wrists begin to "uncock."

underclub *v.intrans. & reflexive.* To select (for oneself) a club giving too little distance for a particular shot.

1900 Harold Hilton *The Outing* (Sept.) 654: A besetting sin of nearly all golfers is what may be termed "underclub themselves"; that is, to take a club with which they cannot possibly reach the distance they require.
1931 Henry Cotton *Golf* 56: There are more shots lost through underclubbing than anything else.
1977 Arnold Palmer *New York Times* (June 18) 15: "... then on the 10th, I underclubbed and put it in a trap for another bogey."

underspin *n.* Backspin.

1911 James Braid *Advanced Golf* 225: Now let us see what this underspin is and what it does.
1948 Ben Hogan *Power Golf* 80: You can hit a ball with a maximum of underspin and a minimum of underspin and several variations somewhere in between the two. Underspin is also sometimes referred to as backspin.

unplayable *adj.* (Of a lie or ball) too difficult to be worth trying to play as it lies, so that the player may opt for relief and penalty under Rule 29.

1926 A.T. Packard *Golf Illustrated* (Dec.) 32: There was no unplayable lie rule in those days [1905], and Warren hacked away until the ball was out.
1976 *Rules of Golf* 29.2.a: The player is the sole judge as to whether his ball is unplayable.

up *adv* **1** (In putting) reaching at least as far as the hole.

1857 H.B. Farnie *The Golfer's Manual* 61: In long putting, the player should make it a point always to be up.
1895 (Young) Tom Morris (advice to his father) in H. Dalrymple *Handbook to Golf* 112:

"Aye be up; ye ken the hole canna come tae ye."

1963 Bob Rosburg *The Putter Book* 40: The old cliché of "never up, never in" is not practiced by many pros.

2 (In match play) standing a specified number of holes above one's opponent.

1870 Charles MacArthur *The Golfer's Annual* 132: The first match was gained by the former by 3 up and one to play.
1977 *New York Times* (June 9) D19: Muraskin was 7 up at the turn.

3 On to the green.

1975 Mark McCormack *Golf Annual* 58: He got up at the 17th with two prodigious shots.

up and down. Out of a bunker, or other trouble, and into the hole.

1970 John Jacobs (in Dick Schaap *The Masters* 144): "[Kono]'s a terrific scrambler. He can get it up and down from anywhere."
1977 Dave Hill & Nick Seitz *Teed Off* 100: Gary Player, the best bunker player in the world, actually aims approach shots into bunkers on some holes in the U.S. Open and counts on getting up and down in two shots.

upright *adj.* (Of a club) having a wide angle of lie, so that the shaft at address stands relatively close to the vertical.

1881 Robert Forgan *The Golfer's Handbook* 62: UPRIGHT.—A club is said to be "upright" when its head is not at a very obtuse angle to the shaft.

upswing *n.* Backswing.

1913 R.E. Howard *Country Life* (Sept. 13) 369: . . . the short up-swing of the veteran . . .
1931 Bernard Darwin *The Game of Golf* 120: Mr. Bobby Jones's up-swing has an indolent, almost drowsy grace.

Vardon grip. The overlapping grip.

1916 P.A. Vaile *The New Golf* 6: The Vardon grip was not introduced by Harry Vardon. It was known and used before Vardon took it up, but he undoubtedly set the fashion for it.
1976 J.C. Jessop *Golf* 19: There are three main grips in golf. Most popular by far is the "Vardon grip," or the overlapping grip.

W

waggle *n. & v.* **1** *n.* The preliminary flourish of the club behind and over the ball at address.

1890 Horace Hutchinson *Badminton Golf* 89: ... the preliminary 'waggle' is a means of seeing that all the machinery is in proper working order.
1962 Sam Snead *The Education of a Golfer* 109: The waggle is supposed to be a tension-breaker which loosens up the wrists and also gives you the feel of the clubhead.
1977 Tom Watson *Golf Magazine* (June) 113: Let's say you are now waggling 15 times before every shot. If you follow my program exactly, you should be able to get down to three waggles.

2 *v.trans. & intrans.* To flourish (the club) behind and over the ball as preliminary to making a stroke.

1890 Horace Hutchinson *Badminton Golf* 90: Even such a brilliant player as young Tommy Morris used to 'waggle' his driver with such power and vehemence in his vigorous young wrists as often to snap off the shaft of the club close under his hand before he ever began the swing proper at all.
1919 Robert K. Risk *Songs of the Links* 29:
Day by day the game expands, day and
  night, the golfer stands,
A-waggling on the Universal Tee ...
1950 Dai Rees *Golf My Way* 16: ... the loosening-up feeling developed by the waggle.
1961 Tommy Armour *How to Play Your Best Golf All the Time* 91: Cultivate a wood waggle, for, as the old Scotch saying goes, "As ye waggle so shall ye swing."

walk *v.intrans.*, or **walk round** or **around** *phr.v.* (Of a nonparticipant) to accompany a golfer or group of golfers during a game.

1890 Horace Hutchinson *Badminton Golf* 240: To what extent it is advisable for a medal player to converse with friends who may be walking round with the match ...
1915 Alexander H. Revell *Pro & Con of Golf* 104: Taylor's brother walked round with him during the last round and prevented anyone speaking to him.
1922 P.G. Wodehouse *The Clicking of Cuthbert* (repr. 1956) 10: Adeline was looking up at him tenderly. "May I come, too, and walk round with you?" Cuthbert's bosom heaved. "Oh," he said, with a tremor in his voice, "that you would walk round with me for life!"
1969 Jack Nicklaus *The Greatest Game of All* 104: She walked around Hershey that day—she was always very obliging when I asked her to come out and follow me.
1971 Tommy Bolt *The Hole Truth* 19: Bing Crosby followed us during the playoff. I was tickled to death he thought enough of golf to walk eighteen holes with us.

water, casual. See **casual water.**

water hazard. A body of water or channel defined under the rules as a hazard.

1976 *Rules of Golf* Definition 14.b: A "water hazard" is any sea, lake, pond, river, ditch, surface drainage ditch or other open water course (regardless of whether or not it contains water), and anything of a similar nature.

water club. Any of various iron clubs of the period 1880–1930, specially designed for playing the ball from water, all now banned under Rule 2.2 *See also* **president, rake.**

water club
The "Deadun" water
mashie, Jack White-
Gibson, Kinghorn,
1920

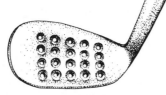

wedge n. & v.   **1** n.   A pitching wedge or sand wedge, sometimes classed as a number ten iron; also a shot played with a wedge.

1952 Henry Cotton *History of Golf in Britain*: . . . the club generally used was a wedge—a broad-soled niblick with a flat sole, the back edge of this club not riding as high as the "sand wedge."
1969 Jack Nicklaus *The Greatest Game of All* 152: . . . played what was rather a good wedge under the circumstances—25 feet past and to the right of the cup.
1978 Advertisement *Golf Magazine* (May) 5: The full set includes . . . Pitching Wedge, Dual Wedge, Sand Wedge . . .

2 v.trans. & intrans.   To play (the ball) with a wedge.

1969 Paul D. Peery *Billy Casper: Winner*

wedge
(1-2) concave-faced
    wedge (now
    illegal), Walter
    Hagen, 1930
(3-4) sand wedge, Tony
    Lema, c. 1960
(5-6) pitching wedge,
    Ben Hogan, c.
    1970

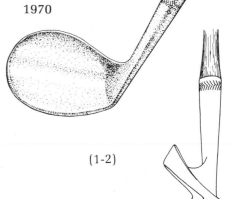

(1-2)

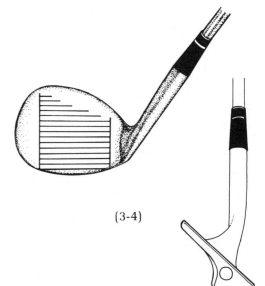

(3-4)

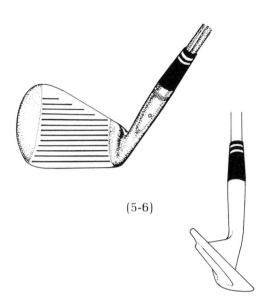

(5-6)

138: . . . Billy wedged ten feet from the pin for a birdie four.
1977 Max Conrad letter to *Golf Digest* (July) 12: He knocked the ball 185 yards up the fairway, wedged onto the green and made birdie.

whiff *v. & n.* [*Origin:* probably borrowed from baseball.] **1** *v.trans. & intrans.* To make a stroke at (the ball) and miss entirely.

1950 Sam Snead *How to Hit a Golf Ball* 72: WHIFFING—This is an aggravated case of topping in which you don't even touch the ball.
1977 Hubert Green *Golf Magazine* (July) 37: I could skull it, scoop it, hit it fat, top it or even whiff it by swinging up and over.
1978 Dave Anderson *New York Times* (June 18) S5: Trying to hit it high, he swung and his wedge went completely under the ball, nudging it a few inches. "My wife thought I took a practice swing . . ." Jerry Pate says, "but I told her, 'No, honey, I flat whiffed it.' "

2 *n.* A stroke that misses the ball.

1977 George Peper *Scrambling Golf* 36: If the ball is sitting up high on top of the rough, you should guard against hitting under it, causing a pop fly, or even a whiff.

whins *n.pl.* Gorse bushes.

1773 *Regulations* (in Clapcott 1935, 24): IX. When a Ball is struck into the Whins or any part where it may be covered . . . no whins must be laid aside excepting such as he shall set his foot upon when playing the Ball.
1853 *Unidentified newspaper clipping* (in Allan Robertson's album at the R. & A. 45): . . . Sir Thomas having driven a ball wild, which Allan had some difficulty in extracting from whins.
1976 *Rules of Golf* 17.2: If a ball lie in long grass, rushes, bushes, whins, heather or the like, only so much thereof shall be touched as will enable the player to find and identify his ball.

whip *n.* Flexibility of a clubshaft.

1911 James Braid *Advanced Golf* 33: Whip in the shaft [of an iron] is apt to make the club run away with you.
1975 Henry Cotton *History of Golf* 206: . . . the new carbon-graphite shaft . . . has offered as many as seventeen different whips.

whipping *n.* The binding of thread around the neck of a wooden club.

1673 *Wedderburn's Vocabulary* [(in O.E.D.) giving Latin equivalents for golfing terms]: *Baculi manubrium,* the handle where the wippen is; *Baculi filum,* the wippen. [Latin *filum* = thread.]
1881 Robert Forgan *The Golfer's Handbook* 62: WHIPPING—The pitched twine uniting the head and handle.
1907 J.R. Gairdner in Leach *Great Golfers in the Making* 219: We afterwards put on string or proper tarry "waupin," if we were fortunate enough to have a piece of it.
1973 *Bartlett's World Encyclopedia of Golf* 365: Nylon whipping is added where the neck and shaft meet.

windcheater *n.* A shot played low against the wind; especially, such a shot played with strong backspin such that it starts low and rises only toward the end of its flight.

[**1858** *Unidentified newspaper clipping* (in Allan Robertson's album at the R. & A. 90): It is thus evident that the driving-putter sends 'skimming' balls, and so 'cheats the wind,' a most desirable virtue in boisterous weather.]
1915 Cecil Leitch in Revell *Pro & Con of Golf* 69: "For example, necessity taught me how to play what are commonly called 'wind-cheaters.' "
1960 Rex Lardner *Out of the Bunker and Into the Trees* 108: . . . using a 3-wood, I hit a beautiful wind-cheater into the face of a stiff breeze.
1977 George Peper *Scrambling Golf* 162: . . . one of those low, delayed-rising "wind-cheaters."

winter rules. Local rules used at some courses during the winter, and sometimes also at other times of year, permitting the improvement of lies through the green in order to protect the turf from divots.

1929 *Golf Illustrated* (Apr.) 19: . . . some of these infringements have developed from the abuse of "winter rules"—some sort of mythical rules that no one can explain.
1961 Tommy Armour *How to Play Your Best Golf All the Time* 45: . . . don't get into the habit of using "winter rules." If you do, you'll never learn to play the shots you need to be a decent golfer. "Winter rules" are generally an amusing delusion. They aid neither in the development of the turf nor of the player.
1977 *Newsweek* (May 9) 26: Nixon tends to play "winter rules" year round, moving his ball to favorable lies and ignoring the two-stroke penalty for out-of-bounds infractions.

wood *n. & adj.* **1** *n.* Any club having a wooden head or, if of a material other than wood, having the head and general design characteristic of wooden-headed clubs; now usually included in a numbered set of five (or more) having graduated lofts, lies, and lengths of shaft; the driver (or number one wood), number two wood, number three wood, number four wood, number five wood, and sometimes half-numbers and higher denominations.

1915 A.W. Tillinghast *A Woman's Way* (in *Cobble Valley Golf Yarns* 75): Hodge couldn't quite get there with two from his wood.
1937 P.G. Wodehouse *There's Always Golf* (repr. 1976) 118: "No, darling. You know how shaky you are with the wood, darling. Take your iron, darling."
1975 Henry Cotton *History of Golf* 27: Woods became squatter, and apple, pear and beech replaced the unyielding thorn for club heads.

2 *adj.* Having a head made of wood or, if of material other than wood, having the general form characteristic of wooden-headed clubs.

1976 *Rules of Golf* Definition 36: A "wood" club is one with a head relatively broad from face to back, and usually is made of wood, plastic or a light metal.

wooden *adj.* (Of clubs) wood.

1890 Horace Hutchinson *Badminton Golf* 59: Nowadays the array of wooden clubs is commonly much curtailed.
1969 Tom Scott & Geoffrey Cousins *The Golf Immortals* 46: . . . Hagen could never be regarded as a consistent player with wooden clubs.

wry-necked *adj.* *Chiefly British.* (Of a club) having a somewhat crooked neck or hosel so that the clubhead is set slightly off the line of the shaft; offset.

[**1895** W. Dalrymple *Handbook to Golf* 75: Mr. F.A. Fairlie . . . has invented what is known as the "wry neck"—in which, by a sudden twist at the neck while the metal is still malleable, the side of the club to be presented to the ball is, so to speak, reversed.]
1919 Robert K. Risk *Songs of the Links* 25:
  The Old Gang at St. Andrews never
    heard of wry-necked clubs . . .
1975 Henry Cotton *History of Golf* 81: . . . his wry-necked putter did the trick.

wood

(1) short spoon, Hugh Philp, c. 1860
(2) driver or play club, c. 1880
(3) baffy, Spalding, 1906
(4) "bap" spoon, George
    Richard, 1924
(5) three-wood, Ben
    Hogan, 1979.

(1)

(2)

(3)

wry-necked
putter, c. 1930

(4)

(5)

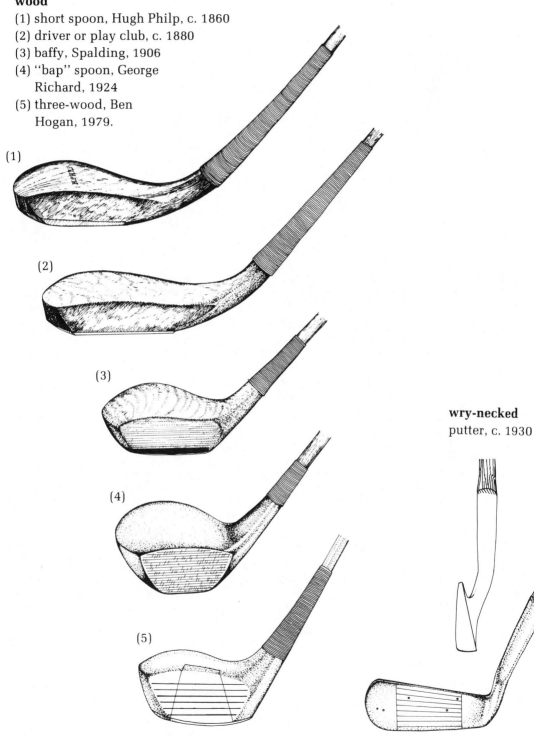

Y

yardage *n.* Distance through the green, or length of a hole or course, traditionally given in yards.

1929 A.W. Tillinghast *Golf Illustrated* (June) 42: ... the average yardage of a trifle under sixty-eight hundred will be the route ...

1970 Charles Price *Golf* 25: The yardage of a hole is measured, on the flat, from the middle of its tee area through mid-fairway to a point halfway from the front edge of the putting green to its back edge.

1977 Dave Hill & Nick Seitz *Teed Off* 50: My caddie's week starts when he gets his yardages on Monday and Tuesday. He paces off the course and computes the yardages from the landing areas for tee shots.

yip *v.trans. & intrans.* To mishit (a putt) from an attack of yips.

1962 Sam Snead *The Education of a Golfer* 134: I tried cross-handed putting ... and I still yipped everything.

1977 Desmond Tolhurst *Golf Magazine* (Aug.) 58: One time he yipped a four-footer right off the green. ... "I concluded that as long as I initiated the putting stroke, I would continue to yip."

yips *n.pl.* Chronic nervousness in putting or other play.

1968 Stephen Potter *Golfmanship* 65: Readers are reminded that the word 'yip' was invented by T.D. Armour the great teacher of golf. ... Armour defines 'yips' as a 'brain spasm which impairs the short game.' 'Impairs' is a euphemism.

1970 Dick Schaap *The Masters* 54: Hebert is discussing his problems with his game. "I've got the yips," he says. "Not with my putter. With my wedge."

1977 Dave Hill & Nick Seitz *Teed Off* 159: He's played so long, his nerves are gone on the greens. He has a terminal case of the Yips.

Peter Davies was Executive Editor of the first edition of *The American Heritage Dictionary of The English Language* (1969), and co-author of *The American Heritage Word Frequency Book* (1970). A classical scholar, linguist, and lexicographer, with wide-ranging interests in anthropology and history, he was the author of popular books on language including *Roots: Family Histories of Familiar Words* (1981) and *Success With Words: A Guide To The American Language* (1983).

Historical sources are especially prominent in all Davies's work. To discover the origins of golf and its special language he combed little-known archives on two continents. A superb natural athlete and games enthusiast, Davies' prowess as a golfer is in some dispute, but his unique contribution to the game and its enjoyment is stamped on every page of this authoritative book.